D0339705

The Working Class Foodies Cookbook

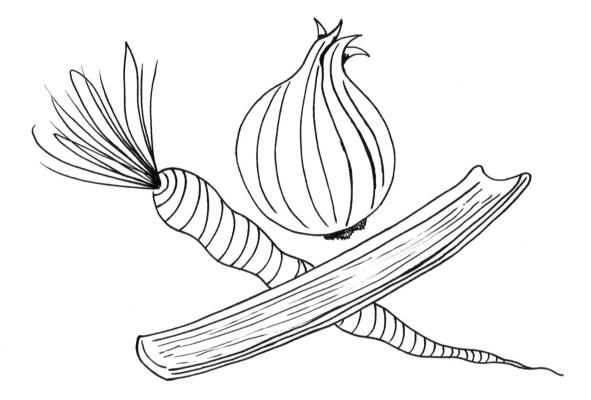

THE WORKING CLASS FOODIES COOKBOOK

100 Delicious Seasonal and Organic Recipes for Under $8 per Person

REBECCA LANDO

GOTHAM BOOKS

GOTHAM BOOKS
Published by the Penguin Group
Penguin Group (USA) Inc., 375 Hudson Street,
New York, New York 10014, USA

USA | Canada | UK | Ireland | Australia | New Zealand | India | South Africa | China
Penguin Books Ltd, Registered Offices: 80 Strand, London WC2R 0RL, England
For more information about the Penguin Group visit penguin.com.

Copyright © 2013 by Rebecca Lando
All rights reserved. No part of this book may be reproduced, scanned, or distributed in any printed
or electronic form without permission. Please do not participate in or encourage piracy of
copyrighted materials in violation of the author's rights. Purchase only authorized editions.

Gotham Books and the skyscraper logo are trademarks of Penguin Group (USA) Inc.

LIBRARY OF CONGRESS CATALOGING-IN-PUBLICATION DATA
Lando, Rebecca.
The working class foodies cookbook : 100 delicious organic dishes for under $8 / Rebecca Lando.
pages cm
Includes bibliographical references.
ISBN 978-1-592-40753-8
1. Natural foods. 2. Low-budget cooking. I. Title.
TX369.L355 2013
641.3'02—dc23   2012043512

Printed in the United States of America
1 3 5 7 9 10 8 6 4 2

Set in Fairfield LT Std   Designed by Elke Sigal
Photographs by Kit Pennebaker
Illustrations on pages ii, xiv, 4, 9, 10, 11, 72, 132, 234 by Daisy Edwards;
all other illustrations by Rebecca Lando
EWG chart on page 23 copyright © Environmental Working Group, www.ewg.org.
Reprinted with permission.
Storing Fresh Fruits and Vegetables for Best Flavor chart on page 261 courtesy
of Produce for Better Health Foundation.

While the author has made every effort to provide accurate telephone numbers, Internet addresses,
and other contact information at the time of publication, neither the publisher nor the author
assumes any responsibility for errors or for changes that occur after publication. Further, the
publisher does not have any control over and does not assume any responsibility for author or
third-party websites or their content.

To my family, for raising me to love good food,
humoring my obsessive tastes, and always
encouraging me to follow my passions;

to Kathleen for being the first and best
champion of Working Class Foodies;

to my Next New Networks family for
their support and encouragement;

and to Kit for putting up with my insistence
on always seeking out good food . . . and being willing
to taste every dish and experiment along the way.

Contents

Part 1 • Evolution of a Working Class Foodie

Chapter One • My Quest to Eat Well on a Tight Budget   1

Chapter Two • How to Be a Working Class Foodie   5

How to Shop Like a Working Class Foodie   5

How to Cook Like a Working Class Foodie   12

Being a Working Class Foodie Is a Lifestyle   14

Sample Day as a Working Class Foodie   14

Chapter Three • Your Pantry   17

Cooking from the Pantry   17

Basics of the Pantry   18

How to Stock a Pantry for $60 to $80   25

How to Stock a Pantry for $80 to $100   26

Chapter Four • How to Use This Book   29

$8 per Person   29

Part II • Recipes

Chapter Five • Basics: Cooking from the Pantry   33

Stocks

Basic Vegetable Stock   34

Meat Stock   35

Jar It!: Sauces, Dressings, Condiments, and Pestos

Basic Tomato Sauce   37

Bolognese Sauce   39

Basic Vinaigrette   41

Ketchup   42

Mayonnaise   43

Peanut Butter   45

Indonesian-Style Peanut Sauce   46

Basic Grains

Polenta   47

Basic Risotto   50

Basic Pasta Dough   51

Baking Basics

Basic Whole Wheat/White Blend Bread   54

Pâte Brisée (All-Butter Pie Crust) for Sweet and Savory Dishes   56

Spoiler Alert: Two Seemingly Random Recipes Using Food with a Short Shelf Life

Herb Butter	58
Homemade Ricotta	59

Chapter Six • Appetizers and Snacks   61

Roasted Broccoli	61
Surprisingly Vegan "Caesar Salad" Kale Chips	63
Lemon-Pepper-Poppy Beet Chips	64
Sesame Sichuan Snap Peas	65
Chicken and Bacon Pâté	66
White Bean and Bacon Dip	68
Roasted Onion Dip	70

Chapter Seven • Sides, Soups, and Salads   73

Grammy's Stuffing	73
Zucchini Pancakes with Seasoned Ricotta	75
Brendan's Israeli Couscous	78
New Potatoes with Butter and Herbs	82
Carl's Latkes	83
Spicy Sweet Potato "Fries" with Maple Butter	86

Salads

Butter Lettuce and Radishes with Lemon-Poppy Yogurt Dressing	88
Green Beans and Hazelnuts with Tarragon-Cider Vinaigrette	91
Cucumber, Jicama, and Seaweed in Sesame Oil	93

Spicy Watermelon and Feta Salad | 94
Thirty-Second Tomato Salad | 96
Tricolor Summer Salad | 97
Kale and Quinoa with Roasted Tomatoes | 98
Roasted Carrot Salad | 101
Grilled Radicchio with Kumquats | 103

Soups and Stews

Chilled Cucumber Soup | 106
Gazpacho | 107
Roasted Tomato Soup | 110
Roasted Red Pepper and Corn Soup with Cilantro-Lime Cream | 111
Borscht | 114
Grandma Shirley's Mushroom Barley Soup | 116
French Onion Soup | 120
Spiced Squash Soup | 122
Collard, White Bean, and Kielbasa Soup | 126
Escarole, Black Bean, and Chorizo Soup | 127
Curried Spinach, Lentil, and Sweet Potato Soup | 128
Early Fall Chickpea Stew | 130

Chapter Eight • Main Dishes 133

Breakfast

Granola | 133

Traditional Cheese Blintzes   135

Pumpkin Waffles   137

Eggs *en Cocotte* with Tomato and Shallot   139

Pizzas and a Calzone

Margherita Pizza from Scratch   142

Cherry Tomato and Burrata Pizza   147

Fresh Kale and Tomato Calzone   148

Pasta

Sweet Potato Gnocchi   150

Ricotta Ravioli in Brown Butter with Sage   152

Beet Ravioli in Lemon Butter   155

Pappardelle with Lamb Ragu   157

Almost Completely Homemade Lasagna with Bolognese   159

Feta, Red Onion, and Tomato Pasta Salad

    (Or How I Spent an Un-Air-Conditioned Summer in New York)   161

Polenta, Grits, and Risotto

Polenta with Mushroom Ragu and a Poached Egg   162

Max's Cheddar Shrimp 'n' Grits   165

Grits and Sausage in Tomato Sauce   167

Asparagus Risotto with Lemon   168

Roasted Root Vegetable Risotto   170

Pancetta, Squash, and Shallot Risotto   172

Vegetables and Meats

Rustic Ratatouille — 175

Lamb Shanks — 178

Indonesian Chicken Wings with Peanut Noodles
and Spicy Sesame Slaw — 181

Golabki (Polish-style Stuffed Cabbage) — 185

Brendan's Moroccan-Spiced Lamb Meatballs — 188

Tzimmes (Short Ribs and Fruit) — 192

Our Mom's Brisket — 195

Maple-Mustard Roasted Pork — 199

Spice-Rubbed Pork Tenderloin — 203

Cider-Brined Pork Chops — 204

Roast Chicken and Vegetables with Mustard Jus — 206

Whole Roasted Trout with Potatoes, Tomatoes, and Lemon — 210

Mussels with Ale and Garlic — 212

Spice-Rubbed Salmon — 213

Chinese-style Leek and Pork Dumplings (*Jiaozi*) — 215

Between Crusts

Veggie Burgers — 218

Sweet Potato and Corn Empanadas with Chipotle Dipping Sauce — 220

The Sandwich that Tastes like Summer — 223

Apple, Gouda, and Spinach Quesadilla — 224

Butternut Squash and Mushroom Tart — 226

Mustard Greens, Apple, and Cheddar Quiche — 229

Thanksgiving Leftover Pot Pies — 231

Chapter Nine • Desserts 235

Pumpkin Whoopie Pies	236
Jumble Berry Pie	238
Toaster Pastries	240
Apple Cake	244
Southern Fruit Cobbler	245
Cranberry Dark Chocolate Oatmeal Lace Cookies	248
Honey-Cornmeal Cookies	250
Sea Salt–Honey Caramels	251
Bibliography	253
Resources for Working Class Foodies	259
Acknowledgments	263
Index	265

Part 1

EVOLUTION OF A WORKING CLASS FOODIE

Chapter One

My Quest to Eat Well on a Tight Budget

After my freshman year of college, I vowed never to touch processed food again. I moved to an apartment-style dorm with a kitchen in Union Square. My mom armed me with a heavy-duty Dutch oven and I spent a few dollars on a used skillet at a flea market. There was a Food Emporium supermarket across the park from my dorm, but I quickly learned that the produce sold there was no better than the mealy apples and oranges from my freshman dorm. I tried instant ramen for the first time and found that, even for 15¢ a package, I couldn't bear to eat it. At the same time, it slowly dawned on me that on my Spartan working class budget, my fresh food options would be as dismal as the offerings on my old freshman meal plan. If I wanted to eat good food—fresh vegetables, whole grains, meat that wasn't vacuum-packed in Styrofoam to achieve an unnaturally long shelf life—I would have to learn not only how to cook and how to budget but also how to approach both from a new, creative angle.

One morning, I stepped out of the apartment and saw that Union Square Park had become a tent city. Jostling through the crowds, I allowed the flow of foot traffic to sweep me under one of the tents and found myself surrounded by dusky red, tannic green, and hazy, yellow-freckled pink apples—varieties I never knew existed. I was in the heart of the Union Square Greenmarket. I fingered the $1.50 in change in my pocket and checked it against the acidic ache of hunger in my stomach. The apples smelled lightly of grass and honey, their skins dusty and unwaxed. I grabbed three apples, each from a bin labeled with an unfamiliar name, and approached the cashier. He weighed my apples without caring that one was a Mutsu and one a Pink Lady and one a Fuji. He gave me my apples and my change—75¢.

Everything, suddenly, had changed. I could get three different kinds of apples, each crisp and plump, for less than one mealy, tasteless Red Delicious at the supermarket or in the dining hall. High-quality ingredients were literally right outside my door—and well within my meager price range. I learned that carrots can be purple, that the four or five varieties of radish tasted as different as they looked, that the grass-fed beef was so evenly marbled because it wasn't bulked up on extra fat at the end of its life, the way commercially raised meat is.

Buying my food directly from the farmers who grew it also changed my beginner cooking skills in the kitchen. I learned how much of the woody ribs on the black-soil Tuscan kale would have to be removed before steaming, and to save those ribs for making a better vegetable stock than could ever be found in a grocery store; I learned that red-skinned potatoes coated in butter and chives made a whole meal for a single dollar. But, in the end, I realized that instead of spending at least $20 a week on food, as I had originally budgeted, I could eat fourteen sparse but solid meals a week for about $8. Real local, seasonal, and where possible organic food was affordable, and it was delicious.

Being young, hungry, and broke didn't end after college—and neither did the weekly farmers' market haul. When my boyfriend, Kit, and I moved to an overpriced apartment on the overpriced Upper East Side, we gravitated to the small weekly farmers' market a quarter mile away: Just like in college, the market's produce, fish, and meat were cheaper and better quality than the food at the supermarket closer to our apartment. Too broke to afford to eat in any of the high-profile restaurants we followed obsessively online and in magazines, we did our best to re-create the dishes at home in our tiny galley kitchen. We attempted to chronicle our cooking on a food blog, but after a long day at work, the gym, walking the dog, cooking, eating, and doing the dishes, we were too tired to take good photos of the food or write eloquently about the meal. The food blog faltered and burned out almost as quickly as it started.

Out of the ashes of the food blog, though, rose *Working Class Foodies*. Kit had started to chronicle our farmers' market forays and cooking on camera, and, with the help of Next New Networks (now the YouTube Next Lab) and, most of all, our friend and Next New producer Kathleen Grace, we turned our food philosophy-turned-lifestyle into a weekly series. With my brother, Max, and later our friend Chef Brendan McDermott as cohosts, we've shared our "young, hungry, and broke" guide to shopping, cooking, and eating with millions of people around the world, hopefully inspiring all of them—and now you—to be working class foodies too.

Chapter Two

How to Be a Working Class Foodie

W ith a little planning ahead and a stocked pantry (more on this on page 17), two people can easily eat good food for a week for $30 to $40 a person.

If you've always shopped at the supermarket, or never tried gardening, or are maybe even new to using your kitchen for more than heating up a TV dinner, this list may seem daunting to you. But once you get in the habit of approaching food this way, you'll feel healthier and more connected to the food on your plate.

How to Shop Like a Working Class Foodie

Shop at farmers' markets. The USDA keeps a database of national farmers' markets—including which ones accept alternative payments like the Supplemental Nutrition Assistance Program (SNAP)—at search.ams.usda.gov/farmersmarkets/default.aspx.

Shop early in the morning or late in the day. These are the times when you can get the best deals. When shopping at the Greenmarket in New York, I learned that early in the morning I could eavesdrop on the restaurant scouts buying whole flats of shishito peppers and what a shishito was and what I could do with it. I also learned that the best deals could be had at the end of the day when the farmers were packing up their stand and would gladly sell me two pounds of snap peas for the one-pound price.

Do a lap around the market before you commit to buying anything. The first few times I ventured to the farmers' market, I wiped out my wallet within the first couple of stalls. I let myself be overwhelmed by the bounty facing me—multicolor carrots, five or six varieties of tomatoes, potatoes ranging from the size of your pinkie finger to a softball, and pears that ranged far beyond the supermarket descriptors of "mealy" and "not mealy"—all of which tasted as different as they looked. It's easy to get carried away, but resist the urge to thrust your cash in the face of the first farmer hawking heirlooms. The farmer next to him might have a better price. Slowly but surely, just like me you will learn how to shop not just for your wallet but for the season, for your kitchen, your tastes, and your schedule too.

Talk to the farmers. They can tell you how each variety of produce should look, feel, and smell at its peak, which will help you pick out produce that's neither underripe nor overripe, but ready for you to take home and cook that night. Better yet, ask them what they plan to have at market next week and the week after, and you can plan your meals and budget accordingly. Hands down, farmers are the best resource you can have when it comes to how and when to buy your produce.

Better yet, befriend the farmers. Bring your favorite farmer a hot coffee in winter or an iced tea in summer. Get to know them a little—and give them a chance to get to know you—and eventually you may find them slipping an extra heirloom tomato into your bag or holding aside a few donut peaches for you. Getting to know the person or people who spend their lives growing and cultivating your food will help you better appreciate what you eat—and the money you spend on it.

Shop with the seasons. When you've spent a lifetime eating fruits and vegetables regardless of season, I promise you there's nothing more life-changing than biting into the first Jersey peach of the year, juice dripping down your arm. That is the beauty of eating seasonally: Food, like love, is better after a little time off. Skinny, delicate New York asparagus in June will always taste better, fresher, and healthier than thick-stalked Peruvian asparagus in December.

Don't know what's in season? The U.S. Department of Agriculture website has a great seasonal foods guide. There are also great apps like Seasons and Fresh Fruit that will show you which foods are in season in your area. And, of course, you can always just ask the farmers themselves, who will know best of all when you can expect your corn, kale, plums, and raspberries to appear.

Keep a few things on your regular shopping list. A good list to start from: Eggs, waxy potatoes, a 3- to 4-pound chicken, fresh milk, your favorite seasonal vegetable(s) and fruit(s). Having a list or a strategy to work from will keep you from overspending or getting overwhelmed by all the new choices every week at the market.

Sign up for a Community Supported Agriculture share. In a CSA a farmer or a group of farmers sell advance "shares," or subscriptions, to their produce or products. CSA memberships often offer a few different price levels based on the amount and variety of produce you sign up for as well as discounted or subsidized shares for low-income households. Often membership in a CSA will require a few hours of volunteer work either at the farm helping to pick the produce or at the CSA's stand or distribution center sorting and handing out shares to other members.

While the cost of joining a CSA—generally anywhere from $80 to $300, depending on the quantity of your share, your household size, and income level—can seem steep, the benefits of joining a CSA are almost innumerable: You get ultra-fresh produce, often picked that morning; an intimate knowledge of where the food comes from and even how it's grown; an introduction to new foods you might never try otherwise; and fantastic value for your money. CSAs also directly support local farms: Your up-front payment gives the farmers seed money for the next season's crops by taking out the overhead and risk of bad weather, poor sales at the farmers' market, and the cost in time and money of lugging produce to and from the market every week.

Interested in joining a CSA? Want to learn more? Check out localharvest.org and the Rodale Institute, both of which have searchable CSA databases.

Join a co-op. A co-op is a member-owned store that offers produce, groceries, and other products to its members at discount after they pay relatively low dues and/or commit to a set number of volunteer hours to help work the store. Dues and volunteer times will vary from co-op to co-op, but they are well worth the investment for getting a discount on foods and products that are healthy for both you and the environment.

Join a buying club. A buying club is essentially a private CSA made up of your friends, family, and/or coworkers. Members of the club join together to buy in bulk directly from a farmer or distributor and take care of the purchase, transport, and distribution of food themselves. Like a CSA, the farmer gets immediate cash in hand for her labor, and the club participants get a discount on natural, local, organic food. You can ask a farmer at your local market about buying from her privately in bulk or you can go through a co-op or, sometimes, a natural food store.

Get the best out of your food. Long-lasting fruits like apples and pears and vegetables like potatoes, onions, garlic, turnips, parsnips, carrots, and beets can go weeks if stored in a cool, dry place. Dry ingredients like whole spices, flours, grains, lentils, and—to a lesser degree—nuts will also last for a few weeks or even a couple of months if stored in a cool, dry place. For more information check the resources section on page 259.

Buy meat judiciously. Whole steaks are unhealthy for you (high in fat and cholesterol), your wallet, and the environment. Think of meat as more of a seasoning than a main ingredient most of the time: Chop a slice or two of bacon, fry in a dash of oil, and add the bacon to a soup of white beans and escarole. Ditto chorizo with black beans and potato or chickpeas and kale. Buy quality meat in small quantities and you'll find the taste to be richer and more satisfying than a big hunk of crap meat. You'll appreciate the flavor of whatever meat you're cooking with more when it's spread out across a dish or meal.

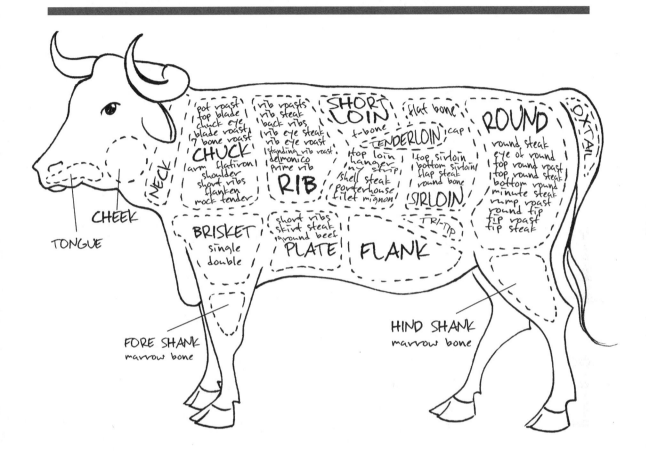

Likewise, experiment with off-cuts like beef tongue and try to get as much use as possible out of every cut you buy. Paying for the bone weight of lamb shanks can actually be cheaper than a butterflied leg of lamb, which factors in the butcher's time and skill in removing the bone; what's more, those picked-clean shank bones will be the base of a beautifully rich lamb stock, giving you a whole second use for your money.

NECK

SHOULDER
Arm Chop Blade Chop
Whole Shoulder
Boned and Rolled
steaks
cubes
ground

RACK
crown
rib roast
Frenched
rack
rib chop
cutlet

LOIN
loin chop
double loin
loin roast
tenderloin
cannon
noisettes

LEG
half leg   shank
boneless joint
bone-in steaks
kebabs   strips
sirloin chop   top round
center slice center leg
whole leg American roast
Frenched roast
sirloin roast

FORE SHANK

BREAST
belly spare ribs
flank   riblets
boned and rolled

HIND SHANK

Get the most beef (and pork and lamb) for your buck.

Beef tongue, top blade and top round roast, sirloin tip steak, tri-tip, flank steak, eye of round, beef back ribs and short ribs, ground beef, pork shoulder, pork spare ribs, ham hocks, lamb breast, lamb shoulder, lamb shanks, unboned leg of lamb, lamb tongue, and lamb neck all provide a ton of flavor for relatively low cost.

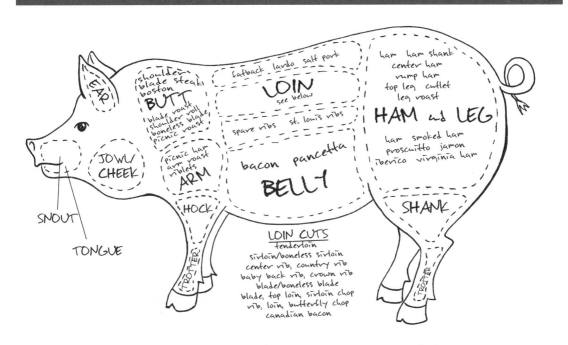

WHAT IS PASTURED MEAT
AND WHY IS IT SO EXPENSIVE?

The typical factory-raised cow is fed eight pounds of grain a day, a huge strain on the environment as well as on the cow's well-being. By contrast, pastured livestock graze on open farmland—which is usually organic, too. Farmers rotate their herds through different fields throughout the year to keep the symbiotic relationship between animal and environment balanced: Pastured animals get more nutrients, more exercise, and fewer illnesses than their factory feedlot brethren, and the land they graze benefits from natural fertilization (not to mention requiring less farmland and resources dedicated to growing grain to feed the livestock). The meat from pastured animals is generally lower in fat and cholesterol and higher in vitamins and omega-3 and omega-6 fats. Pasturing livestock is more space- and time-consuming for the farmer, thus making this higher-quality meat more costly than conventionally raised meat.

Choose sustainable but affordable seafood. Because seafood is hard to farm and harder to catch, it is, of course, generally pricier per pound than chicken, beef, or pork. This can make it tempting to buy the cheapest fillets or even canned fish, which, generally, are the least healthy, fresh, and environmentally friendly options.

Depending on where you live, though, it is possible to find affordable, healthy, and sustainably caught or raised fish that won't break your budget. If there's no fishmonger at your farmers' market, seek out a fish market or, barring that, the fish counter at your local supermarket. Line-, pole-, troll-, and harpoon-caught are the most environmentally friendly forms of fishing; recirculation tanks and cultured shellfish currently are the most sustainable methods of fish farming.

If you're willing to test your taste buds, try less popular fish like mackerel and whole sardines. These oilier fish generally need stronger seasoning—think lots of olive oil, lemons, capers, and parsley—but are full of healthy fats and have a lower environmental impact than popular fish like tuna and sea bass. The best resource for fish and shellfish sustainability and environmental impact is MontereyBayAquarium.org/SeafoodWatch.

When you are faced with having to spend a lot of money on fish or meat, remember that quality food will always taste better than high-quantity but cheap food and will stretch a lot further in the long run. It's all worth it in the end!

Mix and match. This may be the closest thing to a working class foodie motto: Be flexible! When you're short on money, split your shopping between the farmers' market, co-op, CSA, a supermarket, or wherever you can get great fresh, local, seasonal, or organic food. You'll learn through taste, time, and budget what's worth splurging on and where you can find the most affordable—yet still fresh and tasty—items. Can't imagine living without hydroponically grown lettuce or that expensive fair-trade, single-origin, organic, cold-pressed, extra virgin olive oil? Balance your budget by baking your own bread, buying apples by the bushel, or growing your own tomatoes.

How to Cook Like a Working Class Foodie

Just cook. We all need to eat, and cooking can be the healthiest, most affordable, and most gratifying way to do so. As M.F.K. Fisher says in *How to Cook a Wolf,* the goal of cooking is to fill empty bellies, but the joy of cooking is discovering what "you yourself like best," to dig deeper into your tastes, develop new ones, discover new ingredients and techniques and skills. And cooking doesn't have to be—and shouldn't even be—a solitary experience. Whether it's to help you chop vegetables, clean dishes while you cook, or just to keep your glass of wine full, making cooking social is a great way to better connect with family, roommates, and friends. The trick is to see cooking as not just a necessary part of our lives but a necessary part of ourselves. Cooking is human and personal and can connect us with the world around us as much as it connects us to our loved ones and ourselves.

Manage your time. In basic scientific terms, cooking is the application of energy and time to transform raw ingredients into finished dishes. This applies as much to you, the cook, as it does to your stove, oven, or grill. If you're going to boil pasta, use the water first to steam broccoli or parboil potatoes. Make kale chips in a preheating oven. Shave sweet zucchinis into a batter of flour and seltzer water and lightly pan-fry while your curds and whey separate into ricotta, then eat your zucchini fritters with a dollop of fresh ricotta while beans slowly simmer in the ricotta's leftover calcium-fortified whey. Maximize your time in the kitchen and multitask as much as possible; every time you turn on a burner or preheat your oven, get the most out of your time, energy, and money by cooking as many dishes or dish bases as possible. This will not only save you time during the week when work, family, and life in general have taken over your schedule, but it will also help you use all of your fragile produce before it starts to go bad. It might even stop you from reaching for the takeout menu when you get home at night.

Be creative. Be adventurous with your cooking and you'll save money: Try new vegetables, fruits, and meat. That's the only way you will learn to cook and become comfortable with your kitchen skills. This was how I learned that carrot greens are mildly sweet and earthy and make for a delicious chimichurri-style dressing (page 102) and that papalo is like a stronger cilantro both in flavor and divisiveness but that it can be great in guacamole, salsas, and cemita sandwiches. These are lessons you'll never learn from buying packaged food from a supermarket or ordering food through a window.

Know that a well-stocked pantry can go a long way. Your pantry is such an important part of being a working class foodie that it deserves its own section (see page 17). Being a working class foodie means a lot more than buying heirloom tomatoes and pasture-raised chickens; the ingredients in your pantry—from olive oil and flour to jarred tomatoes and honey—are not only time- and money-saving building blocks for hundreds of dishes but can also provide whole meals in themselves in a pinch.

Use everything. Bones and vegetable scraps make stock. Extra strips of pie dough can be balled together, wrapped in plastic, and frozen for future use or sprinkled with cinnamon and sugar to make quick flaky cookies. Even the water from steamed or boiled vegetables can be reused for boiling pasta. Fruit scraps, eggshells, and coffee grinds make compost for your garden—or your neighbor's garden, your friend's garden, your farmer's garden.

Grow your own. Creating a garden is the best way to know where your food comes from. Grow your favorite herbs (easy), vegetables (mostly easy), and fruits (easy, if you've got space). Basil, dill, mint, sage, rosemary, thyme, cherry tomatoes, and jalapeño peppers can thrive in a sunny window box almost as easily as in a spacious garden, and leafy vegetables like lettuce, spinach, kale, and chard are some of the easiest ingredients to grow. Do some research on the type of produce that can grow in your area and enjoy the freshest ingredients you can get your hands on. For more information check out the resources section on page 259.

Being a Working Class Foodie Is a Lifestyle

Being a working class foodie is about changing the way you think about food. It's about defining "good food" as food that is raised and/or grown with care and respect and is as fresh as possible and has a positive impact on the local community and the environment. It's believing that good food shouldn't just be available to the upper classes, but to all. That the prepared foods available to us in our daily lives—from public school cafeteria pizza infamously (but somewhat mistakenly) counting as a vegetable to microwave dinners that are bad for the environment (all that packaging!) and for us—are not the best option. We all deserve to eat healthily and well.

And, above all, it's about firmly believing that the best meals come from fresh ingredients prepared simply and shared with loved ones—even when the loved one is just oneself.

Sample Day as a Working Class Foodie

This can all seem like quite a lot to consider before even heading to the market. How do you apply all of these ideas for shopping, cooking, and even *being* into your daily life?

If you can, do all your shopping—CSA pickup or farmers' market, co-op or grocery store, local butcher—in one day. For a household of two, you should be able to shop for the following for no more than $20. Then spend a few uninterrupted hours either that day or the next turning your raw ingredients into the basis for a week's worth of meals.

Boil a large pot of water with twice as much salt as seems right and steam torn-up kale or chard leaves with whole cloves of garlic. When the greens are done, parboil a pound of small whole potatoes in the pot. Store them in the fridge and either eat them tossed with olive oil and mustard, or smash them down a little in hot oil in a skillet until brown and crisp on the outside and top with a fried egg.

Wash and slice your vegetables, toss them with olive oil, salt, and pepper, and lay them flat on baking sheets. Roast your veggies in big batches, then store them in the fridge once they've cooled. This works for almost every type of vegetable. They're even more delicious cold the next day, tossed with a little extra olive oil and some fresh parsley—or even just straight out of the container.

Any time you fire up the grill, pull out all the vegetables in your fridge and grill them with olive oil, salt, and pepper and store them for salads or sandwiches. Cook up extra proteins, too, whether chicken, steak, or seafood, and use them throughout the week. Toss your leftover herbs or salad greens in the food processor with garlic, olive oil, salt, pepper, a little Parmesan, and your favorite nut. Ta-da: instant homemade pesto for sandwiches, pastas, or as a nice side sauce for almost anything you can make. You can even mix and match: Think about parsley and dill as a pesto for chicken or salmon; chives and arugula for steaks and hamburgers; Thai basil or tarragon and a hot pepper for shrimp, steak, or corn on the cob.

Stock up on French canning jars or Ball jars; they're about $1 to $2 apiece new, depending on size, and will last a lifetime if properly cared for. Whenever you know you won't have time to get to a vegetable or fruit before it gets soft, preserve and can it. Make tomato sauce; confit peppers, onions, tomatoes, artichokes; turn peaches and berries into preserves, apples and pears into butter. Boil clean jars and lids to sterilize them, then, when filled, boil them again to seal your food inside. Store unopened in a cool, dry, dim place for months. For extra instructions on pressure canning, check at the National Center for Home Food Preservation website at nchfp.uga.edu.

Anytime you cook with vegetables and fresh herbs, toss the scraps and peels into a saucepan with enough water to cover, a bay leaf, a few peppercorns, and a dash of salt. Simmer until a golden broth forms (anywhere from 30 minutes to 6 hours, depending on how concentrated you want it), then let cool, strain through cheesecloth, and freeze the stock in ice cube trays, plastic containers, or gallon-size freezer bags (for flat storage). When you next need veggie broth—say, to make a more flavorful soup with your beans—toss a big veggie broth ice cube in a pot and slowly melt it before adding reconstituted dried beans.

Proof a packet or 2¼ teaspoons of active dry yeast in a cup of warm water with a tablespoon or so each of honey and olive oil. When the cup is domed in froth, mix the contents into a large bowl of flour, some salt, and one raw egg. Knead this into a dough, cover the bowl with plastic wrap, and forget about it for an hour or two while you do something else. Punch the dough down, knead it again, put it back in the bowl, and forget about it for another hour or two. Watch a movie. Go to the gym. Grab a drink with friends. Study. Bake the dough in a lightly oiled Dutch oven or on a baking stone spattered with cornmeal until the dome is golden brown and the bottom sounds hollow when tapped. Now you have fresh bread.

Make a sandwich on your hot, fresh bread with your cold roasted vegetables: Press the veggies down into the bread, drizzle with olive oil and maybe some balsamic vinegar, and smash the sandwich together. Top the veggies with cheese if you want, but you'll see it isn't necessary.

Heat a gallon of milk to a rough simmer—almost a boil—and curdle it with distilled white vinegar. Strain out the whey in a colander lined with cheesecloth to reveal creamy ricotta. Save the whey for boiling potatoes, pasta, or beans. Use the ricotta on pasta, on pizzas, with vegetables, as dessert.

Briefly simmer berries with just enough water to cover them, a dash of sugar or honey, and a squeeze of lemon juice. When the berries break down, kill the heat. Stir in a quarter cup of cream, if you like, and pour the mixture into prefrozen ice pop molds. Core apples, fill them with brown sugar and cinnamon, stud them with cloves, and bake them until the skins are wrinkled and browned. Poach pears in a few cups of cheap prosecco with vanilla and ginger. Serve the apples or pears alone or with a scoop of ricotta drizzled with honey.

And, perhaps, above all, save your stale bread either for breadcrumbs (blend, then freeze) or for French toast.

Next week, you can go back to the market again. There probably will be something new for you to take home, transform, and enjoy.

Chapter Three

Your Pantry

Cooking from the Pantry

What do I mean by "cooking from the pantry"? It's not just fancy code for microwaved baked beans or instant organic oatmeal. A well-stocked pantry will save you time and money and enhance all the lovely local, seasonal, organic perishables you bring home: Think of how a good sea salt brings out the summery essence of an heirloom tomato garnished with a single basil leaf or the difference in quality of a pumpkin pie made with freshly ground whole spices instead of a prepowdered, half-stale spice mix.

A working class foodie's pantry extends beyond the cabinet above your stove or the dark little closet where cans of soup go dusty over time. It includes the organic olive oil you keep next to the stove and the hunk of Parmesan in your fridge; anything you use in dish after dish. So think of your pantry as your kitchen arsenal and stock it with the things you love best: Maybe the only seasoning you like is salt and pepper; maybe you prefer maple syrup to every other kind of sweetener; maybe you hate dried herbs but love ground spices. I've included a few inches of space at the bottom of this section for you to fill in your own pantry staples. (I mean it when I say I want you to make this *your* cookbook!)

In the recipe section called Basics: Cooking from the Pantry (page 33), I will show you how to make things like peanut butter, mayonnaise, and granola so you can save money at the supermarket on these and other staple items.

PANTRY AND COST

When I calculate the cost of a dish or meal, I rarely include the price of pantry items. Items like olive oil, flour, salt, and seasonings are bought infrequently and in large quantities—not in small amounts as called for in a specific recipe. To calculate the few cents used here and there would have a negligible effect on the overall cost of most recipes, and, beyond that, these items are generally kept in stock in most homes. The exceptions are recipes like Homemade Ricotta (page 59), which uses a full gallon of milk in one go, or the Sea Salt–Honey Caramels (page 251), which call for an unusually large amount of honey.

Basics of the Pantry

When it comes to pantry staples that can be bought locally and/or organically, there are a few good bits of information to keep in mind:

Sugar and other sweeteners: From sugar cane, palm trees, beets, agave, and maple, there are a ton of products to sweeten food. The health and environmental effects of these sweeteners vary greatly.

Sugar is a simple carbohydrate with a complex relationship to our diets and the world. Here are some of its many forms:

- Natural brown sugars are pure sugar cane extracts with hard crystals. Varieties include muscovado, demerara, and turbinado. Unlike white sugar, turbinado, or "raw," sugar is always vegan, never processed with chemicals, and retains many of the raw sugar cane's nutrients, like potassium and calcium.
- Conventional white sugar, by contrast, is highly refined with chemicals that

strip away all nutrients except for calories and is often whitened with bone char, making it unhealthy and non-vegan.

- Softer, commercially produced brown sugars are just refined white sugar combined with molasses, another by-product of sugar cane refinement.
- Confectioners' or powdered sugar is white sugar ground to a smooth powder and sifted with a small amount of cornstarch to prevent caking.
- Date sugar is made from finely chopped dried dates. It is richly sweet and less harmful to the environment than cane sugar but clumps easily and doesn't melt; it's fine on yogurt or fruit and in some baking but useless in coffee and tea. It's sweeter than brown sugar.
- Agave nectar is sweeter than sugar or honey, dissolves easily, and is vegan. However, it is higher in refined fructose than high-fructose corn syrup and generally is processed in much the same way—meaning with chemicals. Fructose is processed by the liver, which means it doesn't affect your blood sugar levels; instead, it's converted into triglycerides, which contain twice as many calories as carbohydrates and proteins and are stored in your body's fat cells. High amounts of triglycerides have been linked to heart disease and stroke.
- Honey is as sweet as white sugar, but it can have a more nuanced flavor depending on the honey's flower source. It contains traces of amino acids, vitamins, nutrients, and antioxidants; the nutrients and their amounts vary based, again, on that honey's flower source. And when I say honey, I mean the expensive kind at your farmers' market, natural foods store, or co-op. Honey that you buy from the supermarket can be highly processed, which can kill many of honey's natural nutrients. Buy local and you'll never go back!
- Maple syrup is obtained by carefully boiling the water out of maple tree sap. In addition to having a distinctly sweet flavor, it is high in iron and manganese. It's higher in calcium than honey and lower in sodium. Antioxidants in maple syrup may even inhibit an enzyme related to type 2 diabetes. No other sweetener is as complexly flavorful as maple syrup, which can be citrusy, smoky, herbal, or have hints of creamy vanilla. Be wary of products with brand names that don't include "maple" or products called "pancake syrup":

While cheaper than real maple syrup, these are sugar water imitations of the real deal and have no nutritional significance beyond their calories.

Another thing to consider, according to a 2004 World Wildlife Fund study, sugar may be the most environmentally damaging crop in the world owing to habitat loss to make space for sugar cane plantations and the amount of water used and polluted in the growth and processing of sugar cane. If you want to help the environment and your health, you're better off buying locally produced honey or maple syrup, both of which are pricier but will provide more nutrients than natural brown sugar, and have more nuanced flavor than the granulated stuff.

Flour: Different flours provide different levels of protein for varied taste and nutrition; bread flour, which contains at least 4 grams of protein per ¼ cup, has a soothing density to it, while "leaner" flours like Italian 00 are light and chewy and perfect for pizza and pasta. If you like to bake, it's a good idea to keep some whole wheat flour on hand; mix a little into your doughs for extra texture and a pleasing color. Niche flours like buckwheat, bran, rye, oat, and corn are excellent for combining in various amounts with regular all-purpose, bread, or pastry flour—and some are even gluten-free. If you've only ever baked with supermarket flour, then good, organic, and, if possible, fresh flour is a revelation. No joke; studies have found they make hardier and tastier breads. One of many reasons you might consider buying organic or, if possible, local flour.

Eggs: Eggs may be one of the most important ingredients to buy from a local farmer. Supermarket labels like "organic" and "free range" are purposefully misleading: Even these eggs can come from chickens crowded into factory farms, debeaked to prevent pecking, and limited to a tiny porch that counts as the outdoors but which most chickens will never see. These chickens might be cage-free, but their living conditions are often no better than any other factory farm.

Beyond chicken welfare, eggs from your local farmer will always be the best for you too. Most small farms either pasture-raise their chickens (meaning the birds peck the ground for seeds and worms and get regular exercise) or at least feed them an organic and high-quality meal while housing them in coops, henhouses, and penned enclosures. Eggs from these birds—who eat and exercise as chickens should—are higher in nutrition, lower in cholesterol, and have an amazingly fresh taste. Don't believe me? Compare the raw egg yolks from an egg fresh from the farmers' market with one you just brought home from the supermarket. The farm egg is more likely to have a tight, almost fluorescently bright yolk. No matter how hard or soft you like your yolk, a fresh egg from a local chicken should taste creamy compared to the supermarket standard. And because the protein and fat content of farmers' market eggs are usually higher, you can buy large eggs instead of the supermarket's jumbo for about the same price.

Dried beans: Dried beans are dried and packaged. Supermarket beans are less likely to have an errant pebble in the mix, but beans grown and dried closer to home may have better texture and flavor—not to mention variety.

Dairy: There is no way around spending extra for organic and local dairy products, but the cost is well worth it. Fresh milk—even if you can't easily get it raw in most of America—is a treat regardless of how much fat you prefer skimmed off. Better yet, some local dairies still bottle in glass, meaning you can return the empty bottles to the farmer for a deposit return so he or she can clean and reuse them. Good for your wallet, good for customer loyalty, and good for the environment.

Salt: There may be no ingredient more important or useful than salt.

- Table salt, which probably is already living in your pantry, almost always contains iodine, a heavy element that can prevent mental retardation and thyroid conditions.
- Kosher salt, a large- and flat-grained, additive-free salt used to cure meats, pickle vegetables, and season dishes, is a good one to add to your pantry.
- Sea salts vary greatly in color, grain size, flavor, and price: The gray fleur de sel, generally from the coast of Brittany in France, has a lightly mineral taste from high levels of magnesium and potassium; Australia's peach-hued Murray River flake salt is almost sweet; and the crunchy red crystals of Alaea Hawaiian sea salt are fantastic when grilling fish and meat, to name a few.
  Sea salts are minimally processed—they're obtained by evaporating seawater—

and therefore retain many naturally occurring nutrients like magnesium and potassium. Table salt has no flavor beyond "salty" and is processed heavily to remove impurities; for these reasons as well as the additions of nutrients such as iodine, many people prefer sea salt to table salt, although the amount of sodium chloride is the same in both types.

• Specialty salts, like naturally smoked sea salt, which adds a subtly smoky flavor, and sea salt infused with red wine (great with meat) or bits of dried truffles (transformative on runny eggs) are a treat to have on hand.

Olive oil: I like to keep two olive oils on hand: a glass liter bottle of regular organic virgin olive oil by the stove for cooking and a smaller bottle of organic extra virgin olive oil for making dressings and finishing dishes. Both extra virgin and virgin olive oils come from cold-pressed olives—no heating or chemicals have been used to extract the oil. As a result, both extra virgin and virgin olive oils are high in antioxidants. The difference between extra virgin and virgin is flavor (extra virgin has a purer taste) and fatty acid content (in the United States extra virgin must have a fatty acid content of .8% or less, whereas virgin olive oil can have a fatty acid content as high as 2%).

Garlic: Did you know that supermarket garlic is often shipped in from China? Local garlic can be comparatively expensive, but the taste—sharp, grassy, and spicy—is more than worth the extra dime or two.

Vegetables and fruit: If you can, buy most of your vegetables and fruits locally and when they are in season. Remember the Working Class Foodie motto, mix and match!

Here is a useful list published yearly by the Environmental Working Group, a nonprofit environmental advocacy group that can help you choose when to buy organic and when not to. Of course, when price and selection allow, it is generally better for your health and the environment to shop organically.

Please check the Environmental Working Group's website, www.ewg.org/foodnews/, for the 2013 Dirty Dozen chart.

A WORD ABOUT ORGANIC FOODS

Most small, local farms practice organic methods but can't afford to pay for organic certification. Outside the farmers' market, organic can mean grown naturally, with no pesticides or hormones and with care for the environment the produce is grown in as well as the produce itself—or it can be a vague marketing price-up for food that's grown with as much chemical enhancement and protection as a conventional food item. Not to get too political, but unfortunately the image of organic foods coming from small farms run by happy farmers who care about the environmental impact and natural quality of their food has been co-opted by some of the world's biggest corporations. These days, most products labeled organic are manufactured by huge corporations (think Kraft, PepsiCo, Dole, ConAgra, and the quiet mastermind behind them all, Monsanto) whose intentions are to make money (duh) and not to uphold the idea of producing chemical- and pesticide-free food. It's a sad state of affairs made sadder by the fact that it's all too easy for the well-meaning but unsuspecting consumer to fall prey to the gimmick. On packaged goods, this corporate hijacking extends to adding ingredients like chemically based food dyes, lab-grown stabilizers, and more to foods labeled organic. At the end of the day, local, fresh, and seasonal produce and meats from your local farmer, CSA, or co-op are the best bet for those who care about how their food is grown, made, and packaged. And when you do buy packaged goods at the grocery store, be sure to check the ingredients: Anything that contains more chemicals—or simply multisyllable, unpronounceable words—than real food should go back on the shelf and not into your cart. My best advice for how and when and where to shop organic is simple: Buy as much as you can at the farmers' market, CSA, or co-op, grow as much of the rest as is possible, and read labels carefully on everything else. Above all, trust your taste and wallet to guide you: You may not be able to taste the difference between a supermarket apple and its organic farmers' market cousin, but you can pick a vine tomato from the farmers' market out of a lineup blindfolded. That will always be more important than how something was grown.

How to Stock a Pantry for $60 to $80

Not every item listed here is necessary; pick and choose as you see fit for your personal tastes, cooking needs, and budget. Depending on which of these items make sense for you and which ones you already have on hand, plan to spend between $60 and $80 at most to round out your pantry with some or all of these items.

This might seem like a lot to spend at once, but remember that everything below will last for at least a week (and in most cases over a few months) and can be used multiple times before needing to be replaced.

Olive oil (see page 22)
$6.00 to $24.00

Canola oil or vegetable oil
$4.00 to $8.00

Kosher salt *$2.50*

Sea salt *$2.50 to $8.00*

Whole peppercorns and a refillable peppermill *$1.50 to $6.00*

Dried herbs and spices—preferably whole, as they'll last longer and taste better (toast and ground as needed), but preground is fine in small amounts
$1.50 to $3.50

All-purpose flour *$2.00 to $6.00*

Rolled and/or steel-cut oats
$3.50 to $7.00

Rice (white, brown, black, wild, and/or arborio) *$2.50 to $8.00*

Polenta or coarse cornmeal
$2.00 to $4.00

Dried and/or canned beans, chickpeas and/or lentils *$1.25 to $3.50*

Dried pasta *$1.00 to $4.00*

Natural brown sugar *$3.00 to $5.00*

Honey *$3.50 to $8.00*

Maple syrup *$8.00 to $22.00*

Baking powder and baking soda
$1.50 to $3.00

Milk *$2.50 to $6.00*

Eggs *$2.50 to $4.00*

Butter *$2.50 to $6.00*

Bacon *$4.00 to $8.00*

Parmesan *$5.00 to $15.00*

Peanut butter (homemade, page 45)
$4.00 to $5.00

Distilled white vinegar (also great for cleaning) *$2.00 to $4.00*

Cider vinegar	$2.50 to $4.50
Balsamic vinegar	$3.50 to $12.00
Onions	$1.00 to $2.00
Garlic	50¢ to 75¢

Potatoes—a pound of your favorite kind, including sweet potatoes, means a last-minute dinner is never out of reach $1.00 to $2.00

Canned or boxed tomatoes	$1.75 to $3.75
Your favorite hot sauce	$2.00 to $3.00
Homemade stocks	(pages 34–36)
Lemons	50¢ to $2.00

How to Stock a Pantry for $80 to $100

Have room for more? One or all of the following additions to your pantry will give you more range in cooking and baking.

A nice "finishing" salt (gray, smoked, pink, Hawaiian)	$4.00 to $12.00
Whole wheat, bread, and/or 00 flour—for anyone who bakes their own breads, pizza dough, or pasta	$3.50 to $7.50
Good mustard	$2.00 to $5.00
Dried mushrooms	$7.00 to $20.00
Rice vinegar	$3.00
Dried fruit	$2.50 to $7.00
Good olives	$2.50 to $9.00
Oil-packed sardines and/or anchovies	$1.50 to $9.00
Specialty flours: buckwheat, rye, pastry flour	$2.50 to $6.00

Dried coconut (unsweetened)	$3.00 to $4.00
Chocolate for baking	$3.00 to $6.00
Specialty salts	$3.00 to $8.00
Grapeseed oil—a neutral oil with a high smoke point, equally great for salad dressings or french fries	$4.00 to $6.00
Specialty oils like pumpkin seed, sesame, citrus, walnut, or hazelnut oil	$3.50 to $12.00
Truffle oil—check the ingredients to make sure the truffle flavor comes from real truffles and isn't synthetically derived	$12.00 to $20.00

Now your pantry's stocked and you can make a completely satisfying meal just from there: olive oil + tomatoes + salt + time = marinara sauce; rehydrate your beans, then simmer them for 2 to 3 hours in a covered pot until tender. Season them, and top with your marinara or toss with buttered rice. With beans, rice, pasta, and good canned tomatoes, you've got at least half a week's worth of meals taken care of.

2 x 2 ‹ $20 (2 PEOPLE, 2 MEALS, UNDER $20)

Not sure where to start? Assuming you have basics like olive oil, salt and pepper, vinegar, mustard, and garlic on hand, the items below should total under $20 and can easily provide lunch and dinner for two people:

One 3- to 4-pound chicken
Fresh thyme and/or chives (bonus points: grow them yourself!)
1 pound small waxy potatoes
Celery and carrots
Arugula or another salad green
Loaf of bread (best choice: keep active dry yeast and flour on hand
    and make your own)

From these humble beginnings you can make a perfect roast chicken (page 206); new potatoes with butter and herbs (page 82); roasted carrot salad (page 101); and an arugula salad with a mustard dressing for dinner the first night. The next day for lunch, you can make a garlicky aioli for a roast chicken sandwich and a mustardy potato salad spiked with more arugula, thinly sliced celery, fresh thyme and chives, and, as a bonus, a hearty and golden chicken stock from your chicken's bones and the leftover bits of celery and carrots.

ANATOMY OF A CHEF'S KNIFE

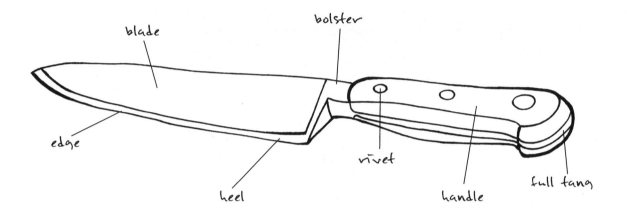

blade

bolster

edge

heel

rivet

handle

full tang

Chapter Four

How to Use This Book

$8 *per Person*

When I started my show back in 2009, $8 was the median price for a takeout lunch in midtown Manhattan (it's now more like $10 to $11). Three years on, $8 a person still gives the show and its viewers a pretty comfortable cushion: Most of the food I cook, on the show and at home, comes in under $8 for the whole dish or meal.

The prices in the book for each ingredient are accurate and the lowest that I paid in the year from 2011 to 2012. Of course, prices for local, seasonal, and, where possible, organic produce will vary depending on demand and availability and on the success of the harvest for that year, so there might be variations in price on the produce you buy. Depending on where you live, food may cost more or less than the numbers I've included here. Consider my advice in the past couple of chapters as a resource to help you shop, cook, and eat as affordably and healthfully as possible, and the delicious yet simple recipes in this book are here to help you make the most of every ingredient.

In most cases, cost breakdowns for the recipes take into account the amount of an ingredient used rather than the whole box, jar, or the like and generally don't include the cost of basic pantry items (see page 25). In many places I've included notes on other uses for leftover amounts of an ingredient so you can get the most out of every ingredient you purchase.

At the end of the day, what matters most in the kitchen is *you*: whatever brought you to the stove in the first place, be it passion, curiosity, an addiction to the smell of garlic hitting hot oil, the basic utilitarian need to put food on the table for your family, or a simple desire to save money and eat more healthily.

I hope that through this book you will get a real feel for how you like your food. I want you to taste things often as they cook to get a sense of what heat and time and fat and salt do to food. You will learn more about the ingredients this way, but you will also learn about yourself: what flavors you like, what cooking methods make the most sense to you, at what point in the process foods are cooked to your satisfaction.

You know that old adage, "Give a woman a fish and she'll eat for a day; teach her to fish and she'll never go hungry"? It's corny, but it's also pretty much the thesis behind this book. If you know how to make risotto, you can make whatever kind of risotto you want. If you know how to braise, you can cook anything from lamb shanks to vegan chili. If you are able to get to the farmers' market, the grocery store, or your CSA pickup, go fill your basket with abandon so you can turn these random raw ingredients into delicious meals and save money. Then we have shown you how to be a rock star: Make the kitchen your stage, and get in there and own it.

Now let's get cooking.

Part II

RECIPES

Chapter Five

Basics: Cooking from the Pantry

These recipes share a theme: Whether they require fresh ingredients or pantry items, they're all recipes that can be made ahead and stored in your pantry or fridge for later use. Some of the recipes you'll find in this section will be used in whole dishes later in the book.

Stocks

Whether or not you cook frequently, there is almost no excuse for not making your own vegetable stock. A quart—a measly quart—of good, organic vegetable stock can cost as much as $4, more if you get suckered into buying "homemade": stock from a gourmet grocery store. Trickery, people.

Anytime I cook with vegetables, I either toss the scraps immediately into a saucepan with water to start stock or store the scraps in a container in the freezer until I have enough quantity and variety for a robust stock. Carrot tops and peels, onion and garlic skins, tomato cores, beet tails and skins, old whippy celery stalks, leek roots, parsnip and turnip skins, old fresh herbs, squash skins, and even apple skins or seeded cores, alone or in any combination, make a great base for vegetable stock.

BASIC VEGETABLE STOCK

Different combinations and amounts of vegetables affect the stock's flavor and color, so play around with your stock options (*har, har*); over time, you'll develop a sense of which vegetable scraps and how much of each creates the stock you like best.

Makes about 1 quart

Tops and peels of 4 to 6 carrots	**1 to 2 tomato cores**
1 to 2 stalks celery	**Old whole fresh herbs**
1 to 2 onion skins	**A bay leaf or two**
Small handful of garlic skins	**Pinch of whole peppercorns**

1. Combine everything in a large pot.

2. Add water to cover by 2 inches and bring to a boil over high heat.

3. Immediately turn the heat down to low and simmer, uncovered, for at least 30 minutes but as long as 2 hours, skimming off any impurities or foam that forms on the top. The longer the stock simmers, the more intense the flavor will be.

4. Remove from the heat and let the stock cool for a few minutes. Remove the scraps and strain the stock through a fine-mesh strainer or colander lined with two layers of cheesecloth or paper towels into heatproof containers. Use right away or keep in an airtight container in the refrigerator for up to 1 week or in the freezer for up to 2 months.

MEAT STOCK

Whereas vegetable stock cooks fairly quickly, meat-based stocks require more patience. But it's largely inactive time, and a great way to spend a winter Sunday.

You can start with plain water, vegetable stock, or a mix of water, vegetable scraps, and meat scraps. This is a perfect way to get the last little bits of flavor out of bones.

"Meat" here is a catchall for whatever stock you are aiming to make: Chicken, beef, veal, pork, or lamb scraps all make hearty stocks that can complement and lift the flavor of many dishes. Where you see Meat Stock as an ingredient throughout the book, plan to use a stock that matches that dish's main protein: lamb stock for the Lamb Shanks (page 178), pork stock for the Golabki (page 185), and so on. You can also use vegetable, chicken, or beef stock in any recipe.

1 pound meat scraps (pork, chicken, lamb, veal, or beef), including bones, trimmed of fat

2 bay leaves

1 teaspoon whole peppercorns

2 to 3 cups vegetable scraps, if not using vegetable stock

Basic Vegetable Stock (opposite page) or water

1. Combine all the ingredients in a large pot, adding vegetable stock or water to cover by 2 inches. Bring to a boil over high heat, then immediately turn the heat down to low and simmer, uncovered, for at least 4 hours but as long as 8 hours, checking every 30 minutes or so to make sure the stock maintains a gentle simmer and skimming the surface of foam as needed (but do not stir). Keep a smaller saucepan of water at a gentle steam on a back burner to replenish the stock as needed.

2. Remove from the heat and let the stock cool for a few minutes. Remove the bones and vegetable scraps (compost!) and strain the stock through a fine-

mesh strainer or colander lined with two layers of cheesecloth or paper towels into heatproof containers.

3. Set the containers of stock in your sink, plug the sink, and pour in cold water and ice around the containers to rapidly cool the stock. When the stock is room temperature, refrigerate it overnight. The next day, remove the solidified fat from the surface of the stock. Strain again if needed. The stock will keep in an airtight container in the refrigerator for up to 1 week or up to 2 months in the freezer. Before using, bring to a boil for 2 minutes.

Jar It!: Sauces, Dressings, Condiments, and Pestos

I have a bone to pick with store-bought sauces and dressings. From pasta sauce to Caesar dressing, it's all a smoke-and-mirrors game, a food Ponzi scheme. A jar of roasted-garlic-and-basil sauce for $5 seems reasonable when we're in a hurry, but it doesn't take long for the doors of our fridges to overflow with as much as $40 worth of jars and tubs of sauces, condiments, and dressings used once and then forgotten until rediscovered a month or so later, lids unappetizingly gummed with dried-out residue. The wasted money is a shame in and of itself, but adding insult to injury is the fact that most of these sauces can be made in about five minutes using items you probably already have in your house (the exceptions being Bolognese Sauce, page 39, and Cole's Sriracha, page 183).

A decent olive oil, a bottle of balsamic vinegar, mustard, a lemon, a clove of garlic: these five ingredients alone can create almost as many dressings. A bottle of cider vinegar and an egg yolk give you at least three more recipes. Sriracha and mayonnaise—both of which you can make yourself—increase the possibilities further.

Likewise, a good sauce or dip can be a beginner or hurried cook's salvation. When your hand is either too heavy or too light with the seasoning or a piece of meat is just on this side of overcooked, a grassy pesto or smoky aioli can buy you wiggle room. Dips, pestos, and sauces can also help you plan ahead, cook in bulk, and make interesting use of leftovers.

For example: Roast or grill a giant batch of vegetables. Toss tonight's portion with an aioli of roasted garlic mashed with olive oil. Tomorrow, pack cold leftover roasted vegetables into a sandwich with a generous dollop of tzatziki or Chipotle Dipping Sauce (page 221). For dinner, boil up some tagliatelle and toss the remaining vegetables and pasta with an herby pesto.

If you've made your lasagna with jarred tomato sauce all your life, next time try it with either my Basic Tomato Sauce (page 37) or Bolognese Sauce (page 39). The result, I hope, will be the best lasagna you've ever tasted—until you try Almost Completely Homemade Lasagna (page 159).

In other words, a good sauce, dressing, or pesto is another weapon in your home-cooking arsenal.

BASIC TOMATO SAUCE

This is a simple tomato sauce recipe that you can alter and add to depending on the dish. Adding finely diced carrots with the onions will make for a slightly sweeter sauce; stewing mushrooms, carrots, and celery into the sauce will create a ragu; and a little chile powder, cinnamon, and ginger transforms it into an Indian-style sauce.

PANTRY OR PRODUCE STAND?

Believe it or not, boxed, canned, or jarred whole or chopped tomatoes, packed in their juice and unseasoned, are the perfect base for tomato sauce no matter the season. If you prefer to use fresh tomatoes, only use them in season and use plum (Roma) tomatoes—no need for pricey heirlooms when you're just cooking them down. Figure an extra pound of fresh tomatoes per two pounds of boxed, canned, or jarred.

Makes 1 quart

One 26-ounce box or 28-ounce can whole or diced tomatoes, in their juice, or 2 to 3 pounds fresh plum (Roma) tomatoes

3 tablespoons olive oil

½ medium onion, diced

1 clove garlic, minced

1 tablespoon (a generous pinch) torn or chopped fresh basil leaves

Salt and freshly ground black pepper

1. If you're using fresh tomatoes, core them and set the cores aside in a bowl. Quarter or roughly chop the tomatoes.

2. In a medium heavy, nonreactive saucepan or Dutch oven, heat the oil over medium heat. Add the onion and sauté, stirring occasionally, until lightly browned, 8 to 10 minutes. Add the garlic and sauté for another minute, or until fragrant.

3. Add the tomatoes and their juice. If you're using fresh tomatoes, squeeze the reserved cores over the pot to extract as much juice as possible.

PRICE BOX

Tomatoes: $2.50 to $6, depending on whether you use packaged or fresh

Onion and garlic: 80¢

Basil: 50¢

Total price: $3.80 to $7.30

4. Bring to a simmer, then turn the heat down to low. Cook, stirring occasionally to prevent the bottom from scorching, for about 45 minutes. Gentle pressure with the back of a wooden spoon against larger chunks of tomato will help break them apart.

5. Add the basil and cook for another 2 to 3 minutes. Season with salt and pepper.

6. Remove the sauce from the heat. It can be served as is, or you may puree it in a food mill or blender in batches, or with an immersion blender. If not using right away, let cool completely, then refrigerate in an airtight container for up to 1 week or in the freezer for up to 2 months.

BOLOGNESE SAUCE

It used to seem strange to me that Bolognese is a sauce and not . . . well, what? A braise? A stew? Nearly a confit? Even without pasta, Bolognese is practically a meal unto itself, like chili or a stately Italian version of sloppy Joe sandwich filling. But it is a sauce, and a beautiful one at that.

If your farmers' market or butcher's counter doesn't offer the ground beef, pork, or veal this recipe calls for, you can use stew meat: just trim it carefully and chop it into the smallest uniform chunks you can manage when you get it home.

Unlike braises or stews (aha!), the vegetables used in Bolognese should be invisible in the final dish. You could cook them down in olive oil for hours, but the most efficient way to "melt" the vegetables into a decadent *soffrito,* or thick paste, is to pulse them in a food processor until they're a colorful pulp. It may seem strange and look unappetizing at first, but the result is a sauce that is lightly vegetal but not overly chunky.

Makes 2 quarts, or more than enough for a 10-serving lasagna

1 cup finely diced pancetta or thick slab bacon

¾ pound ground pork

¾ pound ground veal

½ pound ground beef (short rib or brisket, if possible)

1 carrot

1 stalk celery

3 cloves garlic

½ small yellow onion

Leaves of ¼ bunch flat-leaf parsley

2 tablespoons extra virgin olive oil

Salt and freshly ground black pepper

1 teaspoon tomato paste

¾ cup red wine

1 cup Basic Vegetable Stock (page 34) or Meat Stock (page 35), plus more if needed

¼ cup milk

1. Before you do anything else, take all of the meat out of the fridge and let it come to room temperature.

2. Roughly chop all the vegetables and pulse them in the food processor: Put the carrot, celery, and garlic in the processor and pulse; add the onion and pulse; then add the parsley and pulse for just a few seconds. The vegetables should be very, very finely chopped but not an indistinguishable slop.

3. Heat the oil in a large pot over medium heat. When the oil is shiny with heat, add the pancetta or bacon and render it, 3 to 5 minutes. Remove it with a slotted spoon to a plate. Add the ground meats, season with salt and pepper, and cook, stirring occasionally to break up the larger lumps, until there's no pink left on the surface area, about 6 minutes. Don't crowd the pot; if the meat doesn't fit nicely, brown it in batches.

4. Remove the meat with the slotted spoon and add the tomato paste to the fat in the pot. Scrape it around for a minute, then deglaze with the red wine, removing any browned bits from the bottom of the pot. Bring to a boil, then reduce the heat and simmer until the wine is reduced by half, about 5 minutes.

5. Return the ground meat and bacon to the pan and add the chopped vegetables and stock. Reduce the heat to low and cook for at least 1 hour but as long as 6 hours, stirring occasionally to keep it from sticking, until the Bolognese is thick but loose with a shiny surface. Do not allow the sauce to boil. If the Bolognese gets too dry, add more stock in ½-cup increments.

6. Stir in the milk and turn off the heat.

PRICE BOX

Pancetta or bacon: $3
Pork: $4
Veal: $5.25
Beef: $4.25
Carrot: 30¢
Celery: 25¢
Garlic and onion: $1.00
Parsley: 25¢
Red wine: $1.50
Milk: 15¢

Total price: $19.95; per person: about $2.00

7. You may serve the Bolognese right away, but it's best if left to its devices in the refrigerator overnight so the ingredients may become even closer friends. If you're serving it over tagliatelle (long, flat ribbons of egg pasta), reheat the Bolognese in a wide pan over low heat before tossing in the pasta; for lasagna, let the Bolognese come to room temperature before layering it in.

BASIC VINAIGRETTE

This is not a recipe, really, or even a method; it's just a ratio. Once you know that, you can whip together a vinaigrette at anyone's house, with any kind of vinegar. Well, almost any kind of vinegar; the exception is distilled white vinegar, which would not make a tasty vinaigrette. In its place, though, we have lemon juice, which you can pretend is a vinegar for our purposes here.

Makes 1 tablespoon or more, depending on ingredient amounts

1 part vinegar or vinegar blend (balsamic, red wine, white wine, cider, sherry, rice, seasoned, or lemon juice)

3 parts oil or oil blend (extra virgin olive oil, virgin olive oil, nut oil, squash or pumpkin seed oil, vegetable oil, grapeseed oil, peanut oil, sesame oil, etc.)

Pinch of fine sea salt and a few grinds of black pepper

Garlic and minced fresh herbs to taste

1. Whisk the oil(s) into the vinegar(s) in a slow, steady drizzle. Season with the salt and pepper. Serve immediately or refrigerate, then whisk again before serving.

2. To this basic ratio you can add minced garlic (about half as much garlic as vinegar). Minced fresh herbs can be added just prior to serving.

KETCHUP

Look, guys. I'm from Pittsburgh—the home of Heinz. To me, ketchup *is* the 57 blend, no substitutions allowed. But when my friend and frequent *Working Class Foodies* cohost Chef Brendan McDermott and I were planning our "Condiments" episode, I knew we couldn't skip the king of condiments. Brendan assured me his ketchup recipe was good. All I knew was that we had to do a ketchup, so we'd do it, and that would be that.

Except that wasn't that. Because the ketchup we made? It was *delicious*. I mean, it's different from what I grew up on, but way better than any other ketchup or catsup or sweetened-up tomato paste anyone's ever tried to pass off on me. It's like football: I'm never *not* going to root for the Steelers, but if they can't make the Super Bowl every year, then at least maybe the Giants can. That's what this homemade ketchup is for me: the only acceptable alternative.

Makes about 2 cups

1 to 2 tablespoons canola oil

2 shallots, minced

1 clove garlic, minced

2 generous pinches of salt

2 tablespoons white wine vinegar or cider vinegar

1 to 2 tablespoons brown sugar

2 cups chopped tomatoes with juice (I recommend Pomi boxed tomatoes)

1. Heat the oil in a medium saucepan over medium heat. Add the shallots, garlic, and salt and cook just until the shallots and garlic start to go from translucent to browning, about 3 minutes. Add the vinegar and deglaze, stirring to release any browned bits from the bottom of the pan. Stir in the brown sugar until dissolved, then add the tomatoes.

2. Let everything cook down without boiling, about 10 minutes, stirring frequently to keep the bottom from scorching. Taste, and when the tomatoes have lost their acid, take the ketchup off the heat and buzz it to a fine consistency with an immersion blender or by the cupful in a blender or food processor.

PRICE BOX

Shallots: $1
Tomatoes: $1.45

Total price: $2.45

3. Let the ketchup cool completely, then give it a second buzz to puree any remaining chunks. Refrigerate for up to 1 week in a tightly lidded container.

MAYONNAISE

A basic emulsion of fat and acid, homemade mayonnaise is a beautiful thing and a bit of an eye-opener for anyone who's only ever had the viscous jarred stuff. Homemade mayo can be a little tricky the first time you attempt it, but the result is a light, fluffy spread that just begs to be flavored with everything from tarragon to Sriracha to roasted garlic.

Use a neutral oil or pure olive oil (not extra virgin—you need a refined oil to prevent separation in the fridge). It's also important to use the freshest eggs, as fresher egg yolks have higher concentrations of lecithin, the protein that creates and holds the emulsion between the fat of the oil and the acid of the lemon.

But what about salmonella? Salmonella is found in the whites of eggs, not the yolks; besides that, the lemon juice in the mayo will enzymatically "cook" the yolks. But if you're still concerned, you can use pasteurized eggs.

Makes about 3 cups

2 to 3 large egg yolks (see Note)

Generous pinch of fine sea salt

Juice of 1 lemon

1 to 2 teaspoons smooth mustard

2 cups canola, grapeseed, or pure olive oil

¼ cup water, if needed

1. Bring all your ingredients to room temperature.

2. Whip 2 egg yolks in a blender; add the salt, lemon juice, and mustard and whip until creamy. With the blender on high speed, add the oil in a very slow, thin stream—just a little at a time: Whip in some oil, whip whip whip whip in some more oil, whip whip whip; and repeat until all the oil's in. Otherwise it won't emulsify; if you try to add too much oil too quickly, the emulsion will break. And once it breaks, it can't be reconstituted.

PRICE BOX

Eggs: 75¢

Oil: $2.40

Lemon: 65¢

Total price: $3.80

3. The mayonnaise will thicken as it sits, so if it already seems thick after emulsifying, whip in ¼ cup water in a thin, slow stream.

4. Store the mayonnaise in a jar with a clean, tight-fitting lid in the refrigerator for up to 1 week.

Note: If you're worried the emulsion will break, add an extra egg yolk. Extra yolk equals extra lecithin equals extra protein bridges for the emulsion.

EGG WHITES

You can save the egg whites for making egg white omelets or use them to make meringue cookies by whipping them until foamy in a clean metal or glass bowl and slowly whipping in ¼ cup powdered sugar for each egg white and ½ teaspoon baking powder.

Preheat the oven to 250°F. Lightly butter and flour a baking sheet or line it with parchment paper or a silicone mat.

Wipe white vinegar around a clean glass or metal mixing bowl. Add the egg whites to the bowl and whip until foamy with an electric mixer. Slowly whip in the sugar and baking powder and beat until the mixture forms stiff peaks.

Gently spoon the meringue out onto your baking sheet in a 9-inch circle, or pipe into little circles through a plastic bag with the tip cut off. Bake for 1 hour and then let rest in the oven for another 2 to 3 hours to dry out. Let cool completely, then store until ready to use.

PEANUT BUTTER

I like to add a good shot of honey to my peanut butter. Using unsalted roasted nuts allows you to adjust the saltiness of the peanut butter to your liking. Use a mixture of nuts if you like, and add cinnamon, cocoa powder, or vanilla for a flavored nut butter.

Makes a little over 2 cups

1 pound shelled, roasted peanuts

1 to 2 tablespoons honey, maple syrup, or agave nectar (optional)

1 teaspoon kosher salt (or 2 teaspoons for unsalted nuts), plus more if needed

2 to 3 tablespoons neutral oil, preferably peanut or grapeseed oil

1. In the bowl of a food processor, pulse together the peanuts, honey, and salt for about 1 minute. Scrape down the sides of the bowl and add the oil in a thin, slow drizzle through the hole in the lid, processing until smooth. Taste and add more salt if needed.

2. Store in an airtight container in the refrigerator for up to 2 months, stirring before using if it separates.

PRICE BOX

Peanuts: $4

Total price: $4

INDONESIAN-STYLE PEANUT SAUCE

Perfect as a dip for raw vegetables, a marinade for chicken, or a sauce for noodles or grilled vegetables. It doubles or quadruples easily.

Makes about 1½ cups

3 cloves garlic, finely minced

½ cup finely minced scallions

½ cup soy sauce

½ cup rice vinegar

2 teaspoons honey or agave nectar

½ cup Peanut Butter (page 45)

1 to 1½ tablespoons hot chile sesame oil

1 tablespoon toasted sesame oil

1 teaspoon Worcestershire sauce (vegetarians can substitute miso paste)

Pinch of crushed red pepper flakes

Whisk all the ingredients together in a medium bowl or in the bowl of a standing mixer. Taste and adjust the seasoning; a little extra sesame oil doesn't hurt. Cover and refrigerate for up to 1 week.

Basic Grains

If you know how to make polenta and risotto, dinner's never out of reach. With as little as some water, salt and pepper, and an onion, you've got the basis for a slightly boring but completely filling meal (some cheese, homemade veggie stock, and fresh herbs will only improve things).

And for those nights when you don't have the time to cook polenta or risotto, you'll be glad to have homemade pasta in the freezer. If you've never made pasta before, it can seem daunt-

PRICE BOX

Garlic: 75¢

Scallions: $1.50

Soy sauce: 75¢

Rice vinegar: $1

Peanut butter: $1.20 (or 50¢ if homemade)

Total price: $4.50 with homemade peanut butter, $5.20 with store-bought

ing, but it's actually quite easy (if a little messy). Toss your fresh pasta with a little flour and pack it in your freezer in an airtight container; your frozen pasta can then go straight into boiling water and onto your dinner plate in about three minutes because fresh pasta, even when frozen, cooks in about one third the time of dry pasta.

Not everyone has the time or inclination to make their own bread, but I encourage anyone who routinely buys costly loaves of organic, whole wheat, multigrain, seeded bread to give baking their own a try. The recipe on page 54 will show you the ropes; after that, consider playing with the types and amounts of flours, grains, and seeds for different flavors, textures, and nutrients.

POLENTA OR GRITS?

Polenta and grits are essentially the same thing: coarse cornmeal. Generally polenta is made from yellow corn and grits from white corn, but they are otherwise completely interchangeable.

POLENTA

Polenta is as democratic as it is affordable: You can make it with chicken stock, milk and butter, vegetable stock, or water; serve it wet as porridge or bake, fry, or grill it in slabs or cakes; serve it sweet with maple syrup, cinnamon, and currants, or as an herb-flecked bed for vegetables, poached eggs, or a rich meat stew.

Serves 8 as a side or 3 or 4 as a main

5 cups water, Basic Vegetable Stock (page 34), or Meat Stock (page 35), plus more as needed

Kosher salt

1¾ cups polenta, preferably coarse-ground

½ cup heavy cream or milk

Freshly ground black pepper

1. Bring the water or stock to a boil in a heavy-bottomed pot or Dutch oven over high heat and season with salt.

2. Add the polenta in a steady stream, whisking constantly. Turn the heat down and cook at a simmer, stirring often with a wooden spoon, until done, 30 to 45 minutes, depending on how coarse the polenta is. The polenta will bubble and spit as it cooks and will pull away from the sides of your saucepan when it's done. After 30 minutes, start tasting frequently (carefully—it's hot!) for doneness. If the polenta starts to stick to the bottom of the pot, add more water or stock in ¼-cup increments.

3. Keep cooking to your desired doneness and consistency: You can keep cooking the polenta as long as you keep adding liquid. Loose polenta should coat the back of your spoon; thicker polenta should hold its shape in the bowl of the spoon without dripping out. Finish the polenta by stirring in the cream. Season with salt and pepper; you'll need more than you think, as polenta is a bit of a seasoning black hole. Omit the pepper and halve the amount of salt if you intend to use your polenta for a sweet breakfast.

4. Eat right away, or, while the polenta is still hot, prepare it for storing in the fridge: Pour it into a container or bowl or pour and gently smooth it into a buttered baking dish for baking later. Cover and refrigerate the polenta until you're ready to use it, for up to 1 week.

PRICE BOX

Polenta: 50¢ to 75¢
Cream or milk: 50¢ to $2.50
(local cream costs a lot more than local milk)

Total price: $1 to $3.25;
per person: 13¢ to 41¢ (side),
33¢ to $1.08 (main)

IDEAS FOR COOKING POLENTA

The beauty of this basic polenta is its plainness: Think of it as a blank canvas for your favorite combinations, which can be served either on top of the polenta or mixed in, as you see fit (and depending on the polenta's thickness). In addition to the three recipes noted above, here's a list of just a few ways I like to fancy up my basic polenta, regardless of its thickness:

Topped with Basic Tomato Sauce (page 37) or Bolognese Sauce (page 39) with mozzarella and fresh basil

Topped with roasted corn and poblano peppers, scallions, and cheddar or Jack cheese

Topped with black beans, chorizo, cilantro, and sour cream

Topped with shredded leftover short ribs (page 192) and caramelized onions

Topped with chopped-up leftover Rustic Ratatouille (page 175) and mozzarella

Topped with white beans or chickpeas with garlic, rosemary, and thyme

As a bed for braised lamb shanks (page 178) with a red wine reduction

Drizzled with honey or maple syrup and with a dollop of Homemade Ricotta (page 59) for a sweet breakfast

Topped with chopped apple or pear, drizzled with honey, and dusted with cinnamon as a sweet breakfast

Topped with chopped olives, olive oil, and burrata cheese

Sprinkled with cheddar, Gruyère, or whatever your favorite cheese is, and plenty of it

BASIC RISOTTO

With rich stock, white wine, onion, butter, salt, and Parmesan, my Basic Risotto is a comforting side or meal. Fold in anything from fresh thyme to spring peas or shredded chicken for a heartier meal; or continue to Asparagus Risotto with Lemon (page 168), Roasted Root Vegetable Risotto (page 170), or Pancetta, Squash, and Shallot Risotto (page 172).

Not using white wine? No problem, just replace with the equivalent amount of stock.

Serves 4 to 6

3 cups Basic Vegetable Stock (page 34) or Meat Stock (use chicken; page 35)

2 tablespoons extra virgin olive oil

½ medium onion, minced

1 cup Arborio rice

1 cup dry white wine

1 tablespoon unsalted butter

¼ cup grated Parmesan or pecorino cheese

Kosher salt and freshly ground black pepper

1. In a medium saucepan, bring the stock and wine to a low simmer and maintain it.

2. Heat the oil in a large, high-sided sauté pan over medium heat. Sweat the onion until soft and translucent but not browned, 6 to 8 minutes.

3. Fold the rice into the onion and cook, stirring, for 2 to 3 minutes, until the pan is dry and the rice gives a toasted aroma.

PRICE BOX

Arborio rice: $1.50
White wine: $1 to $2
Parmesan or pecorino cheese: 75¢

Total price: $3.25 to $4.25;
per person: 54¢ to $1.06

4. Ladle some stock into the rice and cook, stirring constantly, until the rice has absorbed the stock. Continue this process, letting the rice absorb all the liquid before adding more and tasting frequently, until the dish is creamy and rich and the rice grains are tender with a pleasant chew. Remove from the heat and fold in the butter and Parmesan. Taste and adjust the seasoning with salt and pepper and serve immediately.

BASIC PASTA DOUGH

00 flour is a very lightweight flour with good elasticity. It can be hard to find and costly, so you may wish to use all-purpose flour, which will make for a heavier but perfectly fine pasta. The Brooklyn Kitchen in Brooklyn carries 00 flour, or you can order it online from KingArthurFlour.com.

Makes enough for 4 to 6 servings

2½ cups 00 flour or all-purpose flour

2 large eggs

1 tablespoon extra virgin olive oil

¼ cup water

1. Make a mound with the flour on a board (you can use a large bowl to start if you don't want to get flour everywhere) and form a well in the center deep enough to fit the eggs and oil. Make sure the sides are tall enough to hold the eggs or it will spill all over your table.

2. Add the eggs and oil to the well in the flour. Using a fork, whisk the eggs and oil together as if you were making scrambled eggs. As you whisk, begin to incorporate the outside walls of the flour, slowly transforming this mess on your board (or in your bowl) into a dough.

3. Once you've got about one third of the flour mixed into the eggs and it's starting to look like pancake batter, slowly add the water. Keep mixing in the

flour. When the mixture returns to the pancake batter consistency again, scrape in the rest of the flour with your hands or, ideally, a bench scraper. Fold together; the dough should take on a flaky consistency.

4. Now begin to gently knead the dough. Push down with the palm of your hand and fold over. Repeat. Do this for 8 to 10 minutes; this is important for developing the gluten in your dough, which will give it a nice chewy texture. Don't try to force the dough to take more flour than it wants to take; it will absorb as much flour as it needs. If the dough is too wet, you can add more flour little by little, but don't let it become dry and crumbly.

5. After kneading for 10 minutes, your dough should be solid and smooth. Wrap it tightly in plastic wrap and leave it to rest at room temperature for about 15 minutes.

6. When you unwrap your dough, you'll notice it has become smoother and more elastic in texture. From here, the sky's the limit for all the pastas you can form, from simple linguine to decadent raviolis (Ricotta Ravioli in Brown Butter with Sage, page 152; Beet Ravioli in Lemon Butter, page 155) to hearty lasagna (Lasagna with Bolognese, page 159). It all starts here.

PRICE BOX

Flour: 50¢ to $1.25
Eggs: 75¢

Total price: $1.25 to $2.50; per person: 21¢ to 62¢

Baking Basics

If you're still hesitant to try bread baking, let me appeal to your practicality: Making a basic bread or flatbread won't cost you more than $2. A loaf of bread or package of flatbreads at the store will run you at least $2.50. Simple economics says give it a shot. The only thing you have to lose is a couple of cups of flour.

Unless, of course, like me, you become a bread-baking fiend and find it next to impossible to stop baking. There is that slight risk. But it's a risk worth taking.

True, even the natural baker's first few loaves may be dense, misshapen things, but that's one of bread's charms: The heaviest, most rustic loaf can still make excellent sandwiches. Or, at least, breadcrumbs.

Even with just all-purpose flour you can make pretty excellent bread. But play with different flours: Go half all-purpose, half whole wheat. Compare all-purpose bread to bread made with bread flour. Throw in some rye flour or buckwheat flour. Sprinkle whole grains and seeds into your dough. Mix in chopped nuts and dried fruits, chocolate, herbs, garlic, olives, cheese. Don't be afraid to experiment wildly and freely; even if one of your crazier breads doesn't turn out, you're only out the cost of some very basic and affordable pantry items.

As far as *how* to bake your bread, I follow the advice of New York's unofficial bread guru, Jim Lahey, he of the famed "no-knead" method. Lahey suggests that the best way to replicate the sealed-in, steam-friendly heat of a traditional domed brick oven is to preheat a large ovenproof pot in your oven and bake the bread in that. Use the largest cast-iron, ceramic, or enameled steel Dutch oven you own. Preheat the lid too, but take notice of the lid's handle: If it's the sort that screws into the lid rather than one that is forged on, it may not be able to withstand the high heat of the oven required for baking bread. If that's the case, slide your raw dough onto a preheated baking stone and, carefully, with pot holders, invert your preheated Dutch oven over the bread to approximate Lahey's "oven within an oven."

BASIC WHOLE WHEAT/WHITE BLEND BREAD

My basic bread recipe is a blend of whole wheat and unbleached white bread flour; the white bread flour gives the loaf a lightness and elasticity and helps it to rise, while the whole wheat gives it a toasty, nutty flavor in the character of fire-baked artisan bread.

Makes 1 large loaf

1 cup warm (100 to 110°F) water

1 packet (2¼ teaspoons) active dry yeast

1 tablespoon honey

2½ cups bread flour

½ to 1 cup whole wheat flour

2 teaspoons fine sea salt

All-purpose flour for dusting

1 tablespoon extra virgin olive oil

1. In a small bowl, stir together the water, yeast, and honey and let proof until the mixture has formed a puffy "crown." Meanwhile, combine the bread flour, ½ cup of the whole wheat flour, and the salt in a large bowl.

2. Using your hands or a wooden spoon, stir the proofed yeast and liquid into the flour until a sticky dough forms and pulls away from the sides of the bowl. Knead in the bowl for 2 minutes, adding more whole wheat flour in ¼-cup increments until the dough won't take any more. Take note of how much whole wheat flour you added in total so you can decide how much of it you like in your bread.

3. Dust a clean work surface with all-purpose flour and turn the dough out onto it; let the dough rest for a couple minutes. Meanwhile, clean and dry the large bowl, then wipe it with the oil and set aside.

4. Dry and flour your hands and knead the dough gently using the heels of your palms to push it away from you, then fold the edges back toward the center.

Repeat pushing and folding for 5 to 7 minutes, until the dough is smooth and silky. Then fold all the edges toward the center, tuck the dough into a tight ball, and roll it around in the oiled bowl to lightly coat it. Place the dough seam-side-down in the bowl. Drape a dishcloth over the bowl and let it rest in a warm spot for 1½ to 2 hours, until doubled in size.

5. Carefully scrape the dough out of the bowl in one piece back onto your floured surface. Gently punch the dough down and fold it in on itself again, forming it into a tight ball. Place it back in the bowl, seam-side-down, and cover. Let rise for another 30 to 60 minutes.

6. While the dough completes its second rise, preheat the oven to 475°F. If you are going to use a baking stone, set it on the bottom of your oven (for a gas oven) or on a rack positioned in the lower third of an electric oven. Place an ovenproof pot on the middle rack.

7. If using a pot with a lid, remove it from the oven using pot holders. Dust the surface of the dough with flour and carefully invert it into the pot (remember—the pot will be very hot). Pop the lid on the pot and return the pot to the oven. If you aren't using the pot's lid, generously flour a pizza peel. Place your dough seam-side-down on the peel and slide the dough into the oven. Using pot holders, carefully invert the pot over the dough.

8. Bake the bread for 30 minutes, then uncover and bake for another 20 to 30 minutes, until the crust is a deep brown. You can also test the bread by giving it a tap on the bottom: If it sounds hollow, it's good to go.

9. Carefully move the bread to a cooling rack. Resist the urge to break into it right away and let it cool for 30 to 60 minutes, until it's just warmer than room temperature.

PRICE BOX

Yeast: $1
Bread flour: 55¢
Whole wheat flour: 12¢ to 44¢

Total price: $1.67 to $1.99

PÂTE BRISÉE (ALL-BUTTER PIE CRUST) FOR SWEET AND SAVORY DISHES

This is my go-to, as-failproof-as-it-gets recipe for pie crust. Mix it quickly, knead it gently, and give it time to rest in the refrigerator before you roll it out and I bet it will become your go-to pie crust too.

Makes two 9-inch pie crusts

2 cups all-purpose flour, plus more for the work surface

1 tablespoon sugar (or 1 teaspoon sugar for savory crusts)

1 teaspoon salt

1 cup (2 sticks) cold unsalted butter, cubed

1 large egg, plus 1 egg, beaten, for egg wash

1½ tablespoons milk

1 tablespoon vanilla extract

1. Whisk together the flour, sugar, and salt in a large bowl. Work the butter in with your fingers or by pulsing in quick bursts in a food processor until the mixture forms pea-size crumbs. Whisk together 1 egg, the milk, and vanilla in a separate bowl and work into the flour-butter mixture just until the dough comes together.

> **PRICE BOX**
>
> Flour: 50¢ to $1
> Butter: $3.15 to $4.70
>
> Total price: $3.65 to $5.70; per slice of double-crust pie: 46¢ to 71¢

2. Knead the dough gently and briefly on a clean, floured work surface. Then divide the dough in half and form each half into a ball; wrap the balls tightly in plastic wrap. Refrigerate for at least 30 minutes or up to 2 days; store in the freezer for up to 1 week if you're not using it within 2 days.

3. Soften the dough a little by letting it rest on the counter for about 15 minutes before rolling it out.

PLAY (WITH YOUR) DOUGH

I love using buckwheat flour in pie crusts because it has an earthy, nutty, subtly sourdough-like flavor, a gorgeous rustic beige color, and no gluten. Because buckwheat flour is gluten-free, it's a great flour to use if you're just learning how to make pie crusts from scratch. It's easy to overwork a pie dough the first few times, resulting in a dry, tough, unpleasant pie crust. In a normal pie dough, gluten giveth elasticity; when a pie dough is overworked, though, that same gluten taketh away the elasticity. So blending a gluten-free flour like buckwheat with gluten-containing all-purpose flour gives you a little (but just a little) room for error. Take it. Use it until you're comfortable enough with your dough-kneading skills to give all-purpose another shot.

If you're not gluten-free, try a 50-50 blend of buckwheat and all-purpose flour in your next crust. It's amazing with quiches and, with a little sugar, is an excellent crust for apple pie.

Spoiler Alert: Two Seemingly Random Recipes Using Food with a Short Shelf Life

Herb butter is a great way to give wilted or drying herbs one last chance—especially useful for those who are going to start that window garden next weekend, dammit, and are dropping $5 on fresh herbs just this one last time.

And, okay—ricotta isn't really a way to preserve milk, but good fresh ricotta ain't cheap and homemade ricotta is a good way to use up (a lot of) extra milk. Besides that, it's ridiculously delicious and may change your life. I'm serious.

HERB BUTTER

I hate when food goes bad because I didn't get to it in time. This is most aggravating with herbs: Outside of pesto, it's always a challenge for me to use an entire bunch of herbs before they wilt into compost. Even when you grow your own herbs, sometimes you can end up with more than you know what to do with. And this is when you make herb butter.

You can use any herbs, alone or in combination. Finely mince them for a super-smooth butter and fully integrated flavor, or leave them roughly chopped for a more rustic spread and individual pops of flavor: chive here, tarragon there.

Now that you've made yourself a little pot of herb butter, what to do with it? Heap it on thick bread and broil for a uniquely flavored garlic bread; toss it with hot pasta and Parmesan for a quick dinner, or with just-cooked fish and shellfish; slip a pat of it into a baked potato or on grilled or roasted vegetables or steak; spread it on toast with thinly sliced radishes and good flaky sea salt; or add a smidge to a fried egg still in the pan, just after you kill the heat.

Makes 1 cup

1 cup (2 sticks) unsalted butter, softened

Fine sea salt

1 clove garlic, finely minced

¼ cup minced or chopped fresh herbs (a single herb or combination)

In a medium bowl, cream the butter with salt and fold in the garlic and herbs. Use immediately or store in an airtight container for up to 2 weeks.

PRICE BOX

Butter: $3.15 to $4.70
Herbs: $1

Total price: $4.15 to $5.70

HOMEMADE RICOTTA

A quart of ricotta will keep for a week and can be an integral part of break-fasts, lunches, dinners, and even desserts.

Homemade ricotta, even made with skim milk, is creamy and smooth; using milk from pasture-raised cows will give the cheese a subtle and soft grassy flavor—a far cry from the bland and often grainy mass-produced ricotta. Combining milks of varied fattiness—a gallon of 2% and ¾ cup heavy cream is my go-to—will yield different flavors and textures. Experiment to figure out which combination of milks you like best.

Season your ricotta lightly with sea salt and white pepper for a basic soft cheese, perfect for lasagna; spike it with roasted garlic, caramelized onions, and fresh thyme for a decadent, thick onion dip; season with lemon zest, pecorino, and fresh herbs as a filling for ravioli; or make it the base for the best Italian cheesecake you've ever had.

Whether you curdle your whey once or twice, consider saving it: The lightly flavored liquid can be used for boiling pasta, as a base for soups, or steaming or boiling vegetables.

You can use a candy thermometer to monitor the milk's temperature, but I've found that it's not necessary. You want the milk at a hard simmer, just before boiling; this you can eyeball. On a thermometer, you want the milk to be at least 185°F and no higher than 200°F.

Makes 1 heaping quart; about 8 servings

1 gallon milk

¾ cup heavy cream

⅓ cup plus 2 tablespoons distilled white vinegar

1 tablespoon kosher salt

1. Rinse a large, nonreactive stockpot with cold water (this will help keep the milk from scorching). Pour in the milk and cream and stir together. Heat over medium-high heat, stirring occasionally, until the milk comes to a simmer, then remove it from the heat and gently stir in the vinegar and salt for 1 minute. Let rest, uncovered, for 5 to 8 minutes while the curds form.

2. Meanwhile, dampen a piece of cheesecloth in cool water and line a colander or mesh strainer with it. Set over a large bowl. Ladle the ricotta into the cheesecloth with a slotted spoon to drain; you may have to do this in batches depending on the size of your colander/strainer.

3. The longer you drain the ricotta, the firmer it will be; drain just a few minutes for very soft ricotta or 2 hours to overnight (in the fridge) for very firm cheese. I like to reserve some of the whey for storing the ricotta to keep it from drying out in the fridge. It will keep refrigerated for up to 1 week.

PRICE BOX

Milk: $4 to $8
Cream: $1.75

Total price: $5.75 to $9.75; per person: 72¢ to $1.22

WHAT'S IN A NAME?

Technically, this is "ricotta" because the milk has been curdled only once; to make true ricotta (and increase your yield), reheat the whey to a hard simmer and stir in more vinegar. Strain as above.

Chapter Six

Appetizers and Snacks

ROASTED BROCCOLI

Lemon. Parmesan. Breadcrumbs. Those three ingredients, alone or in combination, are usually enough to breathe life into a dish. Here, though, they play mere supporting roles to broccoli batons that are crisp and caramelized on the outside yet juicy and mild within. Serve broccoli this way instead of steamed and your kids might even ask for seconds—just consider omitting the crushed red pepper and possibly the lemon the first time you serve it to kids.

Serves 2 as a main or 4 as a side; double for delicious leftovers

Keep as much of the stems as possible; peel off any scarred or woody skin, then slice the broccoli into batons so each piece has both florets and stem for a textural contrast.

1 head broccoli

3 cloves garlic, thinly sliced

2 to 3 tablespoons olive oil

Good pinch of fine sea salt

Freshly cracked black pepper

1 tablespoon crushed red pepper flakes (optional)

1 tablespoon lemon zest

1 tablespoon fresh lemon juice

2 tablespoons breadcrumbs

¼ cup grated Parmesan cheese

1. Place a rimmed baking sheet in the oven and preheat to 425°F. Use 2 baking sheets for 2 heads of broccoli if you're doubling the recipe.

2. Rinse the broccoli and pat it dry. It's important that the broccoli be nice and dry or it will steam instead of caramelize. And everyone will be very, very sad.

3. Trim the woody ends off the broccoli stems and peel any tough skin, but keep as much of the stems intact as possible. Cut the broccoli into batons—a ½-inch-thick slice of stem with one or two florets attached.

4. Place the broccoli and garlic in a large bowl and toss with the oil, salt, pepper to taste, and crushed red pepper. Arrange the broccoli in an even layer on the preheated baking sheet. Make sure the broccoli doesn't overlap or it will steam instead of caramelize. And everyone will be very, very sad.

5. Roast the broccoli for about 20 minutes, tossing the pan occasionally to prevent sticking or burning. Add more oil if necessary.

6. The broccoli's done when it's just fork-tender

PRICE BOX

Broccoli: $3
Garlic: 50¢
Parmesan: 75¢

Total price, $4.25; per person: $1.06 (side), $2.13 (main)

and the florets are browned but not burnt. Transfer everything back to your big bowl; make sure to scrape all the seasoned oil and garlic off the baking sheets. Season with the lemon zest, lemon juice, and Parmesan and toss to combine. Wipe your baking sheet dry and spread the breadcrumbs on it in a single layer; return to the oven and and toast for about 5 minutes, until golden. Sprinkle the toasted breadcrumbs over the broccoli and serve.

SURPRISINGLY VEGAN "CAESAR SALAD" KALE CHIPS

Somehow olive oil, sea salt, garlic powder, and a little hot paprika make kale taste like it's coated in rich Parmesan. This is my favorite recipe for veggie chips, so much so that I have to stop myself from making a batch every night for fear of . . . what? An awesome-flavor overdose? Too much healthiness?

Makes 2 large snack portions

1 large bunch lacinato or curly kale

1 tablespoon olive oil

1½ teaspoons garlic powder

1½ teaspoons hot paprika

1 teaspoon fine sea salt

1. Place 2 rimmed baking sheets in the oven and preheat the oven to 250°F.

2. Stem the kale, saving the stems for either a slow braise in olive oil or for making stock. Wash the kale leaves by repeatedly submerging them in cold water in a large bowl, then draining until the water at the bottom of the bowl runs clear and free of dirt. Pat the kale bone dry between two clean dishtowels.

3. Remove the center ribs and tear or cut the leaves into big pieces. In a large bowl, toss the kale with the oil, garlic powder, paprika, and salt, massaging everything into the leaves with your hands.

4. Arrange the kale leaves in even layers on the baking sheet—use the second one if necessary to make sure none of the kale overlaps. Bake for 20 minutes, or until the leaves are crisp but not burnt. Let cool, then devour, or store in an airtight container for 3 to 4 days.

PRICE BOX

Kale: $2.50

Total price: $2.50; per person: $1.25

LEMON-PEPPER-POPPY BEET CHIPS

Makes 2 snack portions

1 bunch (3 or 4) golden or red beets or a mix of both

1½ teaspoons olive oil

1½ teaspoons fresh lemon juice

½ teaspoon fine sea salt

½ teaspoon cracked black pepper

½ teaspoon poppy seeds

1. Place 1 or 2 rimmed baking sheets in the oven and preheat the oven to 275°F.

2. Scrub the beets under cold running water until free of dirt. Tip and tail them so they're flat on both ends and slice them as thinly as possible into rounds (slice larger beets in half first if they're too unwieldy).

PRICE BOX

Beets: $2.50
Poppy seeds: 25¢

Total price: $2.75; per person: $1.38

3. In a large bowl, toss the beet slices with the rest of the ingredients, then arrange in a flat, even layer on the baking sheets and bake until crisp, about 15 minutes, flipping over once halfway through.

SESAME SICHUAN SNAP PEAS

The first time I ate a Sichuan peppercorn, which looks like a tiny shriveled brown grape, I thought something was wrong. The taste was fine, even interesting: tangy and heated, a little citrusy, but not traditionally peppery. And then my tongue went numb. Thinking I had burnt my taste buds on a chile pepper, I chugged my water; slowly, the numb sensation went away. But after a few bites—and another Sichuan peppercorn—I had become hooked.

This is based on a recipe in Molly Stevens's fantastic *All About Roasting*.

Serves 2 as a side or 4 as a snack

1 pound sugar snap peas

Good splash of vegetable or canola oil

¼ cup sesame seeds

2 tablespoons Sichuan peppercorns

1 teaspoon garlic powder

1 teaspoon powdered ginger

½ teaspoon fine sea salt

Pinch of crushed red pepper flakes

1. Preheat the broiler.

2. String the peas by cutting one stem end off with a knife and pulling the string out of the seam running down the center of each pod. Rinse the peas, pat them dry, and pour them into a large bowl. Toss them with oil until uniformly coated.

3. Heat a small skillet over medium heat; add the sesame seeds and Sichuan peppercorns and toast, tossing frequently, until the sesame seeds are lightly browned and both are fragrant, about 5 minutes.

4. Set half of the toasted sesame seeds and Sichuan peppercorns aside in a small bowl. Combine the other half with the garlic powder, powdered ginger, salt,

and crushed red pepper in a spice grinder (or clean coffee grinder) and grind into a powder.

PRICE BOX

Snap peas: $5
Sesame seeds: $1
Sichuan peppercorns: 50¢

Total price: $6.50; per person: $3.25 (side), $1.63 (snack)

5. Lay the peas out in a single layer on a rimmed baking sheet and sprinkle them with the spice powder. Pop them in the broiler and broil for about 2 minutes, until the tops are lightly browned. Toss the peas and broil for another minute or two, until all the peas are nicely browned all over.

6. Pour the peas into a bowl, sprinkle with the reserved sesame seeds and Sichuan peppercorns, and serve.

CHICKEN AND BACON PÂTÉ

This technically is not a pâté because it is not molded or baked. It also, unlike traditional pâtés, does not contain forcemeat, an emulsion of meat (usually raw) and fat.

But we're not here for definitions. We're here to make delicious things to eat using affordable yet high-quality ingredients. And this fake-pâté, when made with the livers of pasture-raised chickens, is mildly gamey, deceptively rich, and addictively tasty. Generous touches of butter make it mousselike, and white wine keeps it aromatic. Nutmeg imparts a festive zing, while sage, shallot, and garlic soothe the twang of the chicken livers. It has become a holiday season staple for Christmas Eve hors d'oeuvres at my boyfriend's parents' house, where we spread it thickly on grilled baguettes and top it with flaky gray sea salt.

Makes about 2 dozen baguette rounds, or 12 servings

1 pound pasture-raised chicken livers (see Note)

Salt and freshly ground black pepper

2 to 3 slices smoked bacon, diced

4 tablespoons (½ stick) unsalted butter

2 large shallots, diced

1 clove garlic, minced

1 tablespoon anchovy paste (optional but recommended)

1 handful sage leaves (about 10 leaves)

1 cup dry white wine

1 heaping teaspoon freshly grated nutmeg

About ¼ cup good extra virgin olive oil

1 baguette, sliced into ½-inch rounds, for serving

Flaky sea salt for serving

1. Thoroughly rinse and dry the livers. Trim any sinew. Season with salt and pepper on both sides and set aside.

2. In a large nonreactive saucepan, brown the bacon over medium heat just until the fat renders, about 3 minutes. Remove the bacon with a slotted spoon to a plate and add the butter to the pan. Melt the butter into the bacon fat, then add the shallots and sauté for 2 minutes, or until softened. Add the garlic and sauté until fragrant, about 2 minutes. Add the anchovy paste, if using, and the sage and cook for another 3 minutes. If the shallots begin to stick, deglaze with a splash of the wine.

3. Add in the livers in a single layer and sear them for 3 minutes. Flip them over and brown on the other side, another 3 minutes. Add half the wine and stir to combine everything, breaking up the livers with your wooden spoon.

4. When the wine has reduced almost completely, add the nutmeg and the rest of the wine. Cook until the livers have cooked through and the wine has reduced again by half. Remove from the heat.

5. Transfer to a food processor, add the bacon, and process until very smooth, drizzling in up to 2 tablespoons oil if necessary. Taste and adjust the seasoning.

6. Brush the baguette slices gently on both sides with oil and broil for about 2 minutes per side, until nicely browned. Spread the pâté on the toasted rounds, drizzle with oil, and sprinkle with flaky sea salt.

Note: If the poultry stand at your farmers' market doesn't offer liver, ask for a pound of them a week ahead of when you will need them. If your farmer can't provide them for you, use free-range and/or organic chicken livers from your supermarket.

PRICE BOX

Chicken livers: $4
Bacon: $2
Butter: 85¢ to $1.18
Shallots: $1
Anchovy paste: 50¢ (optional)
Sage: 25¢
Wine: $1
Baguette: $2.25

Total price: $11.35 to $12.18; per person: 95¢ to $1

WHITE BEAN AND BACON DIP

If I could, I'd carry around an emergency vial of this dip for whenever a meal needs a kick in the pants. Gently earthy white beans and smoky bacon are so fantastically delicious together that I have, on more than one occasion, made a full lunch of this dip with crackers and grassy watercress. The dip also makes a great base for creamy soups—just imagine how nicely it would play with potatoes and leeks or parsnips—and a perfect spread for roasted vegetable or fish or chicken sandwiches.

Makes about 2 cups, or 8 servings

2 tablespoons extra virgin olive oil, plus more for drizzling

2 slices good smoked bacon

1 clove garlic, minced

¼ cup chopped scallions (whites and greens separated)

¼ cup white wine

1½ cups cannellini or white beans, rinsed and drained if canned

½ teaspoon crushed red pepper flakes

½ teaspoon minced fresh rosemary

Fine sea salt

¼ cup Basic Vegetable Stock (page 34) or Meat Stock (use chicken; page 35)

1½ teaspoons fresh lemon juice

½ teaspoon minced fresh thyme

Crackers or crudités for serving

1. Heat 1 tablespoon of the oil in a large sauté pan over medium heat, add the bacon, and cook until it has rendered its fat but is still soft, 3 to 4 minutes. Remove the bacon to a plate and set aside.

2. Add the garlic and the scallion whites to the fat in the pan and cook until softened, about 1 minute. Deglaze the pan with the wine, then add the beans, crushed red pepper, and rosemary. Season with salt. When the wine is steaming and has reduced visibly, 6 to 8 minutes, add the broth, bring to a boil, then turn down the heat and simmer for 10 minutes, or until the broth is reduced by about half.

3. Crumble or roughly chop the bacon and place it in the bowl of a food processor. Add the lemon juice, thyme, and the contents of the pan to the processor and puree, drizzling in the rest of the oil through the hole in the top of the machine, until the mixture is smooth. Taste and adjust the seasoning. If the dip is too thick, add more oil or water in a thin stream.

PRICE BOX

Bacon: $1.70
White beans: $1.75
Scallions: 50¢
Wine: 50¢

Total price: $4.45;
per person: 56¢

4. Transfer to a bowl, cover, and refrigerate for at least 15 minutes or until ready to serve to let the flavors settle and combine. Serve topped with the scallion greens and a drizzle of good extra virgin olive oil and scoop up with crackers or crudités or spread on vegetable, fish, or chicken sandwiches.

ROASTED ONION DIP

Makes about 2 cups, or 8 servings

A good splash of olive oil

1 medium sweet onion, chopped

2 shallots, minced

2 cloves garlic, minced

Salt and freshly ground black pepper

¼ cup dry white wine or stock, plus more if needed (Vegetable Stock, page 34; or Meat Stock, page 35—use chicken or beef)

2 tablespoons fresh thyme leaves

1 cup sour cream

1 cup thick plain yogurt

1. Heat the oil in a medium skillet over medium-low heat. Add the onion, shallots, and garlic, season with salt and pepper, and sauté, stirring less often than you think you should (leaving them alone will help them caramelize), until nicely browned and reduced by about one quarter, 15 to 20 minutes.

2. As the onions begin to stick to the pan, pour about half of the wine in and scrape the pan to deglaze. Let the wine cook down until nearly evaporated. Repeat as necessary to keep the onions from sticking and burning.

PRICE BOX

Onion: $1
Shallots: $1
Wine: 25¢
Sour cream: $1.85
Yogurt: $1.25
Thyme: 75¢

Total price: $6.10;
per person: 77¢

3. Add the thyme and cook for another 2 to 3 minutes. Turn off the heat.

4. Let the onions cool for a moment while you stir together the sour cream and yogurt in a medium bowl. Fold the onions into the sour cream and yogurt; taste and season with salt and pepper if necessary. Cover and refrigerate for at least 1 hour or preferably overnight before serving.

Chapter Seven

Sides, Soups, and Salads

GRAMMY'S STUFFING

My grandmother Shirley makes what is hands down the best Thanksgiving stuffing—and yes, everyone in my family calls it "Grammy's Stuffing." To get the texture right, cook in a bain marie (see instructions below), as if it were a custard: It's a thick stuffing, and without the bain marie, it will dry out and be unappetizing.

How to describe the flavor of this stuffing? It is unlike any stuffing I've had anywhere else. It's almost more like a soufflé. Instead of a base of cornbread or croutons, it uses matzoh meal—as much as a box. This is very much an "eyeball it" kind of recipe, even for Shirley, who has some sort of mystically alchemical relationship with her stuffing.

If you're using this in a chicken or turkey, roast for an extra 10 to 15 minutes per pound.

Serves 6 to 8

4 tablespoons (½ stick) unsalted butter, plus more for the casserole

1 pound button mushrooms, sliced

1 stalk celery, chopped

2 medium onions, chopped

2 to 3 medium carrots, grated

1 tablespoon powdered ginger

Salt and freshly ground black pepper

6 large eggs

1 cup Meat Stock (use chicken; page 35) or Basic Vegetable Stock (page 34)

Leaves from ½ bunch fresh parsley, minced

1 box matzoh meal

1. Melt the butter in a large skillet or sauté pan over medium heat. Add the mushrooms and sauté until they've released their juices and softened, 12 to 15 minutes. Add the celery and cook for 2 minutes, then add the onions and cook for another 2 minutes. Fold in the carrots, add the ginger, and season with salt and pepper. Remove from the heat and cool.

2. While the vegetables are cooling, whip the eggs in a blender. Working in batches, blend in the vegetables, just a little at first to temper them into the eggs. Pour the mixture into a large bowl.

3. Pour the stock into the blender and pulse the machine to remove any stuck bits, then pour the stock into the bowl. Fold in the parsley. Working in ½-cup increments, add matzoh meal to the egg mixture. You might only need ½ cup; you might need the whole box. It's never the same twice. The final consistency should be very runny and not at all dry. Better to add too little than too much for now.

4. Cover the bowl and refrigerate for 2 to 3 hours, until the mixture has thickened but is still loose. If it's too thick, whisk in water in ¼-cup increments; if it's still too runny, whisk in more matzoh meal in the same measurement.

5. Preheat the oven to 350°F and butter a casserole dish. Bring a kettle of water to a boil.

6. Pour the stuffing into the casserole and set up the bain marie: Place the casserole in a larger roasting pan and pour enough boiling water around the casserole to come one third of the way up its sides. Cover the roasting pan tightly with aluminum foil and bake for 50 to 65 minutes, checking once halfway through to make sure the water is neither boiling over into the stuffing nor evaporating; add more boiling water if necessary and recover and continue baking. The stuffing is done when a toothpick inserted in the center comes out clean; it should be moist and soft but not gummy.

7. Let cool for 10 minutes, then slice and serve.

PRICE BOX

Butter: 85¢ to $1.18
Mushrooms: $4
Celery: 30¢
Onions: $1.50
Carrots: 50¢
Eggs: $2.25
Parsley: 50¢; free if homegrown
Matzoh meal: $2.50

Total price: $11.90 to $12.73; per person: $1.49 to $2.12

ZUCCHINI PANCAKES WITH SEASONED RICOTTA

At a certain point I just can't stand to look at another grilled zucchini, even if the vegetable is just hitting its seasonal peak. But at the same time, I don't want to regret not enjoying zucchini enough come winter. The solution? Pan-fried zucchini pancakes. By using seltzer water instead of an egg to bind the dough together, the pancakes are airy, and, if you omit the ricotta, vegan. With a chilled soup or a nice salad, it makes the perfect summer meal.

We've made them with asparagus, and they'd be delicious stuffed with leeks, shallots, and onions as a riff on Chinese scallion pancakes. Think how pretty a platter of carrot pancakes would be; a little radish grated into them would give your sweet, earthy pancakes a nice spicy zing. Zach Bernstein, who, as the one-man band known as Bicycats, writes and performs most of the music we use on the show, adds crumbled cooked bacon, which is just brilliant.

Serves 4 as an appetizer or side

PANCAKES

2 medium zucchinis

1 cup all-purpose flour

1 cup seltzer water

Sea salt and freshly ground black pepper

1 tablespoon minced fresh dill or oregano (optional)

Olive oil as needed

SEASONED RICOTTA

1 cup Homemade Ricotta (page 59)

Zest of 1 lemon

¼ cup grated Parmesan or pecorino cheese

Sea salt and freshly ground black pepper to taste

1. Place a rimmed baking sheet in the oven and preheat the oven to 250°F.

2. Make the pancakes: Tip and tail the zucchinis and grate them with a mandoline or box grater. Transfer to a large bowl.

3. In a second bowl, combine the flour and seltzer. Season with salt and pepper and fold in the zucchini and herbs, if using. At first it may seem like you have way too much zucchini, but it will work out fine: You just want to coat the zucchini with the batter.

4. Heat a thin, even layer of oil in a large, high-sided skillet or sauté pan over medium-high heat. When the oil is hot but not smoking, scoop out some zucchini batter with a wide, shallow spoon and slide it into the oil. You want the pancakes to be as flat as possible, but don't smash them down into the oil or they'll just get, well, oily. Don't overcrowd the pan; do about 4 pancakes at a time, making sure the edges don't touch. Fry for 4 to 5 minutes, until golden brown, then gently flip and fry for another 4 to 5 minutes. If the pan becomes too dry, add more oil in between batches and let it heat up before continuing to fry the pancakes.

PRICE BOX

Zucchinis: $2.50

Seltzer: 25¢

Homemade Ricotta: $1.45 to $2.45

Lemon: 70¢

Parmesan/pecorino cheese: 75¢

Total price: $5.65 to $6.65; per person: $1.41 to $1.66

5. Transfer the cooked pancakes to a cooling rack set over a baking sheet. Immediately season with a little salt and pepper. Transfer the drained pancakes to the preheated baking sheet in the oven to keep warm.

6. When the pancakes are all in the oven, make the seasoned ricotta by combining all the ricotta ingredients.

7. Serve 2 or 3 pancakes per person, passing the bowl of ricotta around.

BRENDAN'S ISRAELI COUSCOUS

Chef Brendan McDermott is a frequent presence on "Working Class Foodies." He's a fantastic instructor—just watch any of our episodes with him—and just as great a chef.

Although not a vegetarian himself, Brendan had noticed that many restaurants drop the ball on vegetarian entrées, offering only a grilled or steamed vegetable dish. So Brendan set out to make a vegetarian dish that he himself would eat, and this colorful, hearty, healthy Israeli couscous is the result.

And it's become one of my go-to dishes whenever I need to make something for a mixed crowd. Topped with Crispy Roasted Chickpeas (page 81) and slices of creamy goat cheese, it's delicious and filling enough on its own, but in smaller portions it's also an excellent side for chicken and fish.

COUS-C-WHO?

Couscous is actually a semolina pasta, not a grain. And Israeli couscous is more like orzo than traditional couscous. But Israeli couscous cooks like a grain—it absorbs its cooking liquid—so I like to group it with other grain-based dishes. It stands up nicely to any seasoning, is delicious hot or cold, and makes for a lovely cold salad. You should be able to find Israeli or pearl couscous in the pastas and grain section at your grocery store; if not, substitute with orzo.

Serves 4 to 6

VEGETABLES

1 bell pepper

Olive oil, as needed

1 carrot, diced

1 stalk celery, diced

½ medium onion, diced

2 cloves garlic, minced

1 zucchini, diced

Salt and freshly ground black pepper

1 tablespoon ground cumin

1 tablespoon curry powder

1 tablespoon paprika

1 teaspoon ground cinnamon

1½ cups cooked chickpeas

COUSCOUS

2 tablespoons extra virgin olive oil

1½ cups Israeli couscous

3 cups water or Basic Vegetable Stock (page 34)

Kosher salt

GARNISHES

1 tablespoon grated lemon zest

Crispy Roasted Chickpeas (page 81)

4 ounces goat cheese, cut into 4 to 6 equal slices

1. Wash the bell pepper and dry it thoroughly. Using tongs, hold it above an open burner flame on a gas range and carefully blacken the skin on all sides. If you have an electric oven, preheat it to 450°F and char the pepper on a lightly oiled baking sheet for about 15 minutes per side, or until the pepper's

skin is blackened and wrinkled and the pepper has collapsed slightly. Put the pepper in a bowl, cover tightly with a lid or plate, and shake vigorously for 60 to 90 seconds, until the skin starts to come off and most if not all of the seeds have burst out.

2. Split the pepper open (if it didn't split open already) and rinse away the blackened skin and seeds. Pat dry and roughly chop. Set aside.

3. Make the couscous: Heat the oil in a medium saucepan over medium-high heat. Add the couscous and cook, stirring occasionally, until lightly browned and fragrant, 4 to 5 minutes. Add the water, season with salt, and bring to a boil. Immediately reduce the heat and simmer until the liquid has been absorbed, 10 to 12 minutes. Fluff gently with a fork or wooden spoon, cover, and set aside.

4. Heat a good splash of oil in a large skillet or sauté pan over medium heat. Add the carrot and cook for 2 minutes; add the celery and cook for 2 minutes; add the onion and cook for 2 minutes; add the garlic and cook for 2 minutes; finally, add the zucchini and cook for 2 minutes. Season with salt and pepper and add the cumin, curry powder, paprika, and cinnamon. Cook until the carrots are softened, about 5 minutes, then add the chickpeas and the chopped roasted bell pepper.

5. Toss the couscous into the vegetables. Taste and adjust the seasoning. Remove from the heat, fold in the lemon zest, and serve each portion topped with the Crispy Roasted Chickpeas and a slice of goat cheese. Serve hot or chilled.

PRICE BOX

Bell pepper: $1
Carrot: 30¢
Celery: 30¢
Onion: 50¢
Zucchini: $1.25
Chickpeas: $1.25
Israeli couscous: $2
Crispy Roasted
Chickpeas: $1.25
Goat cheese: $3.50

Total price: $11.35; per person: $1.90 to $2.84

CRISPY ROASTED CHICKPEAS

Makes about 1½ cups

    One 15-ounce can chickpeas
    1½ teaspoons fine sea salt
    Freshly ground black pepper
    1½ tablespoons olive oil
    2 tablespoons spice mix (optional; see suggestions below)

1. Preheat a rimmed baking sheet in a 400°F oven. Rinse the chickpeas in a colander under cool running water, then dry them thoroughly between 2 clean, dry dishcloths. If you like, you can use the dishcloths to rub off the chickpea skins and discard them, but it isn't necessary.
2. In a large bowl, toss the chickpeas with the salt and pepper to taste, the oil, and spice mix, if using. Roast the chickpeas in a single layer on the baking sheet, tossing occasionally to keep them from sticking, for 25 to 30 minutes, until browned and crunchy. Set aside to cool for 5 minutes, then enjoy hot or cold.

SPICE MIX SUGGESTIONS

    2 tablespoons curry powder, 1 tablespoon paprika, and 1 teaspoon ground cinnamon
    1 tablespoon curry powder, 1 tablespoon flaked coconut, 1 tablespoon crushed peanuts, and 1 teaspoon ground cinnamon
    2 tablespoons chopped fresh rosemary and ½ teaspoon crushed red pepper flakes

NEW POTATOES WITH BUTTER AND HERBS

As a poor vegetarian in college, I fell in love with potatoes. They are just as filling as pasta and infinitely less fussy (in that you can forget about a potato while it's baking in a not-too-hot oven for two hours while you go to the gym, meet with a study group, or take a much-needed movie break with your roommates, until suddenly your stomach reminds you that you are quite hungry). And while there certainly are more types and shapes of pasta than varieties of potatoes, each kind of potato has its own flavor and its own favorite way of cooking. Russian banana and baby fingerling potatoes, no bigger than a pinkie finger, practically beg to be roasted whole and tossed with good olive oil or butter. Big, grainy-skinned russets refuse to cooperate if not boiled and mashed or slow-baked into submission. Golf-ball-size new potatoes, in skins of gold, maroon, and deep purple, want to be gently boiled, whole or in chunks, then either tossed with butter and herbs or pan-fried into crispy-edged oblivion.

GET AHEAD BY THE SKIN OF YOUR . . . POTATO

Life will be so much simpler if you keep a pound or two of preboiled potatoes in your fridge, ready to go.

This is my favorite spring potato recipe, when both potatoes and herbs are tender and young. It pairs excellently with simple grilled or steamed vegetables or with fish for a light dinner or weekend lunch.

Serves 4

2 pounds small new potatoes, scrubbed but not peeled

Kosher salt

3 tablespoons unsalted butter, at room temperature

3 to 4 generous pinches of coarse or fine sea salt

Freshly ground black pepper

⅓ cup minced fresh chives or tarragon, or whole fresh thyme leaves

1. Place the potatoes in a large saucepan and cover with water by 1 inch. Season generously with kosher salt. Bring to a boil over high heat, then reduce the heat to medium and simmer until the potatoes just slide off the edge of a knife, 15 to 20 minutes.

2. Place the butter in a large bowl as it softens. Drain the potatoes and add them to the bowl, tossing with the butter until it melts. Add the sea salt, pepper to taste, and herbs and toss well. Serve immediately.

PRICE BOX

Potatoes: $3
Butter: 85¢ to $1.18
Herbs: $1.50

Total price: $5.35 to $5.68; per person: $1.34 to $1.42

CARL'S LATKES

My grandpa Carl freely admitted that he only used russet potatoes in his latkes because they were the cheapest. Of course you can make delicious latkes with russets, but for the perfect ratio of crisp lace edges to creamy centers, the smooth-fleshed Yukon gold potatoes are the way to go. There is one other important latke ratio: potatoes to onions, which should be 3 to 1. You want just enough onion for your latkes to have a little bit of sass, but not so much that they're getting uppity with you. The latkes are a great side dish for roast chicken, corned beef, or salmon.

Serves 6 to 8

5 pounds Yukon gold potatoes (about 12)

3 to 4 small sweet onions (about the size of a tennis ball)

2 teaspoons baking powder

4 generous pinches of kosher salt

2 to 4 tablespoons matzoh meal

4 large eggs

2 to 3 cups peanut oil

1 teaspoon fine sea salt for sprinkling

1 cup Homemade Applesauce (page 197) for serving

1 cup sour cream for serving

½ cup sugar for serving

1. Peel the potatoes and set them in a large bowl of cold water to keep them from oxidizing. Peel the onions.

2. Grate the potatoes and onions. The traditional and oftentimes injury-inducing way to do this is by hand, with a box grater over a very large bowl. The saner way to do this is in batches in your food processor using the grater blade attachment. Dump the grated vegetables, whatever your method, into a very large bowl.

3. Now you must drain all of the excess liquid from the potatoes and onions—and I mean *all*. Working in batches, scoop the potatoes and onions into a thick piece of cheesecloth or a clean, dry dish towel and squeeze the liquid out. Place the drained potatoes and onions into a second large bowl and repeat until the potatoes and onions have been thoroughly drained.

4. Add the baking powder, kosher salt, and 2 tablespoons of the matzoh meal to the potatoes and onions. Mix in the eggs and add more matzoh meal if necessary—the eggs will hold the latkes together and the matzoh meal helps shape them.

5. In a large, high-sided skillet, heat 1 inch of oil to 350°F. A candy thermometer comes in handy here and is worth its price. You can also test the oil

by dropping in a little piece of shredded potato: If the oil immediately forms small, hard bubbles around the potato, your oil is hot enough.

6. Preheat the oven to 250°F and prepare a cooling rack with a few layers of old newspaper underneath to catch the drippings.

7. Form the latkes into patties by pressing them onto a slotted spoon to squeeze out any final excess liquid.

8. Working carefully, slide the latkes into the oil one at a time. Do not over-crowd the pan or the oil will cool down too much. (A good rule of thumb is to count to 30 before you add a new latke.) Likewise, don't smash the latkes down into the oil, and don't flip them over too soon: You only want to flip the latkes once so they only absorb the minimum amount of oil.

9. Fry each latke until the fringes at the edges are crisp and brown, then care-fully flip them over and fry on the other side. Whenever the oil becomes too low, wait until there are no latkes being fried, then add more oil and bring back to the frying temperature before continuing to cook the latkes.

10. Move fried latkes to the cooling rack to drain and sprinkle them with sea salt. Let them drain and rest for a couple of minutes, then transfer to a baking sheet and keep warm in the oven.

11. Serve the latkes topped with the applesauce, sour cream, or sugar.

PRICE BOX

Potatoes: $6
Onions: $2
Matzoh meal: 25¢
Eggs: $1.50
Peanut oil: $4.50
Applesauce: $1.50
Sour cream: $1.85

Total price: $17.60;
per person: $2.20 to
$2.94

SPICY SWEET POTATO "FRIES" WITH MAPLE BUTTER

I love the combination of spicy and sweet. Imagine a heaping pile of sweet potatoes, cut thick and baked until their edges are crunchy and brown and the insides melt on your tongue. Now imagine the sweet potatoes rubbed with a just-this-side-of-hot spice blend and dipped into creamy maple butter. It's the perfect meeting of virtue—sweet potatoes are, after all, good for you—and sin—because butter (crazy Scandinavian diets aside) is decidedly not that good for you. But luckily you don't need much of it, so indulge and enjoy.

You can peel the sweet potatoes if you like, but I recommend leaving the skins on. The skins are nutritious, and they help hold the fries together; rubbed with oil, they crisp into deliciousness in the oven.

Serves 4 generously

3 large sweet potatoes

½ teaspoon paprika

¼ teaspoon ground cinnamon

¼ teaspoon freshly grated nutmeg

¼ teaspoon light brown sugar

Pinch of cayenne powder

1½ teaspoons kosher or coarse sea salt

A few good grinds of black pepper

Olive oil to coat (1 to 2 tablespoons)

Maple Butter (opposite)

1. Preheat 2 rimmed baking sheets in a 450°F oven.

2. Gently scrub the sweet potatoes under cold running water to remove any dirt. Dry the potatoes very thoroughly.

MAPLE BUTTER

I like to think of this as the sweet world's answer to bacon: Just as bacon fat in place of oil or butter adds a hint of meaty smoke, maple butter adds a woodsy sweetness.

Make extra maple butter and save it in the fridge for waffles and pancakes, baked beans, and cornbread.

Makes ¼ cup

2 tablespoons unsalted butter, softened
Fine sea salt to taste
I tablespoon maple syrup (Grade A or B, but *not* imitation)
Dash of ground cinnamon

1. In a small bowl, cream the butter and salt with a fork or hand mixer. Beat in the maple syrup and cinnamon.
2. Use immediately or store in an airtight container in the fridge for up to 2 weeks.

3. Remove the tapered ends of the potatoes, squaring them off. Quarter the sweet potatoes lengthwise, then slice each quarter into ½-inch-wide pieces. Cut these in half widthwise so they're no longer than the length of your index finger.

4. In a small bowl, mix together the paprika, cinnamon, nutmeg, brown sugar, cayenne, salt, and pepper.

5. Put the sweet potatoes in a large bowl and add just enough oil to coat. Toss the sweet potatoes with the oil and seasonings, thoroughly working them over the sweet potatoes with your hands.

6. Arrange the sweet potatoes on the baking sheets in an even layer. Don't let them overlap or they will steam instead of crisp.

7. Bake for about 15 minutes, then flip and bake for another 15 minutes, until crisp and browned. (While the potatoes are baking, you can make the Maple Butter.)

8. Serve with a ramekin of Maple Butter. Try not to get addicted.

PRICE BOX

Sweet potatoes: $3
Maple Butter: 50¢

Total price: $3.50;
per person: 88¢

SALADS

I've always loved salad, but I've also always had strict salad rules: The lettuce must be fresh, crisp, and vivid; the dressing must be homemade and applied with a light touch; and the accoutrements must extend beyond raw carrots and celery (frankly, I prefer if you leave those two out altogether).

Make these salads according to when the key ingredients are in season; the difference in flavor and vibrancy will give your salads new life.

BUTTER LETTUCE AND RADISHES WITH LEMON-POPPY YOGURT DRESSING

Kit and I were at the farmers' market waiting in a long line to pick up our Thanksgiving turkey. Normally, no one is more excited than me about root vegetables: Come fall, I can't get enough of parsnips, carrots, potatoes, and beets. I'll eat them roasted, in soup, even steamed or boiled. As we waited on the turkey line, shivering slightly, I craned my neck to see which farm stands had the best root vegetables. Amid the bins of dirt-smudged carrots, pale parsnips and turnips, dark-green kale and milky-green collards, one bin literally popped out. Its contents: airy, neon-green heads of butter lettuce and radishes as small and bright as rubies. It was like that first blade of grass peeking through the snow at the end of a long, cold winter.

We came home from the market with a big, beautiful turkey and all the root vegetables we could carry, but my prize that day was a delicate head of butter lettuce and a bunch of those baby radishes.

This salad is full of flavor, healthy, transportable, and very quick and easy to whip together. The dressing makes for a salad that is as tasty as it is beautiful.

Serves 2

DRESSING

5 ounces plain thick yogurt (Greek or strained)

1 scallion, thinly sliced

Juice and zest of ½ lemon

1½ teaspoons poppy seeds

3 tablespoons extra virgin olive oil

Fine sea salt and freshly ground black pepper

A WELL-ROUNDED DRESSING

Like a smoother tzatziki, lemon-poppy yogurt dressing also makes a great spread for sandwiches, a dip for crudités, and a marinade for chicken and fish. Although poppy seeds are an important enough component to be featured in the title, you can substitute curry powder, chili powder, or whole toasted cumin seeds if you can't find poppies.

SALAD

1 head butter lettuce

6 to 8 small radishes, trimmed, cleaned, and quartered

1 scallion, dark green part only, snipped

Pinch of poppy seeds

1. Make the dressing: In a small bowl, whisk together the yogurt, scallion, lemon juice and zest, and poppy seeds. Whisk in the oil in a thin, gradual stream. Add a little water as needed to adjust the consistency. Season with salt and pepper. Use immediately or cover and refrigerate for up to 4 days.

2. Make the salad: Trim out the core of the lettuce and separate the leaves, discarding any brown ones. Immerse the leaves in cold water and drain; repeat once or twice more, each time with fresh cold water, until the water drains clean. Gently pat dry with a dish towel. With your hands, tear the leaves into bite-size pieces and arrange them loosely on 2 plates. Sprinkle the radishes over the lettuce, drizzle with the dressing, and top with the scallion greens and poppy seeds.

PRICE BOX

Yogurt: $1.25
Lemon: 50¢
Poppy seeds: 75¢
Butter lettuce: $2
Radishes: $1.50
Scallions: 15¢

Total price: $6.15;
per person: $3.08

GREEN BEANS AND HAZELNUTS WITH TARRAGON-CIDER VINAIGRETTE

I love this dish in spring when green beans are just hitting the market. Early in the season, they're crunchy and slim and sassily bright. The barely blanched beans are tossed with toasted hazelnuts and lightly licorice-scented tarragon for a snappy salad or side.

Serves 2 to 4

1 pound green beans

1 heaping tablespoon kosher salt

Ice cubes for the ice bath

½ cup hazelnuts

¼ cup Tarragon-Cider Vinegar (page 92)

⅓ cup extra virgin olive oil

Fine sea salt and freshly ground black pepper

1. Prepare the green beans by tipping them but not tailing them. Bring a large pot of water to a rolling boil and stir in the kosher salt. Toss in the green beans, stir once, then let the water come back to a boil. Boil for 3 minutes while you prepare an ice bath by filling a large, preferably metal bowl half full with ice cubes and cold water.

2. Drain the green beans and immediately transfer them to the ice bath. Leave to cool for 3 minutes, then drain and pat dry between two clean dishcloths.

3. Put the hazelnuts in a zip-top plastic bag, squeeze out the excess air, and seal it shut. Carefully crush the nuts with a heavy pan or rolling pin.

PRICE BOX

Green beans: $3
Hazelnuts: $2.50
Cider vinegar: 55¢
Tarragon: $1

Total price: $7.05; per person: $1.77 to $3.53

4. Heat a small, dry skillet over medium heat. Add the hazelnuts and toast them for 3 to 5 minutes, until fragrant and lightly browned. Remove from the heat.

5. Put the vinegar in a small bowl and whisk in the oil in a slow, steady stream. Season with salt and pepper.

6. Place the green beans in a large bowl and toss with the hazelnuts and dressing.

TARRAGON-CIDER VINEGAR

This will make twice as much vinegar as you need for the beans; save the extra in an airtight container for up to a month for even more herby flavor.

You can substitute any vinegar and any herb to make endless different combinations.

½ cup apple cider vinegar
½ cup rinsed and thoroughly dried fresh tarragon

1. Bring the vinegar to a boil in a small nonreactive saucepan over medium-high heat.
2. While the vinegar is heating, lightly bruise the tarragon with a few gentle whacks from the back of your knife. Stuff the tarragon into a clean glass jar or bowl.
3. When the vinegar reaches a boil, remove it from the heat and pour it over the herbs. Let cool for at least 30 minutes or to room temperature, then shake and use immediately. To store leftover tarragon vinegar, strain out the tarragon and store the vinegar in your refrigerator, tightly lidded, for as long as a month.

CUCUMBER, JICAMA, AND SEAWEED IN SESAME OIL

Crunchy foods are so refreshing. That is what I love about this salad—that, and how unlike a typical salad it is. Like so many good things, this salad is the result of desperation intersecting with innovation: I had picked up a package of locally harvested and dried seaweed at a neighborhood grocery store and had basically been doing a lot of nothing with it. Knowing it was there, purposeless, at the back of a cabinet was getting on my nerves. The seaweed wanted a purpose.

The seaweed I used that first time was dried wakame, a knotty vinelike tangle that softened in the dressing; you can also use nori, thin, dried sheets of seaweed found at Asian specialty groceries and health food stores. Just add nori after the salad has been dressed to keep the delicate seaweed from disintegrating.

Serve the salad with nutty brown rice and grilled fish or chicken for a light dinner.

Serves 4

SALAD

¼ cup dried wakame or nori seaweed

1½ cups jicama peeled and cut into half moons

1 English (burpless) cucumber, peeled (about 2 cups when chopped)

1 small serrano or jalapeño chile

DRESSING

2 tablespoons rice vinegar

1 tablespoon soy sauce

1 teaspoon honey

2½ tablespoons toasted sesame oil

2 tablespoons grapeseed or vegetable oil

1 teaspoon toasted sesame seeds

1. If your seaweed is thick and ropy, soak it for 15 minutes in a bowl of cold water, then drain. If it's in flat sheets, ignore this step.

2. Place the jicama in a large bowl. Slice the cucumber in half lengthwise. Slice the cucumber halves into thin pieces (the same thickness as the jicama) and place in the bowl.

3. Remove the stem end of the chile. Run a butter or table knife around the inside of the chile to remove the pith and seeds. Julienne the chile and mince it. Add it to the bowl.

4. Cut the seaweed into ½-inch pieces and add it to the salad.

5. In a small bowl, whisk together the vinegar, soy sauce, and honey to dissolve the honey. Whisk in the sesame and grapeseed oils.

6. Pour the dressing over the salad and toss. Sprinkle with the sesame seeds. Serve immediately.

PRICE BOX

Seaweed: 50¢
Cucumber: $1
Jicama: $3
Chile: 20¢

Total price: $4.70;
per person: $1.18

SPICY WATERMELON AND FETA SALAD

If a perfectly ripe tomato is the essence of summer, then a perfectly ripe watermelon is the quintessential summer day: Even at a smoky barbecue in a cramped Brooklyn "backyard," with watermelon juices running uncontrollably down your chin you are a child again.

This is the salad I take to barbecues all summer long. It's sloppy and messy, hot and sweet. It makes its own dressing, something I find miraculous in summer, when you want to extend as little effort as possible to make your food taste good. And the juices it produces should be sopped up with good grilled bread.

Serves 4 to 6 as a side

1 medium seedless watermelon (5 to 6 cups cubed)

½ red onion, thinly sliced

1 jalapeño chile

1 cup feta cheese in brine

Juice and zest of 1 lime

1 cup fresh basil leaves

1. Cutting a watermelon can be messy and laborious, but whole watermelons yield fruit that is sweeter, fresher, and cheaper than precut watermelon. To cube, cut the watermelon in half at its circumference. Cut the top off each end, just enough so each half is flat on both ends. Set one half aside. Set the other watermelon half with the narrow end up on your cutting board. Using a sharp knife, carefully "peel" the skin off the watermelon, following the curve of the fruit with the blade of your knife. Don't worry—the first cut will be the most difficult; after that, it gets easier.

PRICE BOX

Watermelon: $6
Red onion: 50¢
Jalapeños: 40¢
Feta: $4
Lime: 60¢
Basil: $2; free if homegrown

Total price: $11.50 to $13.50; per person: $1.92 to $3.38

2. Slice the watermelon from end to end in 1-inch-thick slices. Then turn it 90 degrees and make a 1-inch-thick cross slice. Chop the slices that come off into 1-inch cubes. Repeat this—make a 1-inch-thick cross slice and chop those slices into 1-inch cubes—until the watermelon half is completely cut up. Then repeat the entire process with the other half. As for the skins? You can compost them or you can peel off the white parts and pickle them.

3. Put the cubed watermelon and its juices in a large bowl. Add the onion.

4. Remove the stem ends from the jalapeño. Run a butter or table knife around the inside of the chile to remove the pith and seeds. Discard the pith and seeds, then finely mince the chile and add them to the bowl.

5. Chop or crumble the feta. Add it and up to ¼ cup of its brine to the bowl. Add the lime juice and zest.

6. Julienne the basil by stacking the leaves, rolling them up like a cigar, and slicing the cigar into thin ribbons. Add to the salad and toss everything together.

7. Serve immediately with grilled bread for sopping up the juices.

THIRTY-SECOND TOMATO SALAD

Okay, the name of this dish is hyperbolic, but only slightly. Really, this dish is a shining example of how sublime high-quality ingredients combined simply and with the smallest bit of preparation can be. Heirloom tomatoes are not cheap, so this recipe lets their flavor shine through unadulterated. Peak-season heirloom tomatoes, sea salt worth splurging on and using judiciously, a good grind of black pepper, and the best grassy-flavored extra virgin olive oil are all you need for this dish—that, and maybe a hunk of crusty bread to sop up the juices.

Serves 4

4 plump and delicate heirloom tomatoes (any variety or mix of varieties)

A generous glug of very good extra virgin olive oil

2 generous pinches of fine sea salt

Cracked black pepper

Core and quarter the tomatoes. Nestle them together in a wide, shallow bowl or baking dish, flesh side up. Drizzle them languorously with oil, sprinkle them evenly with the salt, give them a good crack of black pepper, and gobble indiscriminately.

PRICE BOX

Tomatoes: $9.50

Total price: $9.50; per person: $2.38

TRICOLOR SUMMER SALAD

The colors of this salad are as bold as the flavors: It's a great way to let peak summer produce shine. Smoked mozzarella is criminally underused and is an excellent match for sweet cherry tomatoes and corn.

Serves 4

Kosher salt

3 ears corn, shucked

1 cup green beans, topped and tailed

Ice cubes for the ice bath

1 quart cherry tomatoes (2 pint containers), quartered

1 shallot, cut in half lengthwise and very thinly sliced

8 ounces smoked mozzarella, cut into ½-inch cubes

2½ tablespoons sherry vinegar

¼ cup extra virgin olive oil

Fine sea salt and cracked black pepper

1 small handful fresh basil leaves, julienned

1. Bring a pot of water to a rolling boil. Salt it heavily and add the corn. Bring back to a boil and cook for 10 minutes.

2. Using tongs, remove the boiled corn to a colander to drain. Return the same water to a boil, add the green beans, and cook for 3 minutes. While the green beans are cooking, prepare an ice bath in a medium bowl. Cool the green beans in the ice bath for 2 to 3 minutes, then drain.

3. When the corn is cool enough to handle, shave the kernels off the cobs. Run the back of your knife over the stripped cobs to pare away the sweet, starchy liquid within. Place the corn and its starchy pulp in a large bowl and add the tomatoes. Halve or quarter the green beans and toss them into the corn and tomatoes.

4. Add the shallot and mozzarella to the salad.

5. In a small bowl, whisk together the vinegar and oil. Season with salt and pepper.

6. Add the dressing to the salad and toss. Top with the julienned basil and serve.

PRICE BOX

Corn: $1.50
Green beans: $1.50
Cherry tomatoes: $5
Shallot: 50¢
Smoked mozzarella: $3.50
Basil: 25¢; free if homegrown

Total price: $12 to $12.25; per person: $3 to $3.06

KALE AND QUINOA WITH ROASTED TOMATOES

Raw kale needs a little pampering: Here we give it a little fat (olive oil and Parmesan), a little acid (in the form of lemon juice), and a good massage.

The massage is actually the secret to a fantastic raw kale salad. Unlike virtually every other green, the tough leaves should not be lightly tossed with dressing; kale needs a dressing as assertive as itself, and it needs to have that dressing rubbed into its leaves. The result is a velvety salad that tastes as rich and decadent as any Caesar but is far healthier. Even dressed, this salad will hold up well in the fridge overnight because the lemon juice's acidity is no match for the kale's heartiness.

This salad also makes a great topping for a white pizza: Spread it over a round of pizza dough and cover with cubed or pulled fresh mozzarella before putting it in the oven.

Serves 2 or 3 as a main, 4 to 6 as a side

SALAD

1 quart (2 pints) cherry tomatoes

Olive oil as needed

Fine sea salt and freshly ground black pepper

¾ cup red quinoa, rinsed and drained

1½ cups water

2 bunches lacinato (dinosaur) kale

DRESSING

2 cloves garlic, minced

1 teaspoon kosher salt

Juice and zest of 1 lemon

½ cup extra virgin olive oil

½ cup freshly grated Parmesan or pecorino cheese

½ teaspoon crushed red pepper

Fine sea salt and cracked black pepper to taste

1. Make the dressing. Combine the garlic, salt, and lemon juice and zest in the bowl of a food processor. Blend in the olive oil and cheese in turns. Blend in the crushed red pepper and black pepper, taste and adjust. Let set in the fridge while you prep the rest of the salad.

2. Place a rimmed baking sheet in the oven and preheat the oven to 400°F.

3. Rinse and gently dry the cherry tomatoes between two clean dishcloths and halve them. Line the preheated baking sheet with aluminum foil and arrange the tomatoes on it in an even layer. Drizzle them generously with oil, salt, and pepper and toss gently to coat the tomatoes evenly. Rearrange the tomatoes so they're cut side up and roast in the oven for 20 to 30 minutes, until they've released their juices and the edges are browned.

4. Place the quinoa in a small saucepan. Add the water and a generous pinch of salt. Cover with a tight-fitting lid and bring to a boil, then immediately reduce the heat to low and simmer, covered, for 20 minutes, or until the quinoa has bloomed and absorbed the water (it's okay to take a peek under the lid every 10 minutes or so to make sure the quinoa isn't cooking too quickly and burning). Fluff the quinoa with a fork and set it aside.

5. Prep the kale: Remove the bottom 1 to 2 inches of the stems; these are compost. Remove the thick ribs and set aside (for making stock or for a long, slow simmer with lots of garlic and olive oil). Tear or chop the kale leaves and thinner ribs into bite-size pieces. Then submerge the kale in a large bowl of cold water and move it around to shake off the dirt. Drain and repeat until there's no dirt at the bottom of the bowl. Drain the kale and dry it thoroughly in a salad spinner or by rubbing it gently between 2 clean, dry dishcloths. Put the kale in a large serving bowl.

6. Using your hands, toss and massage about half of the dressing into the kale until each piece of kale is coated in the dressing. Add the quinoa and fluff it into the kale with 2 forks or wooden spoons. When the kale and quinoa are well mixed, gently fold in half of the tomatoes and the rest of the dressing. Top with the rest of the tomatoes and their juices and serve.

PRICE BOX

Cherry tomatoes: $5
Quinoa: $1.25
Kale: $4
Lemon: 70¢
Parmesan/pecorino cheese: $1.50

Total price: $12.45; per person: $2.08 (side), $6.23 (main)

ROASTED CARROT SALAD

Why do carrots and raisins go so well together? I don't know, but the combination of roasted carrots, vinegar-plumped raisins, and a vibrant sauce made from the carrot tops is a fall favorite of mine. Try to find smaller baby carrots—not the skinless, blunt-ended pinkie fingers at the supermarket but actual young carrots with sweet, earthy flesh—at your farmers' market. The skin on these young carrots should be thin enough that you don't even need to peel them first; just give them a good rub under cold running water as you would a potato.

Even most whole-vegetable proponents, people who happily serve their roasted beets on a bed of wilted beet greens, often let carrot tops fall by the compost bin wayside. This is a shame because carrot tops can be edible and are nutritious: They pack a load of potassium, calcium, chlorophyll, and vitamin K. If all the carrots at your farmers' market have had their tops removed, ask the farmer for the greens; they will be happy to give them to you with your carrots. If your carrots come with the greens still attached, remove them as soon as you get home so they won't suck the moisture out of the carrot roots.

Serves 4 as a side

CARROTS

1 large bunch of young carrots (6 to 8), cleaned

2 tablespoons olive oil

A good pinch of fine sea salt

Cracked black pepper

Always buy organic carrots, as carrots are spongelike vegetables that suck up whatever's present in their environment. If that includes chemical pesticides and nitrates, you'll be eating those, too.

Carrots are in the alkaloid family, which includes cocaine and caffeine; eating too much of the greens might cause a temporary increase in heart rate or elevated blood pressure. If you've never eaten carrot tops before, take a little nibble before continuing on with the recipe.

DRESSING

½ cup carrot tops, leaves and top inch of stem only

Pinch of fine sea salt

Cracked black pepper

½ teaspoon crushed red pepper flakes

1 clove garlic, minced

2 tablespoons sherry vinegar

⅓ cup raisins

2 tablespoons extra virgin olive oil

1. Place a rimmed baking sheet in the oven and preheat the oven to 375°F.

2. Tip and tail the carrots, which is just a poetic way of telling you to remove their tops and any scraggly, hairy tails. Halve them widthwise and then again lengthwise. Toss them with the oil, salt, and pepper to taste and arrange them, cut-side-down, on the preheated baking sheet. Roast for 15 to 20 minutes, until a knife slides easily into the carrots.

3. Meanwhile, make the dressing: Submerge the carrot tops in cold water, move them around a bit, and let them settle. Drain and repeat until the water runs clear. Pat them dry and put them in the bowl of a food processor. Add the salt, pepper to taste, the crushed red pepper, and garlic.

4. Heat the vinegar in a small saucepan until just steaming. Add the raisins and remove from the heat. Let the raisins plump for 5 minutes. Remove the raisins with a slotted spoon and set them aside. Pulse the vinegar into the carrot tops, then pulse in the oil in a slow drizzle. Taste the dressing and adjust the seasoning.

5. Slide the roasted carrots onto a serving plate. Drizzle with the dressing, sprinkle the raisins on top, and serve.

PRICE BOX

Carrots: $2
Sherry vinegar: 25¢
Raisins: $1.25

Total price: $3.50;
per person: 88¢

GRILLED RADICCHIO WITH KUMQUATS

Grilling or broiling radicchio tames this vegetable's potent bitterness. The trick is to slick the purple and white plant with enough olive oil to get the thick, white stem to cook before the leaves all char off. But let the leaves char a bit; it'll add another layer of flavor to this already sweet-tart-spicy salad.

If you don't have a grill or it's just too cold out for that nonsense, you certainly can cook the radicchio in your broiler. Don't let equipment or weather stop you!

The spicy honey balances this dish, giving it a nice but not-too-strong kick and a sweetness that complements the radicchio. Best of all, perhaps: Because you've given the radicchio a good rubdown in olive oil, you don't even need to add oil to the honey dressing. It makes this salad as light as it tastes.

Use a good, locally produced honey if you can; if you can't, I recommend using agave nectar instead.

Serves 2 as a main or 4 as a side

SALAD

1 head radicchio

Olive oil

Salt and freshly ground black
pepper

8 to 10 kumquats, rinsed

SPICY HONEY

¼ cup apple cider vinegar

2 sprigs fresh tarragon

¼ teaspoon crushed red pepper
flakes

¼ cup good local honey

1. Preheat your grill (medium for propane, ashy coals for charcoal) or broiler. Remove any wilted leaves from the radicchio, trim the stem, and quarter it. Submerge in cold water for a few seconds, then shake out; repeat once or twice more, until thoroughly clean. Pat the radicchio quarters dry and put them in a large bowl.

2. Give the radicchio quarters 2 good splashes of oil and rub the oil in on all sides. Season with salt and pepper.

3. Grill or broil the radicchio quarters for 4 to 5 minutes. Flip over and grill or broil for about 10 minutes. Be careful not to let the radicchio catch fire; you want it to cook and wilt and char, not burn. The radicchio is done when you can easily slide a knife into the stem.

4. While the radicchio is on the grill, prep the kumquats: Remove any stem fragments from the kumquats and cut them in half lengthwise. Thinly slice

each kumquat half, removing the seeds if they get in your way (they can be slippery). Set aside.

5. Make the spicy honey: Heat the vinegar, tarragon, and red pepper flakes in a saucepan until bubbling. Stir in the honey and immediately remove from the heat; keep warm.

6. Arrange one radicchio quarter on a plate for 4 side servings or 2 to a plate for a lunch entrée. Top each quarter with a few kumquat pieces. Drizzle the spicy honey over the kumquats and radicchio, pouring it through a strainer to catch the tarragon and red pepper flakes. Serve immediately.

PRICE BOX

Radicchio: $2.50
Kumquats: $1
Cider vinegar: 28¢
Tarragon: 30¢; free if homegrown
Honey: $1.08

Total price: $4.86 to $5.16; per person: $1.22 to $2.58

SOUPS AND STEWS

What appeals to me most about soup as a type of cooking is that, unlike just about everything else, there are no rules. A soup can be hot or cold, chunky or perfectly smooth, creamy or brothy, spicy or soothing, thin or thick, a slow work of patience or a quick spin in a blender. Soups can be the homiest and most personal of comfort meals or the most elegant course of a dinner party.

MAXIMUM EFFICIENCY

Anytime you make soup, set up a second pot on a back burner to make a new batch of stock from all the trimmings. Check out pages 34 and 35 for homemade stock recipes.

CHILLED CUCUMBER SOUP

This soup is a lifesaver come August. It's cool and refreshing—like eating ice cream for lunch, except healthy and responsible—and requires zero cooking.

Use cucumbers at their peak freshness, preferably bought the same day. Your cucumbers should feel firm and heavy for their size and have unblemished skins. And because cucumbers are mostly water, be sure to use lots of fresh herbs to flavor the soup. My instructions are to use oregano and mint, but any light, refreshing herb—basil, tarragon, chervil, chives, or any combination—will do beautifully.

Serves 6

2 pounds cucumbers, peeled

½ large sweet onion or ¼ large white onion, chopped

½ jalapeño chile, seeded and minced

1 clove garlic, minced

2 tablespoons fresh oregano leaves

¼ cup julienned fresh mint, plus more for garnish

Kosher salt and cracked black pepper

¼ teaspoon sweet paprika, plus more for garnish

1 to 2 cups Basic Vegetable Stock (page 34)

1 cup sour cream or thick plain yogurt, plus more for serving

Good extra virgin olive oil for serving

Juice and zest of 1 lemon for serving

1. Seed the cucumbers, if you wish, by halving them lengthwise and scooping out the seeds with a spoon.

2. Put the onion, jalapeño, and garlic in a large bowl. Roughly chop the cucumbers and add them to the bowl. Add the oregano and mint. Season with salt, pepper, and the paprika.

3. In a blender, working in batches, puree the cucumber mixture with the stock and sour cream. Make sure each batch contains some of each component. Blend until smooth, pouring finished batches into a separate bowl as you go. When everything is well blended and smooth, taste and adjust the seasoning. Pour the soup into a bowl or container large enough to fit it all. Refrigerate for 30 minutes to set the flavors.

4. Serve each bowl garnished with a dollop of sour cream or yogurt, a drizzle of oil, a squirt of lemon juice and pinch of lemon zest, a sprinkling of mint, and a dusting of paprika. A few slices of thick, crusty toast are a must to scrape the bowl clean.

PRICE BOX

Cucumbers: $2.50
Onion: $1
Jalapeño: 20¢
Herbs: $1.50; free if homegrown
Sour cream/yogurt: $1.25 to $1.85
Lemon: 70¢

Total price: $5.65 to $7.75; per person: 94¢ to $1.29

GAZPACHO

To each their own, but when it comes to gazpacho I just cannot get behind the standard fare: watery salsas that let harsh green peppers and soggy cucumbers overpower the tomatoes. Andalusian-style gazpacho does the opposite: It puts perfectly ripe summer tomatoes on a pedestal where their mellow sweetness can shine.

Serves 3 or 4

2 to 4 inches of a good baguette, plus more for serving

2½ pounds ripe tomatoes, preferably heirloom

2 cloves garlic

1 tablespoon plus ½ cup olive oil

Kosher or coarse sea salt

1½ teaspoons ground cumin

2 tablespoons aged or Spanish sherry vinegar

½ teaspoon sugar (optional)

Good extra virgin olive oil for serving

Flaky or smoked sea salt for serving

1. Remove the crust from the bread. Put the naked bread in a large bowl. Core the tomatoes and quarter them. Squeeze the cores over the baguette in the bowl so the juices drip onto it. Add enough water to just cover the bread. Soak the bread for about 2 minutes, until it's spongy and soft, then squeeze the excess liquid from the bread and set aside. It *will* look like a cross between a wad of old chewing gum and a soggy paper towel. Sorry. I promise it tastes better than it looks.

2. Put the garlic in a mortar and pestle with 1 tablespoon of the oil, a generous pinch of salt, and the cumin. Grind into a rough paste.

3. Put the vinegar and 1 tablespoon water in a blender. Add the bread, the garlic paste, half of the tomatoes, and the sugar, if using (only necessary if your tomatoes are more tart than sweet). Blend together in short pulses; add more water 1 tablespoon at a time as needed to make the blending smoother.

4. Blend in the remaining tomatoes. With the blender running, drizzle in some or all of the remaining ½ cup oil in a slow, steady stream. You may not need the full ½ cup—all the more reason to go slowly. The soup should look creamy and rich.

5. Taste the soup: It should be rich and sweet but slightly tart and spicy. If it's too thick, blend in more water or oil by the tablespoon. If it's not tart enough, blend in more vinegar.

PRICE BOX

Baguette: $1.25
Tomatoes: $5
Olive oil: $1
Sherry vinegar: 25¢

Total price: $7.50; per person: $1.88 to $2.50

6. Although not necessary, you can make the soup even smoother by straining it through a fine-mesh strainer to remove any errant seeds or bread-crumbs. Refrigerate the soup in an airtight container for at least 1 hour or up to 1 week before serving to let the flavors combine.

7. Serve with a drizzle of good extra virgin olive oil, a sprinkling of flaky salt, and a hunk of baguette.

CHOOSING TOMATOES

Heirlooms are the best tomatoes for this soup—they have the right balance of flesh to liquid and pack a ton of flavor. This is the part where you say, "But heirlooms are expensive!" and that's usually completely true. But most tomato farmers will have a bin of "second" tomatoes or "ugly ripes" set aside: These are the bruised, the overripe, the rough-skinned, and all-around-unpleasant-looking heirlooms, yearning to be cored and quartered and turned into gazpacho. And because they are not destined to be part of a beautiful caprese salad, they are sold on the cheap—often cheaper than garden-variety beefsteaks and vine tomatoes. These ugly ripe heirlooms at fire-sale prices are the tomatoes you want. (And if your tomato farmer doesn't subscribe to this policy, perhaps suggest it to him. And then go for a mix of vine tomatoes and beefsteaks, both of which should have bright, glowing skins and should feel heavy for their size. And maybe add an heirloom or two for good luck.)

ROASTED TOMATO SOUP

Sharper, deeper, and with a slight caramel richness, this is the badass, grown-up version of the creamy tomato soup generations of Americans grew up on.

It should obviously be paired with a grilled cheese sandwich for a perfect throwback lunch or dinner.

Makes 1 quart, or four 1-cup servings

4 vine tomatoes (or 5 plum tomatoes), cored and quartered

1 red or orange bell pepper, quartered and seeded

2 shallots, halved

4 whole cloves garlic, peeled

4 whole sprigs thyme

2½ tablespoons olive oil

2 tablespoons balsamic vinegar

Salt and freshly ground black pepper

2 to 3 tablespoons extra virgin olive oil

2 cups Basic Vegetable Stock (page 34)

1. Preheat the oven to 350°F.

2. Toss together the tomatoes, bell pepper, shallots, garlic, thyme, oil, and vinegar in a large baking dish. Season with salt and pepper and arrange in a single layer. Roast for 35 to 45 minutes, tossing occasionally, until the vegetables are soft and lightly browned and have released their juices.

3. Let cool slightly, then buzz everything in a blender, working in batches if necessary to keep soup from rocketing out of the blender. Drizzle in the extra

PRICE BOX

Tomatoes: $2.50

Bell pepper: $1

Shallots: $1

Garlic: 50¢

Thyme: 25¢

Total price: $5.25; per person: $1.31

virgin olive oil and stock through the hole in the lid to soften and expand the soup. Taste and adjust.

4. Serve, preferably with grilled cheese sandwiches or at least some good bread.

ROASTED RED PEPPER AND CORN SOUP WITH CILANTRO-LIME CREAM

While there are few things more satisfying in the summer than preparing a filling meal without ever turning on the stove or oven, this soup is well worth the heat. Roasting the peppers and corn first heightens their sweetness and makes for a luxuriously velvety soup that contrasts nicely with the fresh, bright herbs. I like to save this recipe for the tail end of summer, when grilling has lost its seasonal thrill and the nights are just starting to get that crisp edge.

Serves 6 to 8

SOUP

6 red bell peppers

1 jalapeño or serrano chile

6 tablespoons olive oil

1½ cups fresh, or 1 cup grilled/sautéed corn kernels (see page 113)

Sea salt and cracked black pepper

1 medium onion, diced

4 cloves garlic, minced

4 tomatoes, cored and quartered

3 cups Basic Vegetable Stock (page 34) or Meat Stock (use chicken; page 35)

2 tablespoons sherry vinegar

CILANTRO-LIME CREAM

¼ cup fresh cilantro leaves

Juice and zest of ½ lime

1 cup sour cream or plain strained or Greek-style yogurt

2 tablespoons olive oil

Sea salt and freshly ground black pepper

Good extra virgin olive oil for serving

Thick slices of crusty baguette for serving

1. Rinse the peppers and chile and pat them very dry. Char the skins by holding them directly over a burner flame in a pair of long tongs. When the skins are completely black, put the peppers in a large bowl and cover with a tight-fitting lid or plate. Let steam for 2 minutes, then hold the lid in place and shake the bowl vigorously for 60 to 90 seconds. This should beat off the skin and split the peppers open. Rinse away and discard the blackened skin, pith, and seeds. Set the peppers aside.

2. Heat 3 tablespoons of the oil in a Dutch oven or other heavy-bottomed pot over medium heat. Add the corn and season with salt and pepper. Cook, stirring occasionally, for about 2 minutes, until the corn is just starting to color. Remove to a bowl and set aside.

3. In the same pot, heat the remaining 3 tablespoons oil over medium heat. Add the onion and garlic, season with salt and pepper, and cook for about 15 minutes, until softened but not browned. Add the peppers and tomatoes and toss to combine. Let the peppers and tomatoes cook into the onions and garlic for about 10 minutes, until the tomatoes are soft and have begun to release their juices.

4. Add the stock, increase the heat to high, and bring to a boil. Immediately lower the heat and simmer, uncovered, for 20 minutes.

5. While the soup is simmering, make the cilantro cream: Roughly chop the cilantro. Whisk the lime juice and zest into the sour cream, then whisk in the oil in a steady drizzle. Season with salt and pepper and fold in the cilantro. Taste and adjust the seasoning; the cream should be tangy and light with an herby kick, but not overpowering. If the cilantro is too strong, fold in a little more oil. When you're satisfied with the cream, cover it and put it in the fridge to set.

6. Remove the soup from the heat and, working in batches, puree it in a blender until smooth, pouring the batches into a clean pot as you go. Add the vinegar. Taste and adjust the seasoning.

7. Pour the soup into bowls and top with a few spoonfuls of roasted corn and a generous dollop of the cilantro cream. Drizzle with a little good olive oil and serve with thick slices of crusty baguette.

PRICE BOX

Bell peppers: $6
Chile: 20¢
Corn: $1.50
Garlic: 50¢
Tomatoes: $2.50
Cilantro: $1; free if homegrown
Lime: 60¢
Sour cream/yogurt: $1.25 to $1.85

Total price: $12.55 to $14.15; per person: $1.57 to $2.36

GOT LEFTOVERS?

You can sauté fresh corn or use leftover grilled corn shucked from the cob.

BORSCHT

This vibrant, neon-pink soup is the perfect splash of color and flavor for the darkest winter day; with a touch of zesty ginger, it's also a fantastic way to welcome in spring's palette. If you don't like dill, you can complement the ginger with some freshly grated orange zest. Chives, rosemary, or tarragon are also great dill replacements, and chopped walnuts or toasted pumpkin seeds make wonderful toppings.

This recipe is based on our Polish grandfather Carl's recipe; it's the one I grew up on, and it is different from every other borscht I've ever had: no beans, no meat, no cabbage or potatoes. I love a chunky beet stew as much as the next girl, but I appreciate this recipe as a velvety, minimalistic paean to the beet, and it remains my favorite way to make borscht.

Serves 6

5 large beets

Olive oil as needed

Kosher salt

Cracked black pepper

1 medium onion, chopped

2 cloves garlic, minced

1 tablespoon peeled and grated fresh ginger

Fine sea salt

1 bay leaf

1 quart Basic Vegetable Stock (page 34) or Meat Stock (page 35)

1 tablespoon apple cider, balsamic, or red wine vinegar

3 tablespoons roughly chopped fresh dill, plus a few sprigs for garnish

About 1 cup sour cream, crème fraîche, or thick plain yogurt for garnish

3 tablespoons good extra virgin olive oil for drizzling

Toasted whole-grain bread for serving

1. Preheat the oven to 400°F.

2. Tip and tail your beets, saving the beet greens and stems for another dish. Rub the dirt from the beets, but don't skin them. Halve the beets.

3. Rub 2 beet halves with oil, a good pinch of kosher salt, and a few cracks of black pepper and place cut-side-down in a small baking dish or pie plate. Add 2 to 3 tablespoons of water to the dish, just enough to coat the bottom of the dish. Cover with aluminum foil and seal tightly. Pop the baking dish in the oven and roast for about 35 minutes, until you can slide a knife easily into each beet half. Check in on the beets once or twice as they roast to make sure they're not early achievers; when they're knife-tender, remove the dish but keep it sealed with the foil so the skins loosen as the beets cool.

4. While that beet is roasting, prepare the soup: Place the remaining 4 halved beets in a heavy saucepan or Dutch oven and cover with water by 1 inch. Bring to a boil over high heat, then immediately turn the heat down to medium-low and simmer, uncovered, for 40 minutes, or until the beets are knife-tender. Remove from the pan, and when the boiled beets are cool enough to handle, peel and quarter them. Strain the liquid through a piece of cheesecloth and reserve both the beets and the strained liquid.

5. Heat a tablespoon or two of oil in your heavy saucepan or Dutch oven over medium heat. Cook the onion for 2 minutes, or until softened but not browned, then add the garlic and cook for 2 minutes more, until softened but not browned. Add the ginger and season with sea salt and pepper.

6. Add the boiled beets, the strained beet juice, the bay leaf, and stock. Increase the heat to medium-

PRICE BOX

Beets: $2.50
Onion: $1.00
Ginger: 25¢
Dill: 25¢; free if homegrown
Sour cream, crème fraîche, or yogurt: $1.25 to $2
Bread: $1.50

Total price: $6.75 to $7.50; per person: $1.13 to $1.25

high, bring to a boil, then immediately reduce the heat to medium-low to low and simmer for 15 to 20 minutes, until the beets are fork-tender and the flavors have all incorporated.

7. Meanwhile, peel the roasted beets, cut them into 1-inch cubes, and set them aside for garnish.

8. Remove the borscht from the heat. Let it cool for about 5 minutes, then add the vinegar and dill. Puree with an immersion blender or in small batches in a blender. Taste and adjust the seasoning.

9. Serve immediately, or cool completely, refrigerate, and serve cold. Top each serving with a generous dollop of sour cream, a few roasted beet cubes, a sprig of fresh dill, a drizzle of good olive oil, a sprinkle of salt, and a grind of the pepper mill, with toasted bread slices alongside.

GRANDMA SHIRLEY'S MUSHROOM BARLEY SOUP

I grew up in a family of good cooks. Especially on my father's side, many of our recipes were passed down through the generations, and were archaic or odd in one way or another: Sometimes they called for obscure cuts of meat; often ingredients were referred to by their Yiddish names. I don't recall ever seeing my grandma Shirley use a cookbook, much less a recipe card; everything is stored in her brain, even now, at ninety-six. She cooked from memory and by feel and by smell and taste. I still believe this is the best way to learn how to cook.

As a kid, I did not like mushroom barley soup. I didn't like the texture of the barley or the sultry broth, fortified and fattened with marrow bones. I have since come to my senses; this is the first of her family's recipes I asked Shirley for when I started writing this book. True to our family's style of cooking, her over-the-phone reply wasn't much of a recipe, but more of an oral history with a few ingredients thrown in for good measure. I've translated her recipe into a more recognizable form and added a few touches of my own. Grandma Shirley's way of making this soup is to put everything into a big stockpot and cook it all together on a simmer for about two hours, a neat and efficient method. If you have a little more time, though, I recommend you cook the soup in stages to maximize each ingredient's flavor and texture within the soup. I also like to use one bottle of brown ale or rye beer; Grandma Shirley suggests throwing in a parsnip if you have one on hand. She also suggests taking the parsley out before serving and squeezing it over the soup to get all the juices out of it.

I make this soup in four steps, but they can all be done in just two vessels: one stockpot or Dutch oven and one pan.

Whether you make this Shirley's way or mine, the result is a hearty soup to warm your bones on the coldest winter night.

Serves 6 generously

Olive oil as needed

2 pounds beef marrow bones, shin bones, or mixed soup bones

Kosher salt and cracked black pepper

1 bay leaf

2 quarts Basic Vegetable Stock (page 34), Meat Stock (page 35), or water

1 pound button mushrooms

1½ cups pearl barley

4 cloves garlic, minced

12 ounces dark beer, such as brown ale or rye (optional)

2 large carrots, diced

2 stalks celery, diced

1 medium onion, diced

1 bunch parsley, tied together with kitchen twine (optional)

1 parsnip, diced (optional)

1. First, make a stock with the bones: Heat a splash of oil in a stockpot or large Dutch oven over medium-high heat. Add the beef bones and let any

remaining meat or fat on the bones brown, about 5 minutes a side. Season with salt and pepper, add the bay leaf, and cover with the stock. Bring to a boil, then immediately reduce the heat to low and cook at a gentle simmer, uncovered, for 2 hours, skimming off any foamy impurities as they rise to the surface. Meanwhile, prepare the rest of the soup.

2. Prep the mushrooms: Wipe the mushrooms gently with a damp paper towel, halve or quarter any large mushrooms, and thinly slice them. (A note on the mushrooms: You can make this entirely with button mushrooms, but if you've got a little wiggle room in your budget, replace ¼ pound of the button mushrooms with 1 large portobello and another ¼ pound with oyster mushrooms. The subtle diversity in flavor and texture will make the soup even more complex.)

3. Heat another splash of oil in a large sauté pan. Add the barley and toss to coat. Let the barley toast, tossing occasionally, until fragrant and lightly browned. Remove to a bowl and set aside.

4. Heat a second glug of oil in the sauté pan. Add half of the garlic and cook for about 1 minute, then add the mushrooms and season with salt and pepper. Toss the mushrooms to coat them with the oil and garlic and cook. At first they'll release their liquid; then they'll quickly shrink as the liquid evaporates. When the pan is dry, hit the mushrooms with about half of the beer, if using, stir, and cook down the mushrooms until they've absorbed almost all of the beer, about 10 minutes. Remove the mushrooms, garlic, and any remaining liquid into a second bowl and set aside.

5. Add a little more oil to the pan. Heat it up. Add the carrots and cook for 1 minute; add the celery and cook for another minute; then add the onion and the remaining garlic. Season lightly with salt and pepper and cook for about 5 minutes, until the carrots have just softened slightly. Set aside in a third bowl. Last one, I promise.

6. After the bones have simmered for 2 hours, stir the toasted barley into the pot. Yes, the bones are still in there—that's okay. Bring back to a simmer and cook for 15 minutes. Then add the carrots, celery, onion, and garlic and simmer for another 15 minutes. Now taste the barley: It should be al dente. If not, cook another 5 minutes and taste again. When the barley's al dente, add the mushrooms and the parsley bundle, if using, bring back to a simmer, and simmer for another 30 minutes. If at any point the soup is getting too thick, add the rest of the beer and a little more stock or water.

PRICE BOX

Bones: $8
Mushrooms: $4
Barley: $1.50
Garlic: 50¢
Carrots: 50¢
Celery: 50¢
Onion: $1.50
Beer (optional): $1.75
Parsley (optional): $1.50
Parsnip (optional): 55¢

Total price: $16.50 to $20.30; per person: $2.75 to $3.38

7. When the soup is thick and rich and the barley is soft, remove the soup from the heat. Using tongs, carefully remove the bones, parsley, and bay leaf. If you used marrowbones, stick the clean handle end of your wooden spoon into the bone to slide the marrow into the soup; stir the marrow in so it melts into the soup. Taste the soup and adjust the seasoning—it probably will be on the bland side, as the barley absorbs most of the salt during cooking.

8. Ladle into bowls and serve. The soup will keep in the refrigerator for up to 1 week or the freezer for 2 to 3 months.

Note: If the soup is too fatty for your tastes, you can make it in two stages. First, make the broth with the marrow or soup bones as directed and slide the marrow out of the bones and into the broth. Remove the bones and store the broth in the fridge until cool. Skim the fat off the top of the cooled broth and discard it; bring the broth back to a simmer while you prepare the rest of the ingredients, and continue making the soup as above.

FRENCH ONION SOUP

For me, French onion soup is like heirloom tomatoes or pumpkin pie: It has a season, specifically from the beginning of scarf weather to the last muddy thaw of spring. On a cold Sunday afternoon, there's little better than pulling on my softest sweatshirt and standing in front of a big pot of onions braising slowly in rich broth.

French onion soup is a work of balance: Let the broth go flat and you've got a bowl of watery onions; add too much sugar and it's like onion candy. The thyme and caramelized garlic and shallots suggested to me by the waiter at a little Parisian bistro, where I had the best bowl of French onion soup of my life, provide all the sweetness this dish needs, and I can't recommend enough using homemade beef or veal stock as the base for this soup.

Done right, French onion soup is hearty, luscious, and complex enough to be a satisfying meal unto itself; done right, it can also be quite time-consuming, so I like to make the biggest pot I can and freeze the leftovers for quick reheating throughout the winter.

Serves 4 to 6

3 tablespoons unsalted butter

2 tablespoons olive oil

4 to 6 cloves garlic, minced

2 shallots, minced

3 pounds onions, quartered, sliced, and layers separated

Kosher salt and cracked black pepper

1 bunch of fresh thyme sprigs, tied in a bundle with kitchen twine, 2 sprigs reserved

1 bay leaf

6 cups Meat Stock (use beef or veal; page 35) or Basic Vegetable Stock (page 34)

2 cups beer (brown ale or stout) or 2 cups red wine (preferably burgundy)

1 baguette or other crusty bread   **½ cup grated Gruyère cheese**

1 clove garlic, tip cut off   **½ cup grated Parmesan cheese**

½ cup grated Gouda cheese   **½ cup grated pecorino cheese**

1. Melt the butter with the oil in a large Dutch oven or stockpot over medium-low heat. Add the garlic and shallots and caramelize them, taking care not to let them burn, about 8 minutes. Add the onions and season with salt and pepper. Stir the onions to coat them in the fat. Add the thyme bundle and bay leaf and let the onions caramelize, stirring occasionally to make sure they don't burn, at least 20 minutes.

2. Once the onions have caramelized and cooked down, pour in the stock and beer and bring to a boil. Immediately reduce the heat to low and simmer, uncovered, for at least 1 hour but as long as 3 hours. Taste occasionally and adjust the seasoning as needed.

3. About 20 minutes before you're ready to serve the soup, slice the bread into ½-inch-thick slices, 2 per bowl. (You can use stale bread if that's all you have on hand.) Rub each side of bread with the clove of garlic and toast the bread.

4. In a large bowl, mix the grated cheeses together and set aside.

5. When the soup is done, preheat the broiler. Remove the thyme sprigs and the bay leaf from the soup.

6. Arrange 4 to 6 oven-safe bowls on a rimmed baking sheet or in a baking dish. Ladle soup over the toast, leaving about 2 inches at the top of the

PRICE BOX

Garlic: 75¢

Shallots: $1

Onions: $4

Thyme: $1.50

Beer: $1.75

Baguette: $2.50

Cheeses: $12

Total price: $23.50; per person: $3.92 to $5.88

CHEE$E

Using a variety of cheeses will give your soup extra depth and character, but it won't save you money. Luckily, all the cheeses in this recipe are versatile: for example, the Quesadilla (page 224) demands Gouda; and Parmesan and pecorino are called for throughout this book.

bowl. Top the soup with a second slice of toast. Cover the toast in cheese. Be generous! You want the cheese to seal in the soup and drape over the rim of the bowl.

7. Carefully place the sheet of soup bowls in the broiler and broil for 4 to 6 minutes, until the cheese is brown and bubbling on top. Garnish with a little thyme and serve.

SPICED SQUASH SOUP

This soup plays the sweetness of roasted butternut squash against a ballsy dose of good, kicking curry. It's delicious hot or cold and is relatively healthy despite its creaminess because the soup is based on vegetable broth and finished with just a shot of cream. It can also be made vegan with almond milk instead of the cream (vegans, also omit the yogurt garnish). If your curry powder is exceptionally strong and the soup comes out too spicy, you can tame it with a dash of cider vinegar.

Serves about 6

1 butternut squash

A good glug of olive oil

Kosher salt and cracked black pepper

Fine sea salt

1 quart Basic Vegetable Stock (page 34)

1 large carrot, diced

2 shallots, minced

2 cloves garlic, minced

2 to 3 tablespoons curry powder

1½ tablespoons ground cinnamon

Seeds from 6 cardamom pods (optional)

1 to 2 cups water, if necessary

¼ cup heavy cream (or ⅓ cup milk or almond milk)

About ⅓ cup thick plain yogurt (1 tablespoon per bowl)

1. Put a rimmed baking sheet in the oven and preheat the oven to 400°F.

2. Cut the squash in half widthwise, separating the neck from the body. Cut the neck in half lengthwise, and cut the body in half lengthwise too. Scrape the seeds and stringy flesh from the squash, reserving the seeds.

3. Rub the squash's flesh with oil, kosher salt, and pepper and roast it, flesh-side-down, on the preheated baking sheet until the skin has browned and wrinkled and a knife slides easily into the caramelized flesh, about 25 minutes.

4. Rinse any squash flesh off the seeds and pat the seeds very dry with a clean dishcloth. Arrange the seeds in a single layer on a piece of aluminum foil, place it on the baking sheet, and season with sea salt. Roast them for about 10 minutes, until toasty brown. Remove them and let them cool.

5. Prepare the vegetables and soup base: Heat the stock in a small saucepan over low heat. Don't let it boil or even simmer; you just want it to be hot enough so you can add it to the vegetables without it cooling them down.

6. Heat a good glug of oil in a Dutch oven over medium heat. Throw in the carrot and cook for 2 minutes; add the shallots, stir, and cook for 2 minutes; then add the garlic. Cook for—you guessed it—2 minutes, then season with salt and pepper and add the curry powder, cinnamon, and cardamom seeds if using. If the pan gets too dry, deglaze with a little of the stock.

PRICE BOX

Squash: $3
Carrot: 30¢
Shallots: $1
Cardamom (optional): 75¢
Cream/milk: 55¢ to $1
Yogurt: 42¢

Total price: $5.27 to $6.47; per person: 88¢ to $1.08

7. Once the squash is roasted, remove it from the oven and let it cool until cool enough to handle. Peel the skin off and mash, scoop, or chop the flesh up and add it to the pot. Stir to incorporate it into the rest of the vegetables and get it coated with the seasoning. Try to break the squash down as much as possible while you stir it. Then pour in the stock and add extra water, if necessary, to cover the vegetables in liquid. Bring to a boil, then reduce the heat and simmer, stirring occasionally, for about 20 minutes, until the flavors are combined, the squash has broken down, and the soup is thick but not stewlike.

8. Remove the soup from the heat and puree it in batches in a blender. Work carefully and don't overfill the blender; the steam of the hot soup could pop the lid off your blender, so hold it down with a dishtowel over your hand to prevent getting burned. Return the soup to a clean pan.

9. Stir in the cream and taste. The soup should be a little spicy, a little sweet, and creamy without tasting fatty. Adjust the seasonings as needed.

10. Serve hot or cool completely, refrigerate, and serve cold. Top with a dollop of thick yogurt and a good sprinkling of toasted squash seeds and kosher salt.

CARDAMOM

I like to add the seeds of 6 cardamom pods (which, by the way, is a phrase I love—"the seeds of 6 cardamom pods"—because it sounds like something from a medieval witch's brew). The cardamom offsets the heat of the curry with a very subtly sweet perfuminess. It's totally optional, but if you have cardamom on hand or are curious to try it, it works perfectly here.

A Cruciferous Green, a Bean, and a Sausage Walk into a Stockpot . . .

This is not the start to a bad joke (only because I haven't figured out a suitable punch line . . . yet) but rather the key to an almost endless variety of soup combinations. And it doesn't have to include sausage at all; the goal is to stew together at least one leafy cruciferous or bitter green with at least one mild, starchy legume and at least one hearty ingredient, be it sausage, ground or shredded meat, mushrooms, or root vegetables.

In addition to being packed with healthy vitamins, minerals, and antioxidants, the soup can be made, as demonstrated above, with whatever you have on hand, a welcome prospect when three-foot-tall banks of snow separate you from the grocery store down the block.

HERE'S MUD IN YOUR . . . SOUP?!

The greens in these recipes can be quite muddy or sandy. This is the easiest way to clean them:

Remove the thick stem ends and any brown or discolored leaves, then chop the greens and springier stems into roughly bite-size pieces.

Put the greens in a colander or the strainer insert of a salad spinner and put that in a larger bowl. Submerge the greens in cold water and ruffle them with your hands to separate them and circulate the water through them. Let them settle for a minute, then pull the colander or strainer out of the bigger bowl and discard the water.

Repeat this process of soaking and draining, soaking and draining, until the water left in the bowl is clean and free of dirt.

Dry your greens, either in a salad spinner or by patting them gently between two clean dishcloths.

COLLARD, WHITE BEAN, AND KIELBASA SOUP

Serves 8

4 tablespoons olive oil

1 medium onion, diced

4 cloves garlic, minced, plus 1 whole clove garlic

2 cups kielbasa cut into bite-size pieces

2 bunches collard greens, stemmed and cut into bite-size ribbons

Kosher salt and cracked black pepper

2 cups dried white beans

1 bay leaf

2 quarts Basic Vegetable Stock (page 34) or Meat Stock (page 35)

1½ tablespoons apple cider vinegar

Tabasco or other hot sauce

1. Heat the oil in a stockpot or large Dutch oven over medium-low heat. Add the onion and sweat for 2 minutes. Add the garlic and sweat for another minute. Add the kielbasa and cook until the meat is lightly browned, 4 to 6 minutes. Add the collards and season with salt and pepper. Using tongs, toss the collards to coat them with the oil and cook until they are shiny and bright green, about 5 minutes. Add the beans, bay leaf, and stock. Stir and add water as needed to cover all the ingredients.

2. Bring the soup to a boil, then reduce the heat to medium-low and simmer for about 1 hour, stirring occasionally. Taste the soup; the broth should be rich and slightly thickened, the beans should hold their shape but be soft inside, and the collards should be silky and easy to chew. Continue cooking for up to another hour if necessary—collards can take a long time. If the soup gets too thick, add more broth or water as needed.

3. Remove the soup from the heat and discard the bay leaf. Stir in the vinegar and season with hot sauce. Serve with thick slices of good crusty bread.

PRICE BOX

Onion: $1
Garlic: 50¢
Kielbasa: $8
Collards: $4
White beans: $2

Total price: $15.50; per person: $1.94

ESCAROLE, BLACK BEAN, AND CHORIZO SOUP

You can use fresh or cured chorizo for this soup; if using fresh, remove it from its casing to fry it, which should give your soup a lovely red color.

Serves 6

3 tablespoons olive oil

1½ cups crumbled or coarsely chopped chorizo

½ medium onion, diced

2 cloves garlic, minced

3 plum tomatoes, chopped, or 1½ cups boxed or canned tomatoes with their juice

½ teaspoon ground cumin

1 teaspoon paprika

2 heads escarole, chopped

Kosher salt and fresh cracked black pepper

1½ cups cooked black beans

1½ quarts Basic Vegetable Stock (page 34) or Meat Stock (page 35)

Thinly sliced manchego or pecorino cheese (optional) for serving

1. Heat the oil in a stockpot or large Dutch oven over medium-low heat. Add the chorizo and cook for 5 minutes, or until the meat is lightly browned and has rendered some fat into the pot. Remove with a slotted spoon and set aside on a plate. Add the onion to the pot and sweat for 2 minutes. Add the garlic and sweat for another minute. Add the tomatoes and their juice and the cumin and paprika. Cook for another 3 minutes, then add the escarole and season with salt and pepper. Toss the escarole into the ingredients in the pot and cook for 3 minutes, or until the escarole is bright and shiny.

2. Return the chorizo to the soup along with the beans and stock. Add water to cover as needed. Bring to a boil, then immediately reduce the heat to medium-low and simmer, stirring occasionally, for 20 to 25 minutes, or until the beans are heated through and the soup's flavors have combined.

3. Taste and adjust the seasoning. Serve with a slice or two of manchego or pecorino cheese, if using, along with thick slices of good crusty bread.

PRICE BOX

Chorizo: $3.50
Onion: 50¢
Tomatoes: $2
Escarole: $4
Black beans: 80¢ to $1.30
Cheese (optional): $2.50 to $3.50

Total price: $10.80 to $14.80; per person: $1.80 to $2.47

CURRIED SPINACH, LENTIL, AND SWEET POTATO SOUP

With hot curry balanced by a touch of cinnamon and a squirt of lemon, this soup is delicious and vegan. For a subtle yet decidedly non-vegan touch of decadence, swirl in a tablespoon of butter after you remove the soup from the heat.

Curry powders vary in potency; start with 2 tablespoons and keep going from there. Remember that the spices will strengthen overnight, so leftovers will be more flavorful the second day. You can always tame a suddenly very-spicy soup by reheating it with extra stock.

Serves 4

2 tablespoons olive oil

1 large carrot, diced

1 medium sweet potato, scrubbed clean and diced (about 1 cup)

½ medium onion, diced

2 cloves garlic, minced

Kosher salt and fresh cracked black pepper

2 tablespoons curry powder, plus more as needed

1½ teaspoons ground cumin

1 teaspoon ground cinnamon

1 teaspoon paprika

½ teaspoon ground ginger

Pinch of cayenne powder

1 cup dried lentils, rinsed and drained

1½ quarts Basic Vegetable Stock (page 34)

2 cups fresh spinach leaves

1 tablespoon lemon juice

1 tablespoon butter (optional)

1. Heat the oil in a stockpot or large Dutch oven over medium-low heat. Add the carrot and sweat for 3 minutes; add the sweet potato and sweat for 2 minutes; add the onion and sweat for 2 minutes; then add the garlic and sweat for 2 minutes. Season with salt and pepper and add the curry powder, cumin, cinnamon, paprika, ginger, and cayenne and cook for 2 minutes, or until fragrant.

2. Add the lentils and stock. Increase the heat to high and bring to a boil, then immediately reduce the heat to medium-low and simmer until the lentils are just al dente, about 25 minutes, stirring occasionally.

3. Add the spinach and lemon juice. Bring back to a simmer and cook for about 5 minutes, until the spinach is wilted and the lentils are tender. Remove from the heat and adjust the seasoning and spices as needed; stir in the butter, if using, then serve.

PRICE BOX

Carrot: 30¢
Sweet potato: $1
Onion: 50¢
Lentils: 75¢
Spinach: $2.50

Total price: $5.05; per person: 84¢

USE THOSE LEFTOVERS!

Shred about 1 cup of leftover roasted chicken into the soup along with the spinach; to adjust for this extra volume, add about ½ cup more stock. Oh, and if you're adding chicken, feel free to use chicken stock instead of vegetable stock—obviously the soup isn't vegetarian at this point anyway.

EARLY FALL CHICKPEA STEW

When things go well and it's been a good summer, I can still find good zucchini and tomatoes at the farmers' market even after the air has begun to crisp and cool.

When I have to put on a light jacket to go outside and it's finally cool enough to turn the stove on for longer than it takes to fry an egg, I know it's time to stew chickpeas and zucchini in a light sauce of fresh tomatoes. I make a large pot of it, because as delicious as it is hot that first night, it's even better served at room temperature the next day—which is sure as anything to be another scorcher.

Serves 6

1 to 2 tablespoons olive oil

½ medium onion, diced

1 clove garlic, minced

4 plum tomatoes, chopped

1½ teaspoons dried oregano

¼ teaspoon crushed red pepper flakes

1 tablespoon fresh thyme leaves

¼ cup fresh flat-leaf parsley (leaves and top 1 inch of stems only)

Salt and freshly ground black pepper

2 cups diced zucchini

2 cups cooked chickpeas

Zest of 1 lime

1. Heat the oil in a large saucepan or Dutch oven over medium heat. Sweat the onion for 2 minutes, then add the garlic and cook until fragrant, 1 to 2 minutes.

2. Add the tomatoes and season with the oregano, crushed red pepper, thyme, and half of the parsley. Season with salt and pepper and stir to incorporate. Cook for 12 to 15 minutes, until the tomatoes have released their juices and softened. Stir in the zucchini and chickpeas and cook at a low simmer until the zucchini is soft, about 10 minutes.

3. Remove from the heat. Fold in the rest of the parsley and the lime zest. Taste, adjust the seasoning, and serve over rice or pasta or with strips of grilled flatbread to scoop it all up.

PRICE BOX

Onion: 50¢
Tomatoes: $2.50
Parsley: 75¢
Zucchini: $2.50
Chickpeas: $1.75
Lime: 60¢

Total price: $8.60; per person: $1.43

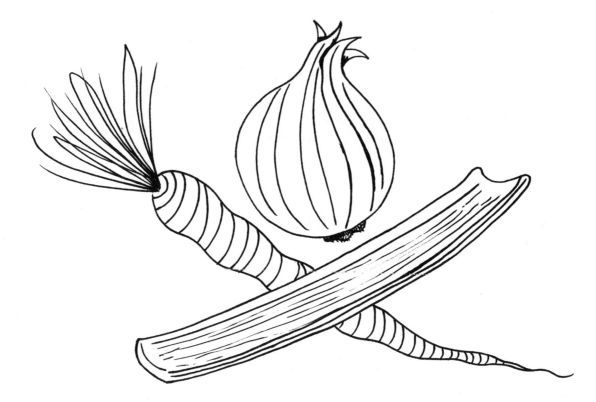

Chapter Eight

Main Dishes

BREAKFAST

GRANOLA

From the stalls of the Brooklyn Flea (more renowned as a hipster foodie food court than a regular old flea market) to bakeries and cafés across the country, everyone seems to be making and hawking homemade granola. Which, I think, means that you should just make some yourself and see what all the fuss is (rightly) about. For breakfast, this granola is delicious topped with thick local yogurt.

Serves 4

This basic granola is super adaptable! Play with the types and amounts of seasoning, nuts, and mix-ins like dried fruit, toasted coconut, flax seeds, and chocolate.

½ cup roughly chopped almonds

2 cups quick oats

Dash of fine sea salt

¼ to ⅓ cup maple syrup

½ cup (1 stick) unsalted butter, melted

1 teaspoon vanilla extract

1. Preheat the oven to 350°F.

2. Heat a small skillet over medium heat and toast the almonds until fragrant, about 5 minutes.

3. Pour the almonds, oats, and salt into a 9 x 9-inch baking dish and shake to combine. In a separate bowl, combine the maple syrup, butter, and vanilla and pour the mixture over the oats and almonds. Stir to coat the oats and almonds in the butter mixture, allowing some big clumps to form.

4. Bake for 30 minutes, stirring once halfway through. Let cool for 5 minutes before serving, or let cool completely and store in an airtight container or zip-top plastic bag for up to 2 weeks.

PRICE BOX

Almonds: $2.50
Oats: $1.05 to $2
Maple syrup: $2
Butter: $1.70 to $2.35

Total price: $7.25 to $8.85; per person: $1.81 to $2.21

TRADITIONAL CHEESE BLINTZES

A blintz is made of two components: a thin egg-batter crêpe and an inner filling of soft, mild cheese that can be made savory with caramelized onions and herbs or sweet with fresh fruit or chocolate. The crêpes are cooked in a pan on one side, filled, rolled up like little burritos, and then browned lightly in butter.

Want savory blintzes instead? Add an extra ¼ teaspoon salt and a few grinds of black pepper. Skip the sugar and vanilla and the toppings.

Serves 4 to 8

CRÊPES

3 large eggs

1 cup milk

4 tablespoons (½ stick) unsalted butter, melted

½ teaspoon salt

¾ cup all-purpose flour

CHEESE FILLING

2 cups Homemade Ricotta (page 59)

1 large egg, lightly beaten

1 tablespoon unsalted butter, melted

2 tablespoons sugar

½ teaspoon salt

1½ teaspoons vanilla extract

FOR SERVING

Powdered sugar   **Warm maple syrup**

1. Make the crêpe batter: Combine the eggs, milk, 2 tablespoons of the butter, and the salt in a blender and blend to combine. Add the flour and blend until just combined, about 30 seconds total, pausing once to scrape down the sides of the bowl. Put the batter in the refrigerator to chill for at least 1 hour or as long as overnight.

2. While you wait, make the cheese filling: Combine the ricotta, egg, butter, sugar, salt, and vanilla in a large bowl. Set aside.

3. Heat a griddle pan or cast-iron or nonstick skillet over medium-low heat. Brush evenly with a tiny bit of the reserved melted butter.

4. Spoon just enough batter into the pan to make a thin film; swirl the pan to coat it evenly. Cook for about 90 seconds, until the bottom is just lightly browned. Carefully remove the crêpe from the pan and set, browned-side-up, on a plate. Cover with a clean dish towel to keep warm.

5. Repeat until the batter is used up, brushing the pan with more melted butter as needed and stacking the crêpes under the towel.

6. Assemble the blintzes: Lay a crêpe on a plate, browned-side up. Spread a thick spoonful of filling in the center. Fold the bottom of the crêpe over the filling, fold in the sides, and roll the blintz away from you to seal in the filling, keeping the seam on the bottom. Set aside and repeat with the remaining crêpes.

PRICE BOX

Eggs: $1.40
Milk: 50¢
Butter: 85¢ to $1.18
Homemade Ricotta: $2.88 to $4.88
Fruit Compote: $2.50 to $4.50

Total price: $8.13 to $12.46; per person: $1.02 to $3.12

7. Turn the burner up to medium and brush again with melted butter. Fry the blintzes until browned on each side, about 3 minutes per side. Top with the compote, dust with powdered sugar, and drizzle with maple syrup.

PUMPKIN WAFFLES

This is a simple, seasonal twist on a favorite brunch dish. Candied pumpkin seeds make an elegant topping.

As with all buttermilk waffle batters, the waffles will fluff up better if the batter is refrigerated overnight, so plan accordingly.

Serves 4 to 8, depending on the size of your waffle iron

1¾ cups all-purpose flour

¼ cup packed light brown sugar

1 heaping teaspoon baking powder

½ teaspoon baking soda

¼ teaspoon salt

1½ teaspoons ground cinnamon

1 teaspoon grated nutmeg

½ teaspoon ground ginger

½ teaspoon ground cloves

2 large eggs

1 cup well-shaken buttermilk (see Note)

1 teaspoon vanilla extract

1 cup pumpkin puree (not pumpkin pie filling)

3 tablespoons unsalted butter, melted

CANDIED PUMPKIN SEEDS

¼ cup hulled pumpkin seeds

1 teaspoon unsalted butter

2 tablespoons maple syrup

Vegetable oil for the waffle iron

Butter, maple syrup, and crème fraîche or whipped cream for serving

1. Put the whisk attachment of your stand mixer or hand mixer in the freezer to chill.

2. In a large bowl, mix together the flour, brown sugar, baking powder, baking soda, salt, cinnamon, nutmeg, ginger, and cloves.

3. Separate the eggs, reserving the whites in a cool metal bowl.

4. In a medium bowl, whisk the egg yolks with the buttermilk, vanilla, pumpkin puree, and butter. Whisk in the dry ingredients until just combined—don't overmix. Any lumps will work themselves out overnight or in the waffle maker.

5. Take your mixer attachment out of the freezer and whisk the egg whites until they hold soft peaks. You know they're there when the whites "stand up" just barely when you remove the whisk from the bowl.

6. Very gently fold the whites into the batter, taking care not to crush the whites. At this point, you can refrigerate the batter overnight or freeze it for up to 1 month.

7. Preheat your waffle iron. If you are making the whole batch at once, preheat the oven to 250°F as well.

8. While your iron and oven are preheating, make the candied pumpkin seeds: Spread a silicone baking mat on your counter or lightly butter a piece of waxed paper. Preheat a nonstick skillet over medium heat. Toast the pumpkin seeds until they start to pop. Stir in the butter. Add the maple syrup and toss or stir until the syrup has coated the seeds, about 2 to 3 minutes. Spread the seeds out on the prepared silicone mat or waxed paper. Cool completely, then break apart with your hands.

9. Brush the waffle iron well with oil and close it again to reheat. Spoon some batter into the center of the iron; put in far less than you think you'll need,

as the waffles will expand voluminously as they cook. Cook the waffles as you normally would; I generally expect them to be done when they stop steaming. It's a rule that the first waffle won't be your best; taste it for seasoning and adjust as needed.

10. Transfer cooked waffles to a cooling rack or onto a baking sheet and keep warm in the oven.

11. Serve the waffles with butter, maple syrup, crème fraîche, and, of course, your candied pumpkin seeds.

Note: Don't have buttermilk? Whisk 1 to 2 tablespoons lemon juice into 1 cup plus 1 tablespoon whole milk and let clabber (curdle) for 10 minutes.

PRICE BOX

Flour: 50¢
Sugar: 50¢
Buttermilk: 75¢
Pumpkin puree: $1.50
Pumpkin seeds: 40¢
Butter, maple syrup,
and crème fraîche: $1

Total price: $4.65;
per person: 58¢ to
$1.16

EGGS *EN COCOTTE* WITH TOMATO AND SHALLOT

Eggs *en cocotte* are an exercise in egg Zen: You can walk away. You don't have to babysit them to make sure they don't go from raw soup to rubbery nothingness in the blink of an eye. It's okay; you can even make eggs *en cocotte* while the coffee's brewing.

Even better, eggs *en cocotte* are a perfect brunch dish because they can be made in batches large or small. Not only that, but each serving is also self-contained and "mix-ins" can be individualized. With a big pile of buttered strips of toast to dip into the lusciously oozing yolks, eggs *en cocotte* are an elegant and luxurious way to start the day. Even on those days when you just can't fathom doing anything more intense than catching up on your movie queue on the couch. Basic eggs *en cocotte* is all well and good, but this variation is hands-down my favorite and it's hardly any extra work.

Serves 4; multiplies easily

3 tablespoons olive oil

1 shallot, minced

½ cup whole cherry or grape tomatoes, halved

Salt and freshly ground black pepper

4 tablespoons plain thick yogurt, crème fraîche, or sour cream

4 large eggs

¼ cup shredded mozzarella cheese (preferably smoked mozzarella)

1. Preheat the oven to 425°F. Wipe the insides of 4 ramekins or custard cups or 4 holes of a muffin pan with the oil. Spread 1 tablespoon shallots and 3 or 4 tomatoes over the bottom of each ramekin and season with salt and pepper.

2. Pop the ramekins into the oven for about 8 minutes, until the tomatoes have burst and released some of their juices. Remove the ramekins from the oven and arrange them in a 9 x 13-inch baking dish. Add enough hot water to the dish to come halfway up the sides of the ramekins, creating a bain-marie.

3. Spread 1 tablespoon per ramekin of the yogurt over the tomatoes and shallots. Break an egg into each ramekin and top with a good pinch of mozzarella. Season with salt and pepper and bake the eggs for 10 to 12 minutes for loose yolks, 15 to 20 minutes for medium-set yolks, and up to 25 minutes for fully set yolks. Serve with buttered toast sliced into batons.

PRICE BOX

Shallot: 50¢
Tomatoes: $1.25
Yogurt, crème fraîche, or sour cream: 40¢ to $1.80
Eggs: $1.40
Mozzarella cheese: $1.75

Total price: $5.30 to $6.70; per person: $1.33 to $1.68

SUBSTITUTIONS AND INSTEAD OFS

As I mentioned in the recipe, eggs *en cocotte* is a great way to use up leftovers with. Just layer a tablespoon or two of any of the following under the eggs:

Beans
Pulled roasted pork
Hash browns
Bolognese Sauce (page 39)
Mushroom Ragu (page 163)
Grits
Chopped-up Roasted Broccoli (page 61)
Steamed kale or Swiss chard
Basic Tomato Sauce (page 37)

And eggs *en cocotte* can be topped with any cheese, from hard Parmesan to a more traditional Gruyère. Crumbled bacon or roasted garlic make great *en cocotte* toppings, as do fresh herbs like thyme, chives, or oregano. And don't forget a good crusty toast with lots of butter for dipping into the creamy yolks.

PIZZAS AND A CALZONE

MARGHERITA PIZZA FROM SCRATCH

To be perfectly honest, you don't need to be able to make your own pizza dough to make good pizza at home; most pizzerias will sell you a round or two of dough for just a couple bucks. But it's never a bad idea to have a good pizza dough recipe up your sleeve, and it can only help you become a better pizzaiolo (that's pizza chef to you) and better baker in general.

Whether or not you make your own crust, get a pizza stone. They cost about $10 and keep your oven heat consistent no matter what you're cooking. Factor in about 15 extra degrees and about 30 minutes of extra preheating time for an oven with a pizza stone. Invest in a large metal spatula or a short-handled pizza peel, the big, flat spatula pizzaiolos use to transfer pies to and from the oven. A peel is better because you can build your pizzas on it and slide them right into the oven.

Start with thicker crusts and work your way up to paper-thin Neapolitan-style crusts. Your pizza stone will need seasoning—and, as a pizzaiolo, so will you. So focus on getting your dough to a uniform thickness without tearing it. Don't be discouraged if a pizza (or two, or six) disassembles itself from the peel to the stone; just flip the toppings back onto the dough and fold it over itself to make a calzone. This is truly a case where you can't get too much practice, and the results of your efforts will most likely always be perfectly tasty, even if they're not, at first, the most Instagram-able concoctions.

Thicker and smoother than a basic tomato sauce, with a touch of sugar

Ready for more? Once you're comfortable making a basic dough, experiment by blending different flours and mixing in seeds, herbs, or even citrus zest.

and oregano, a good pizza sauce is a beautiful thing. Run your sauce through a blender to smooth it out; if it's too wet, slather it on your pizza dough and parbake for about 2 minutes before covering with cheese and other toppings.

Makes two or three 12- to 14-inch pizzas, depending on thickness

DOUGH

1 packet or 2½ teaspoons active dry yeast

1 cup warm water (about 120°F)

2 tablespoons honey

¼ cup olive oil, plus more for greasing the bowls

2½ to 3½ cups 00 or bread flour

2 teaspoons salt

All-purpose flour for dusting

WHICH FLOUR TO USE

00 flour is favored for pizza dough (and pasta). It's a very finely ground and lightweight flour that makes tender, supple dough; the 00 is an Italian classification that denotes how finely ground the flour is. As you can probably imagine, these qualities are reflected in its price.

Bread flour is a high-protein flour that will give your pizza crust a nice chewiness. It's also great for bread, obviously, and for making bagels and soft pretzels.

All-purpose flour is the most utilitarian flour, as you probably know: It works well for cakes, cookies, and breads. Pizza and pasta dough made with all-purpose flour will be heavier than that made with 00 or bread flour but still delicious.

PIZZA SAUCE

16 ounces boxed, canned, or jarred tomatoes, diced

3 tablespoons olive oil

1 clove garlic, minced

1 teaspoon dried oregano

½ teaspoon sugar

Salt and freshly ground black pepper

1 tablespoon tomato paste (optional)

MARGHERITA TOPPINGS

½ pound fresh mozzarella cheese, tightly wrapped in paper towels or a clean dishcloth to drain

Freshly grated Parmesan cheese

Extra virgin olive oil as needed

¼ cup fresh basil leaves

1. Make the dough: In a small bowl, whisk together the yeast, water, and honey until the honey dissolves. Let sit for 10 to 15 minutes, until the mixture is topped with a large, frothy head. Stir in the oil.

2. In a large bowl, combine 2½ cups of the 00 flour and the salt. Stir the proofed yeast and liquid in with your hands until a dough forms, adding more flour in ¼-cup increments as needed. Knead gently for 2 to 3 minutes, until the dough is smooth and shiny.

3. Transfer to a second large bowl lightly greased with oil. Roll the dough around in the bowl to form a ball that's greased on all sides, and drape the bowl with a plastic shopping bag, plastic wrap, or a slightly dampened clean dishcloth. Let rise in a warm spot for 1 to 2 hours, until doubled in size. If you're making the pizzas immediately, continue as below; if you're making the pizzas within the next 24 hours, transfer the covered bowl to the fridge and remove it 3 hours before you want to get the pizzas in the oven.

Lemon-Pepper-
Poppy Beet
Chips

page 64

Butter Lettuce
and Radishes with
Lemon-Poppy
Yogurt Dressing

page 88

Kale and Quinoa with
Roasted Tomatoes

page 98

Roasted Carrot Salad

page 101

French Onion Soup   *page 120*

Top: Borscht   *page 114*
Bottom: Spiced Squash Soup   *page 122*

Cherry Tomato
and Burrata Pizza

page 147

Fresh Kale and
Tomato Calzone

page 148

Polenta with
Mushroom Ragu
and a Poached Egg

page 162

Max's Cheddar
Shrimp 'n' Grits

page 165

Spice-Rubbed
Pork Tenderloin

page 203

Mussels with Ale
and Garlic

page 212

Apple Cake

page 244

Sea Salt–
Honey
Caramels

page 251

4. Divide the dough in half or thirds. Working on a clean, lightly floured surface, shape each piece into a ball, then gently flatten into ½-inch-thick discs. Lightly oil the discs and dust them with all-purpose flour, then cover loosely with plastic wrap and let rest for 2 hours. (You can also coat each ball in oil, double-bag the balls separately in zip-top bags, and freeze for up to 3 months at this point. Thaw in the fridge for a full day before you make your pizza.)

5. While the dough rises, make the pizza sauce: Drain the tomatoes thoroughly in a fine-mesh strainer or colander and set aside. In a heavy-bottomed nonreactive saucepan or Dutch oven, heat the oil over medium heat. Lightly sweat the garlic for 2 minutes, then add the tomatoes. Turn the heat down to low and stir to keep from scorching.

6. When the tomatoes have started to collapse, after about 4 minutes, stir in the oregano and sugar. Cook for another 2 minutes, then taste and adjust the seasoning with salt and pepper.

7. Puree the sauce with an immersion blender or in a blender or food mill. If it's still too liquidy, return it to the heat and whisk in the tomato paste. Use immediately for best flavor and consistency.

8. Make your pizza: Near the end of the dough's second rise, remove the racks from the oven and place a pizza stone on a rack in the lower third of the oven. Turn the oven to at least 450°F or preferably 500°F.

9. Generously dust your pizza peel and the fronts and backs of your hands with flour. Make loose fists with both hands and drape a portion of dough over your knuckles. Gently rotate your knuckles in concentric circles, slowly stretching and bouncing the dough. If things start to get sticky, flour your knuckles again. If the dough springs back and won't hold the stretch, let it rest on a floured surface for 5 to 20 minutes, until you can stretch it again. This will be a long process the first many times. Don't get discouraged. Work slowly

and patiently. If the dough tears, set it down on your floured surface and lightly oil one side of the tear. Seal the flap shut, using the oil as glue. Wait for 5 minutes for the bond to stick, then continue stretching.

PRICE BOX

Yeast: $1
Flour: 75¢ to $1.75 (depending on amount and type of flour used)
Tomatoes: $2.50
Garlic: 25¢
Mozzarella: $3
Parmesan cheese: 75¢
Basil: 75¢

Total price: $9 to $10; per pizza: or $3 to $5

10. When you've stretched your dough as large and uniform as you can without tearing it, gently lay it on your floured peel. If your dough is on the thick side (½ inch thick or more), brush it lightly with oil and slide it in the hot oven for 2 to 3 minutes. This will keep the cooking times of the dough, sauce, and cheese even. If your dough is thinner, or after your thicker dough has parbaked, slide the dough back onto your peel.

11. Lightly brush the dough with a smear of pizza sauce. Slice or tear the cheese into rounds or bits and sprinkle the cheese over the pizza. Slide the pizza into the oven and bake for 2 minutes. Check on the pizza and rotate it if it is browning unevenly. After a total of 5 to 8 minutes, when the crust is a caramel-bronze color and the cheese is melted and bubbling, your pizza is done.

12. Transfer the pizza to a cutting board. Dust evenly with Parmesan, drizzle with oil, and garnish with basil leaves. Let the pizza settle for 3 to 5 minutes, then slice and serve. If you'd like to freeze your pizza, let the pizza come to room temperature without adding the Parmesan, oil, or basil and freeze it; reheat in a 450°F oven for 5 to 8 minutes, then add your toppings and serve.

13. Repeat steps 9 to 12 for the remaining rounds of dough.

CHERRY TOMATO AND BURRATA PIZZA

Burrata is like a mozzarella marshmallow: a thin shell of elastic fresh mozzarella holds within it a ball of oozy-soft, custard-creamy curd. It is delicate and rich and grassy and sweet and, basically, edible perfection.

The trick to this pizza is to bake it cheese-less and add the burrata right when you pull the pie from the oven; baking the burrata will melt it and make it indistinguishable from regular fresh or buffalo mozzarella.

Of couse, if you can't find burrata, you can use fresh or buffalo mozzarella instead: Simply layer it under the tomatoes and bake as normal for a fresh white pizza.

Makes two 14-inch pizzas (serves 4 to 8)

1 recipe pizza dough (see Margherita Pizza from Scratch, page 142)

¼ cup extra virgin olive oil

1 clove garlic, minced

1 pint cherry tomatoes

Good pinch of fine sea salt

Pinch of crushed red pepper flakes

2 balls burrata or fresh mozzarella cheese

6 fresh basil leaves, roughly torn

1. Make the dough according to steps 1 to 4 of Margherita Pizza from Scratch, page 142.

2. Put your pizza stone in your oven and preheat the oven to at least 450°F but preferably 500°F. Remove the burrata from the fridge and carefully wrap each round in a clean paper towel. Set aside.

3. Continue with steps 8 and 9 of Margherita Pizza from Scratch, page 142.

4. When you've stretched your first round of dough on your floured pizza peel, lightly brush it with olive oil. Sprinkle half the garlic over your dough and add

half the tomatoes. Season with salt and crushed red pepper and slide the pizza onto the baking stone. Bake until the crust's edges have lightly browned and the tomatoes have burst.

PRICE BOX

Pizza dough: $1.75 to $2.75

Tomatoes: $2.50

Burrata: $12 to $16

Basil: 50¢; free if homegrown

Total price: $16.75 to $21.75; per pizza: $8.38 to $10.88

5. Remove the pizza from the oven and break the burrata over the pizza, letting it glop thickly around the pie. Let the burrata spread and melt, then sprinkle with the basil.

6. Repeat steps 4 and 5 with the second round of dough, slice, and serve.

FRESH KALE AND TOMATO CALZONE

Serves 2

⅓ recipe dough from Basic Margherita Pizza from Scratch (page 142)

2 heaping handfuls fresh kale leaves

¾ cup cherry or grape tomatoes, halved

2 cloves garlic, minced

¼ cup freshly grated Parmesan cheese

Olive oil as needed

Sea salt and freshly ground black pepper

⅓ pound fresh mozzarella, tightly wrapped in paper towels or a clean dishcloth to drain

1. Make the dough according to steps 1 to 4 of Margherita Pizza from Scratch, page 142.

2. Tear the kale into bite-size pieces. In a large bowl, combine the kale, tomatoes, garlic, and Parmesan. Toss with enough oil to thinly coat and season with salt and pepper.

3. Cut or tear the mozzarella into rounds.

4. Lightly brush the dough with oil. Cover one side of the dough with the mozzarella. Heap the kale mixture over the cheese. Cover with the remaining mozzarella and fold the dough over, pressing the ends together to seal. Lightly brush the top of the calzone with oil.

PRICE BOX

Pizza dough: 75¢
Kale: $1
Tomatoes: $1.75
Parmesan: 75¢
Mozzarella: $2.34

Total price: $6.59;
per person: $3.30

5. Bake for 8 to 10 minutes, rotating once halfway through, until the top crust is a deep mahogany color but not burnt. Remove to a cutting board, let cool for 5 to 8 minutes, then cut in half and serve.

PASTA

The arguments for the practicality of homemade pasta go far beyond the question of getting dinner on the table quickly. Leftover meat and cooked vegetables can be shredded or chopped and folded into Basic Tomato Sauce (page 37) for a hearty sauce; gorgeous ravioli can be made from Homemade Ricotta (page 59) alone or mixed with finely chopped beets; and once you make lasagna with homemade noodles rolled paper-thin, you will never want to go back to the boxed, wavy-edged dried lasagna noodles.

You can stock your kitchen with a pasta roller, ravioli cutter, tree for hanging long pasta to dry, and all sorts of shapers. But for basic noodles and ravioli, none of this is necessary. All you need is flour (preferably 00, but all-purpose will work; see page 143), an egg or two, and a good rolling pin. Actually, you don't even need a rolling pin; a clean, empty wine bottle will work just as well.

SWEET POTATO GNOCCHI

Like reality TV stars, sweet potatoes generally get buried under the weight of cosmetics—way too much sugar and spice, and sometimes, heretically, marshmallows. Can't there be some kind of middle ground? Something interesting, impressive, and elegant? Enter sweet potato gnocchi . . .

Subtly sweet, pillowy, and light despite their butter sauce, sweet potato gnocchi is one of those dishes that makes you feel like a badass just because you made them yourself, even though they're not hard to make in the least. Best of all? You can make a giant batch of gnocchi, freeze them on a baking sheet, then transfer them to freezer bags to store for later use. Pull them out of the freezer and plop them directly into boiling salted water. In 2 to 3 minutes, dinner will be ready with hardly any cleanup.

Serves 6 to 8

1½ to 2 pounds sweet potatoes, scrubbed	**1 large egg**
Kosher salt	**Sauce of your choice (see page 151 for one option)**
2 to 3½ cups all-purpose flour	**Freshly grated Parmesan cheese**

1. Put the sweet potatoes in a large saucepan and cover with water by 1 inch; salt the water heavily. Bring to a boil, reduce to a simmer, and cook for 15 to 20 minutes, until the sweet potatoes slide off the edge of a knife. Drain the sweet potatoes and let them cool until cool enough to handle, then peel them.

2. Mash the sweet potatoes by hand or in a ricer or food mill. Get them as smooth as possible. Season the sweet potatoes with a pinch of salt and add about 2 cups flour. You might need more, but start with 2. Add the egg and mix together until a soft dough forms, adding more flour as needed if the dough is sticky.

3. Gently knead the dough for 2 minutes. Wrap it in plastic wrap and let it rest for 15 to 20 minutes.

4. Flour a clean work surface. Unwrap the dough and gently knead and flatten it into a ½-inch-thick rectangle. Cut the rectangle into equal-size logs and roll each log out from the center, delicately pushing the dough out to the ends to elongate it.

5. Bring another large pot of generously salted water to a boil. While it comes up, roll out the gnocchi.

6. Divide the dough into little pillows about the size of the top third of your thumb with a knife or bench scraper. Gently make an indentation in the center of each gnocchi with your thumb or roll the gnocchi over the back of a fork's tines to give the sauce something to grip to. If you're not making the gnocchi right away, let them rest in the fridge for up to 2 days or arrange in a single layer on a baking sheet, cover loosely with plastic wrap, and freeze. When frozen, move the gnocchi to a ziplock bag and store in the freezer for up to a month.

BROWN BUTTER SAGE SAUCE

Here's a simple but great sauce that you can serve with the gnocchi:

Butter (figure 2 tablespoons per person)
Sage leaves (figure 1 leaf per tablespoon of butter)

1. Melt the butter in a saucepan over medium heat, swirling it to keep the butter cooking evenly, until the butter turns brown.
2. Fry the sage leaves in the butter for 3 to 5 minutes, then turn the heat to very low to keep it warm while you cook the gnocchi.

7. Add the gnocchi to the boiling water in small batches, 10 to 12 at a time. After you drop them in, stir the pot once to keep the gnocchi from sticking. They'll rise to the top when they're done—it takes just 2 to 3 minutes.

8. Toss the cooked gnocchi into the Brown Butter Sage Sauce or the sauce of your choice to coat, then serve with freshly grated Parmesan.

PRICE BOX

Sweet potatoes: $2.50 to $3.50
Flour: 50¢ to 75¢

Total price: $3.00 to $4.25; per person: 38¢ to 71¢

RICOTTA RAVIOLI IN BROWN BUTTER WITH SAGE

A light filling of ricotta mixed with egg and Parmesan and just kissed with a pinch of nutmeg makes for an elegant and filling dinner. Once filled, ravioli can be spread out and frozen on a baking sheet dusted with coarse cornmeal or polenta, then transferred to zip-top bags and frozen for up to 3 months. Like other fresh frozen pastas, the ravioli can go straight into the boiling water, no thawing necessary.

A half recipe of Basic Pasta Dough will make 12 good-size ravioli, or enough for 2 entrées or 3 or 4 appetizers. Make the full recipe, though, and freeze half of your ravioli; the extra few minutes of work now will mean a quick dinner on another night.

Serves 4 as a main or 6 to 8 as a side or appetizer

1 recipe Basic Pasta Dough (page 51)

3 large eggs

¾ cup Homemade Ricotta (page 59)

½ teaspoon freshly grated nutmeg

Sea salt and cracked black pepper

Freshly grated Parmesan cheese

8 tablespoons (1 stick) unsalted butter

8 whole fresh sage leaves

1. Make the Basic Pasta Dough, and divide it into three pieces. On a clean, floured work surface, roll out one piece of dough, elongating it as you go. Continue dividing it into sections if it becomes too long for your work surface. Roll out until the dough is just thick enough not to be translucent, then trim off any raggedy edges and let rest under a damp paper towel. Repeat this rolling and dividing until all your dough is rolled out and trimmed.

2. Whisk 1 of the eggs in a small bowl to make an egg wash. Set aside.

3. Bring a large stockpot of water to a rolling boil.

4. In a medium bowl, beat the remaining 2 eggs. Fold in the ricotta, add the nutmeg, and season with salt and pepper. Fold in about ¼ cup Parmesan; taste and adjust. The filling should be thick and tasty, not pastelike or watery. Set aside.

5. On your floured work surface, set out the pasta sheets one at a time. Make a crease widthwise in the center of each pasta sheet.

6. Hold your left index and middle fingers together and set them at the right edge of the crease in the center of your pasta sheet (switch "right" for "left" and vice versa if you're left-handed). Place about 1 tablespoon of the ricotta filling to one side of your fingers, then move your fingers to the other side of the filling. The idea is that you're using your fingers to evenly space out the ravioli. Repeat until one entire side of your pasta sheet is dotted evenly with

the filling, leaving a two-finger space at the end of the sheet. Leave the other half of your pasta sheet blank. Repeat on the remaining pasta sheets: Crease and add filling evenly spaced on one side until all the filling is used or you run out of pasta.

7. Using your fingers, wipe the egg wash thinly along the borders of the ravioli, painting a box around each scoop of filling. Carefully fold the empty half of each pasta sheet over to the filling side and seal each ravioli, pushing out air bubbles as you go. As with cased sausage, air pockets in your ravioli could cause bursting in the boiling water, resulting in a very sad state of affairs after all your hard work. (Boiled ricotta is not appetizing, I promise you.)

8. Salt your boiling water. Heat the butter in a large sauté pan over medium-high heat until it melts and browns; add the sage leaves and turn the heat down to medium.

9. Separate the ravioli with a knife or bench scraper. Check again to make sure they're all sealed and air-pocket-free. Gently slide the ravioli into the water in batches of 4 to 6. Stir once or twice to keep the ravioli from sticking and cook until they float, 2 to 3 minutes. Transfer the ravioli to the pan with the brown butter using a slotted spoon and toss together, adding pasta water in ¼-cup increments until the sauce thickens and sticks to the ravioli.

10. Plate 6 ravioli and 2 sage leaves per person as a main or 3 to 4 ravioli and 1 sage leaf as an appetizer or side, drizzled with the brown butter and dusted with Parmesan and a sprinkle of salt and a grinding or two of black pepper.

PRICE BOX

Basic Pasta Dough: $1.25 to $2
Homemade Ricotta: $1.08 to $1.83
Butter: $1.70 to $2.32
Sage: 25¢

Total price: $4.28 to $6.40; per person: 54¢ to $1.60 (main), 53¢ to 80¢ (side)

BEET RAVIOLI IN LEMON BUTTER

A gorgeous, tasty, and playful ravioli. When you cook the ravioli, they emanate a diffused ruby glow.

Serves 4 as a main or 6 to 8 as a side or appetizer

2 large red beets

Olive oil as needed

Kosher salt and cracked black pepper

½ cup Homemade Ricotta (page 59)

2 large eggs

½ teaspoon freshly grated nutmeg

Fine sea salt

1 recipe Basic Pasta Dough (page 51)

½ cup (1 stick) unsalted butter

½ cup white wine

Juice and zest of 1 lemon

¼ cup heavy cream

1 tablespoon snipped fresh chives

Freshly grated Parmesan cheese

1. Preheat the oven to 400°F. Tip and tail the beets, saving the beet greens and stems—rinsed well and sautéed in olive oil with fresh garlic, they make a delicious alternative to wilted spinach. Rub the dirt from the beets, but don't skin them. Halve the beets.

2. Rub the beet halves with oil, a good pinch of kosher salt, and a few cracks of black pepper and place cut-side-down in a small baking dish or pie plate. Add 2 to 3 tablespoons of water to the dish, just enough to leave a thin layer on the bottom of the dish. Cover with aluminum foil and seal tightly. Pop the beets in the oven and cook for about 35 minutes, until you can slide a knife easily into each beet half. Check in on the beets once or twice to make sure they're not early achievers; when they're knife-tender, remove the dish but keep it sealed with the foil so the skins loosen as the beets cool.

3. When the beets are cool enough to handle, rub the skins off. Finely grate the beets into a medium bowl. Fold in the ricotta, 1 of the eggs, and the nutmeg. Season with sea salt and pepper and set in the fridge to come together until cooled to room temperature.

4. Make the Basic Pasta Dough and roll it out per step 1 of the Ricotta Ravioli, (page 152).

5. Assemble the ravioli with the beet-ricotta filling following steps 5 to 7 for the Ricotta Ravioli (page 152). Separate the ravioli with a bench scraper and cover with a damp paper towel to keep from drying out.

6. Bring a large stockpot of water to a rolling boil. As it comes up, make the lemon butter sauce: First, cut the butter into tablespoon-size pieces and set aside.

7. In a large skillet over high heat, bring the wine and lemon juice to a boil. Immediately reduce the heat and simmer, stirring occasionally, until reduced by half, about 20 minutes. Whisk in the cream and cook until reduced by half again, 4 to 5 minutes.

8. Turn the heat to a whisper above low and whisk in the butter, 1 tablespoon at a time, until the full stick is incorporated. The sauce should coat the back of a spoon. Whisk in the lemon zest and half the chives and season with salt and pepper; remove from the heat and cover to keep warm.

9. Salt the boiling water and slide the ravioli into it in batches of 4 to 6. Stir to keep them from sticking, and boil until they rise to the surface, 2 to 3 minutes.

PRICE BOX

Beets: $1.25
Homemade Ricotta: 72¢ to $1.22
Basic Pasta Dough: $1.25 to $2
Butter: $1.70 to $2.32
Wine: $1
Lemon: 70¢
Heavy cream: $1

Total price: $7.62 to $9.49; per person: 95¢ to $2.37

10. Transfer the ravioli to the lemon butter sauce with a slotted spoon, then return the sauce to the burner over low heat. Toss together, adding pasta water in ¼-cup increments until the sauce thickens and sticks to the ravioli.

11. Serve 6 ravioli for a main or 3 or 4 as an appetizer or side, drizzled generously with the lemon butter sauce and dusted with Parmesan and the remaining chives.

PAPPARDELLE WITH LAMB RAGU

You can serve this the same night you make it, but it will be even better the next day. Instead of the boned lamb, you can use 2 pounds lamb stew meat on the bone and save the bones for making lamb stock (see Meat Stock, page 35). You can use dried or fresh pasta; for instructions on making pasta yourself, see page 51.

Serves 4

1 tablespoon canola oil

1 pound lamb stew meat, cubed

Salt and freshly ground black pepper

½ medium onion, diced

½ teaspoon anchovy paste

2 teaspoons ground cinnamon

2 sprigs fresh thyme

4 sprigs fresh rosemary

¼ cup pitted and chopped kalamata olives

About 1 cup red wine

1 pound pappardelle pasta

¼ cup julienned fresh mint leaves

Freshly grated Parmesan cheese

1. Preheat the oven to 350°F.

2. Heat the oil in a Dutch oven over medium heat. Season the lamb with salt and pepper and sear until browned on all sides, working in batches if necessary

so you don't crowd the pan. Remove the lamb to a plate or bowl, add the onion to the fat in the pan, and sauté until translucent, 3 to 4 minutes.

3. Stir in the anchovy paste until dissolved, then return the lamb to the pan. Add the cinnamon, thyme, rosemary, and olives and stir together. Pour in enough wine to cover the meat and bring to a boil.

4. Cover the pan and place it in the oven. Braise the lamb for as long as you can: at least 2 hours but as long as 4 hours, reducing the heat to 250°F after the first hour. The longer you cook it, the richer the sauce will be. Check the pot occasionally to make sure the liquid hasn't all evaporated; add a dash of water if necessary to keep things just this side of wet. The lamb is done when it breaks apart easily with the tines of a fork.

5. Shred the lamb with a fork and let rest while you prepare the pasta, or refrigerate overnight (in which case, let the Dutch oven cool to room temperature, then stick the lid back on and pop it into the fridge). Reheat in the Dutch oven over medium-low heat when you are ready to make the pasta.

6. Bring a pot of water to a rolling boil, salt it, and add the pasta. Cook the pasta to al dente: about 2 minutes for fresh pasta or 8 minutes for dried. Using tongs, transfer the pasta to the lamb ragu and toss together. Add pasta water in ¼-cup increments to loosen the ragu if necessary. Taste and adjust the seasoning and serve topped with the mint and Parmesan.

PRICE BOX

Lamb: $15
Onion: 50¢
Anchovy paste: 25¢
Kalamatas: $2.25
Red wine: $2
Pappardelle: $1.25 to $3.50
Mint: 75¢; free if homegrown

Total price: $21.25 to $24.25; per person: $5.31 to $6.06

ALMOST COMPLETELY HOMEMADE LASAGNA WITH BOLOGNESE

Hearty, rich, and satisfying: the ultimate comfort food. In all honesty, I had never had lasagna with Bolognese until the age of twenty-nine. Part of it was because I grew up vegetarian; the other part, I guess, is just a habit carried over from my parents' house, where ground meat is only really used as a main ingredient, never a component in a dish. Plus, the only lasagnas I'd ever seen with Bolognese also included a heavy béchamel sauce, a combination too heavy to pique my interest.

I am thankful, then, to Chef Brendan McDermott for forever corrupting me and showing me how delicious lasagna with Bolognese can be—and how it doesn't need a béchamel at all.

Serves 10

2 recipes Basic Pasta Dough (page 51)

1 tablespoon olive oil

1 bunch fresh spinach

Sea salt and cracked black pepper

1 large egg

3 cups Homemade Ricotta (page 59)

1 recipe Bolognese Sauce (page 39)

1 pound fresh mozzarella

Freshly grated Parmesan cheese

1 clove whole garlic

¼ cup julienned fresh basil leaves

1. Preheat the oven to 400°F.

2. Make the Basic Pasta Dough, divide it in half, and roll out each half on a clean, floured work surface. Keep unused pieces under a damp paper towel

to keep them from drying out. Divide the dough further as you elongate it if it's too long for your work surface and roll out until all the dough is just thick enough to not be translucent. Trim the sides of each sheet of dough to make them straight and let rest under your damp paper towel.

3. Heat the oil in a medium sauté pan over medium heat. Add the spinach, season with salt and pepper, and sauté until wilted, 3 to 4 minutes. Drain and cool.

4. Whisk the egg into the ricotta in a bowl. Season with salt and pepper.

5. Build the lasagna in a large rectangular baking dish or casserole. First, spread a thin layer of Bolognese evenly over the bottom of the dish. Cover with a layer of noodles without letting them overlap. Spread a thin layer of ricotta over the noodles, topped with a few thin slices or torn-off pieces of mozzarella. Dust with Parmesan, sprinkle with some of the sautéed spinach, and season with salt and pepper. Cover with another layer of noodles, being careful not to let them overlap, then repeat, starting from the Bolognese. Continue until your dish is full or you run out of noodles—whichever comes first.

6. Finish with a thick layer of mozzarella and Parmesan. Grate the raw garlic clove over the lasagna with a Microplane zester or fine grater and season with salt and pepper.

7. Bake, uncovered, for 15 to 20 minutes, until the top layer of cheese is bubbling and just browning. Cover with foil and bake for another 10 to 15 minutes to cook through.

8. Remove from the oven and let rest for 10 minutes. Dust with fresh Parmesan, top with the basil, and serve.

PRICE BOX

Basic Pasta Dough: $2.50 to $4
Spinach: $2
Homemade Ricotta: $4.32 to $7.32
Bolognese: $19.15
Mozzarella: $7
Basil: 25¢; free if homegrown

Total price: $34.97 to $39.72; per person: $3.50 to $3.97

FETA, RED ONION, AND TOMATO PASTA SALAD

(OR HOW I SPENT AN UN-AIR-CONDITIONED SUMMER IN NEW YORK)

I spent the summer between junior and senior years at NYU in a dorm on Broome Street, in a strange strip of the city that's not quite SoHo, not quite NoLita, yet not Chinatown. None of my friends were spending the summer in the city. I had two internships and a part-time job that paid under the table and therefore far under the state's minimum wage. My apartment was a small studio with no air conditioner and one window, which my roommate monopolized to blow her cigarettes out of and to line-dry her underwear. I couldn't afford the subway, so I walked everywhere and ate as frugally as possible.

On the other hand, I spent countless hours wandering across the city, whole afternoons in the pay-what-you-wish labyrinth of the Metropolitan Museum of Art, and ate this pasta salad practically every day. Bright, fresh, and more refined than anything else I could afford that summer, it's still one of my favorite dishes when the weather gets hot.

Serves 4

Kosher salt

1 pound bowtie pasta

½ pint cherry or grape tomatoes, halved

¼ red onion, very thinly sliced

1 cup crumbled feta cheese

Extra virgin olive oil

½ teaspoon crushed red pepper flakes

Sea salt and freshly ground black pepper

2 tablespoons julienned fresh basil

1. Bring a large pot of water to a rapid boil. Salt it heavily with kosher salt and stir in the pasta; bring back to a boil and cook for 9 to 11 minutes, until al dente.

2. In a large bowl, toss together the tomatoes, onion, and feta. Toss in about 1 tablespoon oil and season with the crushed red pepper, sea salt, and pepper.

3. When the pasta's done, transfer it to the bowl. Toss everything together; add a little more oil and/or a little more pasta water to create a light dressing. Fold in the basil. Taste and adjust the seasoning; serve hot or cool completely, refrigerate, and serve cold.

PRICE BOX

Pasta: $1.75 to $2.50
Tomatoes: $2
Red onion: 25¢
Feta: $3.50 to $4.50

Total price: $7.50 to $9.25; per person: $1.88 to $2.31

POLENTA, GRITS, AND RISOTTO

POLENTA WITH MUSHROOM RAGU AND A POACHED EGG

This is an easy, elegant, decadent, and filling dish, and it's also a perfect grown-up dish for a weekend brunch. Serve it to a table of your favorite people. Watch their faces as they pierce the eggs and the yolks ooze and burrow through the mushrooms and down to the polenta.

Serves 4

POLENTA

1 quart Basic Vegetable Stock (page 34) or Meat Stock (use chicken; page 35)

1 cup polenta (not instant)

Pinch of fine sea salt, to taste

2 tablespoons unsalted butter

¼ cup freshly grated Parmesan cheese, plus more for serving

2 tablespoons ricotta, blue cheese, or milk (optional)

MUSHROOM RAGU

¼ cup olive oil

2 shallots, thinly sliced

4 cloves garlic, minced

2 cups fresh mushrooms (button, cremini, portobello, oyster, shiitake) cleaned and sliced into ribbons

Salt and freshly ground black pepper

2 tablespoons minced fresh rosemary

2 tablespoons fresh thyme leaves

¼ cup Basic Vegetable Stock (page 34)

¼ cup white wine (optional)

EGGS

4 large very fresh farm eggs

1 teaspoon white vinegar

½ teaspoon fine sea salt

Freshly ground black pepper

Good extra virgin olive oil for drizzling

Fresh rosemary sprigs for garnish

1. Make the polenta: Bring the stock to a rapid simmer in a large, heavy saucepan. Slowly whisk in the polenta until it is incorporated and feels "sludgy" against the whisk or a wooden spoon. Reduce the heat to a gentle simmer so the polenta is only bubbling slightly and cook, stirring often with a wooden spoon, for 30 to 40 minutes, until thick and creamy.

2. Remove the polenta from the heat and whisk in the salt, butter, Parmesan, and ricotta, if using. Taste and adjust the seasoning but keep it on the bland side; the mushrooms will add a lot of flavor.

3. While the polenta is cooking, make the mushroom ragu (but don't forget to stir the polenta often): Heat the oil in a large sauté pan over medium-

low heat. Add the shallots and the garlic and sweat in the oil for about 8 minutes, until the shallots are translucent but not browned. Add the mushrooms, season with salt and pepper, and cook until lightly browned, about 5 minutes. Add the rosemary and 1 tablespoon of the thyme and cook until the herbs become fragrant, about 1 minute. Pour in the stock and wine, if using, and stir, scraping up any browned bits on the bottom of the pan. Cook at a simmer until the broth is thick and rich and the mushrooms have absorbed most of the liquid. Fold in the rest of the thyme and remove from the heat.

4. Poach the eggs: Break each egg into an individual bowl or ramekin. If any of the eggs have broken yolks, set them aside for another dish.

5. Fill a large pot with at least 4 inches of water, add the vinegar and ½ teaspoon salt, and bring to a gentle simmer. If you want to test it with a thermometer, the temperature should read 180°F. A visual guide: Small bubbles on the floor of the pot, no bubbles breaking the surface.

6. Slide 1 egg into the water. It will fall to the bottom and then rise back up, the white encircling the yolk. Once it has done so, you may slide a second egg into the pot, but be careful not to overcrowd. Work in batches. After the whites have set around the yolks and turned opaque, 3 to 4 minutes, gently pull the eggs out with a slotted spoon. Let them rest on a clean dishcloth or a few layers of paper towel to remove the excess water, then season with salt and pepper.

7. Divide the polenta among 4 bowls. Top with a scoop of the mushroom ragu and a poached egg. Dust with Parmesan, drizzle with good olive oil, and top with a sprig of rosemary.

PRICE BOX

Polenta: 75¢
Parmesan cheese: 75¢
Olive oil: 75¢
Shallots: $1
Garlic: 75¢
Mushrooms: $4 to $6
Rosemary: 25¢; free if homegrown
Thyme: 25¢; free if homegrown
White wine (optional): 50¢ to $1
Eggs: $1.50

Total price: $9.50 to $13; per person: $2.38 to $3.25

MAX'S CHEDDAR SHRIMP 'N' GRITS

My brother Max makes a mean bowl of grits, that classic Southern comfort staple. This recipe is perfect for an intimate affair or dinner party or paired with a Bloody Mary for a hangover-curing brunch. All you really need is a little lemon, butter, and good vinegary hot sauce. And, of course, bacon and shrimp.

While stone-ground grits generally are slightly coarser, grits and polenta are basically interchangeable. No need to keep both in the pantry!

Try to buy wild-caught fish from your farmers' market or U.S.-farmed shrimp from your fishmonger or grocery store; according to the Monterey Bay Aquarium's Seafood Watch website, U.S. shrimp farms currently have the lowest environmental impact. They might be expensive, but they are well worth it.

Serves 3 or 4

GRITS

4 cups water or Basic Vegetable Stock (page 34)

1 cup stone-ground grits, or polenta (not instant)

1 cup grated cheddar cheese

2 tablespoons unsalted butter

Kosher salt and freshly ground black pepper

SHRIMP

1 pound medium, large, or jumbo shrimp

1 cup Basic Vegetable Stock (page 34)

2 tablespoons olive oil

½ cup diced thick slab bacon

Sea salt and cracked black pepper

1 clove garlic, minced

1 chile (jalapeño or Fresno), diced

Juice of ½ lemon

1 tablespoon unsalted butter

Hot sauce

2 scallions, thinly sliced

1. Make the grits: Bring the water or stock to a boil in a medium saucepan. Lower the heat to low and whisk in the grits. Cook, whisking often, until the grits are smooth and creamy, about 30 minutes. Remove from the heat and whisk in the cheese and butter. Season with salt and pepper and cover to keep warm.

2. Make the shrimp: Clean and peel the shrimp, reserving the shells.

3. Put the stock in a medium saucepan and add the shrimp shells. Bring to a low boil over medium-high heat and boil until reduced by half, about 10 minutes.

4. Heat the oil in a large skillet or sauté pan over medium heat. Add the bacon and cook, stirring occasionally, until crisp, about 3 minutes per side. Remove bacon to a paper towel–lined plate and set aside.

5. Season the shrimp with salt and pepper and add to the skillet. Cook until just pink, about 2 minutes. Remove from the skillet and set aside.

6. Add the garlic and chile and cook until softened, about 1 minute. Add the reduced shrimp stock and cook until reduced by half, about 5 minutes. Add the shrimp back in and cook until fully cooked, about 3 minutes. Add the lemon juice and stir to incorporate.

7. Remove from the heat, add the butter, and season with hot sauce (I do about 3 good shakes).

8. Serve the shrimp over the grits, topped with the bacon and the scallions.

PRICE BOX

Grits: 50¢
Cheddar cheese: $3 to $4
Shrimp: $15
Bacon: $1.70
Chile: 20¢
Lemon: 40¢
Scallions: 20¢

Total price: $21 to $22; per person: $5.25 to $7.34

GRITS AND SAUSAGE IN TOMATO SAUCE

Cured chorizo and andouille sausage are practically interchangeable here—basically you want a spicy, assertive sausage. Eat this for brunch and you'll be set for the rest of the day.

Serves 4

GRITS

1 quart Meat Stock (use chicken; page 35)

1 cup stone-ground grits or polenta (not instant)

¼ cup heavy cream

2 tablespoons unsalted butter

Kosher salt and freshly ground black pepper

TOPPING

2 tablespoons olive oil

3 cups chorizo or andouille sausage

1 clove garlic, minced

1½ cups Basic Tomato Sauce (page 37)

1 teaspoon paprika

Salt and freshly ground black pepper

Hot sauce

1. Make the grits: Bring the stock to a boil in a medium saucepan. Lower the heat to low and whisk in the grits. Cook, whisking often, until the grits are smooth and creamy, about 30 minutes. Remove from the heat and whisk in the cream and butter. Season with salt and pepper and cover to keep warm.

2. Make the topping: Heat the oil in a large skillet over medium heat. Add the sausage and cook until lightly browned, about 4 minutes. Add the garlic and cook for 1 minute. Add the tomato sauce and paprika and season with salt and pepper. Cook, stirring and scraping up any browned bits from the bottom of the skillet, until the sauce is heated through.

3. Serve the grits with the topping. Pass a bottle of hot sauce around the table for those so inclined.

PRICE BOX

Grits: 50¢
Heavy cream: $1
Sausage: $3 to $5
Basic Tomato Sauce: $1.45 to $2.75

Total price: $5.95 to $9.25; per person: $1.49 to $2.31

ASPARAGUS RISOTTO WITH LEMON

Asparagus is one of my favorite vegetables in the spring when it's fresh and in season, and this is one of my favorite spring dishes: bright, light, and grassy yet filling.

Serves 4 as a side or 2 as a main

1 bunch of asparagus

3 cups Basic Vegetable Stock (page 34)

½ cup white wine

2 tablespoons olive oil

1 small yellow onion, minced

1 cup Arborio rice

½ cup grated Parmesan or pecorino cheese

Zest of 1 lemon

Salt and freshly ground black pepper if needed

1. Rinse the asparagus and pat it dry. Snap off the woody ends of the asparagus stalks and put them in a medium saucepan with the stock and wine. Bring to a low simmer and maintain it.

2. Chop the remaining asparagus stems into roughly ½-inch pieces, leaving the frondy heads intact. Set aside.

3. Heat the oil in a large, high-sided pan over medium heat. Sweat the onion until soft and translucent, 6 to 8 minutes. Do not let it brown.

4. Fold the rice into the onion and cook, stirring, for 2 to 3 minutes, until the pan is dry and the rice gives a toasted aroma.

5. Ladle some stock into the rice and cook, stirring constantly, until the rice has absorbed the stock. Add more stock (leaving behind the woody asparagus stalks) and stir it into the rice. Continue adding stock in this fashion, making sure to let the rice absorb all the liquid before adding more, but don't let it get so dry that it sticks to the pan or burns. Taste the risotto periodically as it cooks to get a feel for how it softens and how long it needs. Cook until the rice is creamy and rich and the grains are tender with a pleasant chew, about 20 minutes. Fold in the asparagus and cook 5 minutes. Remove from the heat and fold in the Parmesan and lemon zest. Taste, adjust the seasoning, and serve immediately.

PRICE BOX

Asparagus: $4
White wine: $1
Onion: 75¢
Arborio rice: $1.50
Parmesan or pecorino cheese: $1
Lemon: 50¢

Total price: $8.75; per person: $2.19 to $4.38

DRESS IT UP

If you're feeling fancy or want to impress, drizzle a little truffle oil over each serving of risotto. Freshly boiled or steamed green peas or sautéed chanterelle mushrooms are great additions to the asparagus as well. If adding chanterelles, sauté the chanterelles and asparagus together lightly before sautéing the onion, remove from the pan, and set aside; proceed with the recipe, adding the asparagus and chanterelles in step 5.

ROASTED ROOT VEGETABLE RISOTTO

Savory, satisfying, healthy, and, best of all, you can roast the vegetables up to a week in advance or even use leftover roasted vegetables—which makes this a great way to use up holiday leftovers. The nutty Gruyère or fontina matches perfectly with the vegetables. As with the Asparagus Risotto with Lemon (page 168), to make it even more impressive, drizzle a little truffle oil over each plate before serving. Whole sage leaves (two per person) fried in butter also make an excellent topping.

You can use any winter vegetables for this and in whatever quantities you like; the ones listed below are meant to be more of a guideline than an actual rule. Adapt! Experiment! Bend the root vegetable universe and turn it on its head! Be as creative as your imagination and farmers' market will allow. Go for sweet vegetables: carrots, parsnips, beets. Think of the palette, not just your palate: Go monochromatic in white with parsnips, turnips, fennel, and celeriac. Dye your risotto purple with beets, red chard stalks, and purple carrots. Stay green with Brussels sprouts and kale. Make it a rainbow: red chard stems, orange sweet potato, yellow carrots, green Brussels sprouts, purple beets (at the time of this writing, there are no naturally blue or indigo root vegetables).

Serves 6

ROASTED VEGETABLES

1 carrot

1 parsnip

1 turnip

½ fennel bulb

1 leek, white and light green parts only, rinsed well

2 to 3 tablespoons olive oil

Kosher salt and freshly ground black pepper

RISOTTO

1 quart Basic Vegetable Stock (page 34) or Meat Stock (use chicken; page 35)

1½ cups dry white wine

2 tablespoons olive oil

1 cup sliced button mushrooms

½ medium onion, minced

1½ cups Arborio rice

1 cup chopped kale or Swiss chard leaves

Kosher salt and freshly ground black pepper

2 tablespoons fresh thyme leaves

¾ cup grated Gruyère or young fontina cheese (or a mixture)

¼ cup grated Parmesan cheese

1. Preheat two roasting pans or rimmed baking sheets in a 425°F oven.

2. Make the roasted vegetables: Chop the carrot, parsnip, turnip, fennel, and leek into bite-size pieces and place them in a large bowl. Toss the vegetables with the oil and season with salt and pepper. Arrange in a single layer in the preheated roasting pans and roast, turning occasionally, for 20 to 25 minutes, until fork-tender and caramelized. Set aside.

3. Meanwhile, make the risotto: In a medium saucepan, bring the stock and wine to a low simmer and maintain it.

4. Heat the oil in a large, high-sided sauté pan over medium heat. Add the mushrooms and cook for 3 minutes, or until they've released their juices. Add the onion and sweat until soft and translucent, 6 to 8 minutes. Do not let the vegetables brown.

5. Fold the rice into the vegetables and cook, stirring, for 2 to 3 minutes, until the pan is dry and the rice gives a toasted aroma.

6. Ladle some stock into the rice and cook, stirring constantly, until the rice has absorbed the stock. Fold in the kale and more stock and stir. Continue adding stock in this fashion, making sure to let the rice absorb all the liquid before adding more, but don't let it get so dry that it sticks to the pan or burns. Taste the risotto periodically as it cooks to get a feel for how it softens and how long it needs. Cook until the rice is creamy and rich and the grains are tender with a pleasant chew, 20 to 25 minutes. Fold in two thirds of the roasted root vegetables just before you add the final ladle of stock. Remove from the heat and fold in the thyme and Gruyère cheese to melt it.

7. Taste and season with salt and pepper. Serve immediately, topped with the remaining roasted vegetables and the Parmesan.

PRICE BOX

Carrot: 30¢
Parsnip: 50¢
Turnip: 60¢
Fennel: $1.75
Leek: 50¢
Wine: $2.50
Mushrooms: $3
Onion: 50¢
Arborio rice: $2
Kale/chard: $75¢
Gruyère cheese: $4
Parmesan cheese: 50¢

Total price: $16.90;
per person: $2.82

PANCETTA, SQUASH, AND SHALLOT RISOTTO

This risotto is real stick-to-the ribs cooking, the perfect bowl of comfort food on a cold winter night. Ask your butcher to cut the pancetta as thick as possible, as if it were slab bacon—you want it thick so its chewiness complements the risotto and contrasts the soft squash.

Butternut, acorn, or kabocha squash or even a sugar pumpkin will work well. Roasting the squash in a hot oven for 20 to 25 minutes will parcook the squash and caramelize it. This step, while not strictly necessary, is highly recommended because it will help the squash keep its shape in the risotto instead of cooking down into mush while intensifying the squash's depth and flavor.

Serves 4

ROASTED SQUASH

1 small (1- to 2-pound) winter squash or sugar pumpkin

1 to 2 tablespoons olive oil

6 fresh sage leaves, cut into julienne

Kosher salt and freshly ground black pepper

RISOTTO

⅓ pound pancetta (double for a richer dish)

1 quart Meat Stock (use chicken; page 35)

1 cup white wine

2 tablespoons olive oil

2 shallots, minced

1 clove garlic

1 cup Arborio rice

6 to 10 fresh sage leaves, cut into julienne

½ cup grated Parmesan cheese

Salt and freshly ground black pepper

1. Make the roasted squash: Preheat a rimmed baking sheet in a 425°F oven.

2. If you're using butternut or kabocha squash or a sugar pumpkin, peel it. If you're using an acorn squash, wash and dry the skin very well. Halve the squash and seed it. Chop the flesh into bite-size chunks and place them in a large bowl. Toss the squash with the oil and sage and season with salt and pepper. Roast on the preheated baking sheet for 20 to 25 minutes, until fork-tender and caramelized, tossing once halfway through to prevent burning. Remove from the oven and set aside.

3. Meanwhile, prepare the pancetta: Remove the waxed paper wrapping and slice the meat into roughly ½-inch-thick strips, then cube into bite-size pieces. The pancetta is likely to lose its rolled-up shape under your knife; that's okay. Just try to keep the ratio of fat to meat in each bite-size piece as even as possible. Let the pancetta come to room temperature.

4. In a medium saucepan, bring the stock and wine to a low simmer and maintain it.

5. Heat the oil in a large, high-sided pan over medium heat. Toss in the pancetta and toss, toss, toss until the sizzle calms down to a low murmur. Let the pancetta cook for 3 to 4 minutes, then add the shallots. Give the pan a good shake to coat the shallots in fat. Cook for 2 minutes, then add the garlic to the pan and give it a good shake to introduce everyone at the party.

6. Fold the rice into the pan and cook, stirring, for 2 to 3 minutes, until the pan is dry and the rice gives a toasted aroma.

7. Ladle some stock into the rice and cook, stirring constantly, until the rice has absorbed the stock. Continue adding stock in this fashion, making sure to let the rice absorb all the liquid before adding more, but don't let it get so dry that it sticks to the pan or burns. Taste the risotto periodically as it cooks to get a feel for how it softens and how long it needs. When the risotto is al dente, about 15 to 20 minutes, fold in the caramelized squash. Fold in the sage. Continue cooking until the rice is creamy and rich and the grains are tender with a pleasant chew, 20 to 25 minutes.

8. Remove from the heat and fold in the Parmesan. Taste, season with salt and pepper, and serve immediately.

PRICE BOX

Squash: $4
Sage: $1; free if homegrown
Pancetta: $4
White wine: $2
Shallots: $1
Arborio rice: $1.50
Parmesan: $1

Total price: $14.50; per person: $3.63

VEGETABLES AND MEATS

RUSTIC RATATOUILLE

For some, summer means grilled hamburgers and steak. For me, it means grilling cherry tomatoes, summer squash, bell peppers, tiny onions, eggplant, and the occasional fennel bulb or pint of shishito peppers—an all-inclusive selection of the produce available at that day's or week's greenmarket.

I love using fairy-tale eggplants in this dish: Small and slender, these finger-shaped fruits can be sliced in half and tossed straight on the grill; unlike full-size eggplants, you don't need to douse them with salt first to leach out bitterness from the seeds. If you can't find fairy-tale eggplants, the lighter-skinned Japanese variety or a smaller regular eggplant will work.

You could call this a grilled antipasto, I suppose, but I've always called it rustic ratatouille, a loose and smoky riff on the classic French vegetable stew. Aside from the fennel and shishitos (generally mild Japanese peppers that are fantastic grilled and tossed with olive oil and coarse salt), the ingredients are the same as a traditional ratatouille, but the preparation—slicing, grilling, and tossing together—is very different. Make a lot; the leftovers are excellent hot or cold, on top of pasta, in an omelet, or broiled under a layer of smoky cheese on thick toast.

If you don't have a grill, you can do this in a broiler; just oil the vegetables well and keep a close eye on them to prevent burning.

Serves 4 as a side

1 pint cherry or grape tomatoes

1 whole head garlic

Olive oil as needed

Coarse salt and cracked black pepper

1 pound fairy-tale eggplants, or 2 small Japanese eggplants, or 1 medium eggplant (1 to 1½ pounds)

3 to 4 summer squash and/or zucchini

1 Vidalia onion

1 or 2 bell peppers (red, orange, or yellow)

¼ cup chopped fresh flat-leaf parsley

¼ cup julienned fresh basil

2 tablespoons fresh thyme leaves

Pinch of crushed red pepper flakes

¼ to ⅓ cup extra virgin olive oil

¼ to ⅓ cup freshly grated Parmesan cheese

Thickly sliced bread, grilled, for serving

1. Set a propane grill to medium, or burn a pile of charcoal on one side of a coal grill until the coals are evenly covered in gray ash but glowing orange within. Soak 1 or 2 wooden skewers in water for the onions, or lightly oil 1 or 2 metal skewers.

2. Make an aluminum foil packet large enough to hold the tomatoes. Cut off the top of the head of garlic, leaving the tops of the cloves exposed, and pop it into a foil packet of its own. Season the tomatoes and garlic with olive oil, salt, and pepper and close both packets tightly. When the grill is ready, put the foil packets of tomatoes and garlic on a medium-hot part of the grill while you prepare the rest of the vegetables.

3. If you're using fairy-tale eggplants, trim the stem ends. Halve lengthwise any that are thicker than your thumb. For a larger eggplant, slice into ½-inch-thick discs or slice lengthwise into ½-inch-thick "steaks." Set larger eggplant slices in a colander and sprinkle generously with kosher salt. Let drain for

10 to 15 minutes while you prepare the rest of the vegetables, then rinse the eggplants and pat them dry. This isn't necessary for the little fairy-tales—just toss them into a large bowl.

4. Slice the squash lengthwise into ½-inch-thick "steaks" too. Set aside in a large bowl (with the fairy-tales, if that's what you're using for eggplant).

5. Quarter the onion, leaving the stem end intact. Press the quarters onto the skewers, spacing them evenly. Set aside.

6. Add the bell peppers (rinsed, dried, and left whole) to the bowl with the squash. Add the drained, rinsed, and dried eggplant (if not using fairy-tales). Give the vegetables a toss with enough olive oil to coat and season with salt and pepper. Rub olive oil, salt, and pepper onto the skewered onion quarters. Take a cutting board and your bowl out to your grill.

7. Check on the tomatoes: They are done when they have burst and released their juices, 10 to 12 minutes. Check the garlic: It's done when the skins and cloves are a rich brown and yield to a gentle squeeze. If they're already done, set them aside; if they need more time, put them back on the grill.

8. Working in batches if necessary, grill the vegetables, flipping as needed, until the outsides are lightly charred and the insides are soft, 7 to 12 minutes, depending on the heat of your grill

PRICE BOX

Tomatoes: $4
Garlic: $1
Eggplant: $3
Summer squash/zucchini: $2.25
Onion: $1
Bell peppers: $1.75
Parsley: 50¢
Basil: 75¢
Thyme: 25¢
Extra virgin olive oil: $1
Parmesan cheese: 75¢

Total price: $16.25; per person: $4.06 (Shave $1.50 off the total price by growing your own herbs. Growing your own cherry tomatoes, too, will bring the total price down to $10.75 or just $2.69 per person.)

and the thickness of your vegetables. As they are done, transfer them to the cutting board and give them a rough chop—you want them to be a little larger than bite-size. Uniformity isn't a big deal. For the onions, just cut off the stem end holding the grilled quarters together.

9. As soon as the garlic is cool enough to handle, pop the cloves into your big oily bowl. Season with salt and throw in half of the parsley, basil, and thyme and the crushed red pepper flakes. Mash the garlic with the back of a fork to form a thick paste, then whisk in extra virgin olive oil in a slow stream until the paste turns into a thick dressing. Fold in the tomatoes and their juices.

10. Add the chopped vegetables to the bowl. Toss everything together, thinning the dressing with more extra virgin olive oil as needed. Toss in the rest of the herbs and the Parmesan. Serve with grilled bread slices to sop up the juices.

LAMB SHANKS

Braising lamb shanks is one of the finest ways you can stink up your house. Simmering beer or wine, melting fat and cartilage, roasting garlic, and that unctuous, unmistakably fragrant lamb combine to create one of the world's most mouthwatering comfort food aromas. And on a cold winter day, the long braise can even help keep your kitchen warm.

Like most braises, the shanks take *forever* to cook, but the longer they cook, the better they'll be. In fact, whether or not you're crunched for time, I'd suggest you make them today for dinner tomorrow; every braise tastes better the next day, after the flavors have spent a night together.

I like to use brown ale as the base of my braising liquid, but you can easily substitute red wine.

Serves 4

4 lamb shanks

Kosher salt and cracked black pepper

Olive oil as needed

1 carrot, diced

1 medium onion, diced

4 cloves garlic, minced

3 to 4 sprigs fresh rosemary

3 to 4 sprigs fresh thyme

1 bay leaf

one 16-ounce bottle of beer

About 1 quart Meat Stock (page 35), Basic Vegetable Stock (page 34), or water

1. Preheat the oven to 375°F.

2. Put the lamb shanks on a plate. Find the end of the tendon on each shank, about ½ inch to 1 inch from the end of the shank. Sever the tendon by scoring the meat from the bone. This will allow the meat to cook down nicely. Season the shanks with salt and pepper.

3. Heat a good splash of oil in a large Dutch oven over medium-high heat. Add the shanks and sear on all sides until golden brown, about 2 minutes a side. Don't crowd the pan; work in batches and don't brown longer than necessary; you're not cooking the shanks, just browning them.

4. Remove the shanks and set aside. Pour out the excess lamb fat from the Dutch oven, leaving just enough to sauté the vegetables in. Add the carrot and cook for 2 minutes, then add the onion and cook for 2 minutes; finally, add the garlic and sauté until the onion is just translucent, about 1 minute. Add the rosemary, thyme, and bay leaf. Return the shanks to the pan and add the beer. Add stock until the liquid just covers the shanks.

5. Bring the liquid to a boil and cover. Carefully transfer the covered Dutch oven to the oven and braise for 2½ to 3 hours, until the liquid has reduced by half and the meat has pulled back from the bone, checking periodically

to make sure there's enough liquid; replenish with water, stock, or beer if needed.

6. When the shanks are done, remove the Dutch oven from the oven. At this point, you can let the shanks and their liquid cool enough to refrigerate, then pop the whole thing (lidded, of course) into the refrigerator overnight. The next evening, stick the Dutch oven on the stovetop over medium heat and, when the shanks are warmed through, pick up at the next step.

7. Remove the shanks to a plate to rest. Put the Dutch oven back on the stove over medium heat, bring to a simmer, and reduce the remaining liquid by half. Strain into a bowl through a colander or mesh strainer lined with cheesecloth. Pour the sauce over the shanks.

8. Serve the shanks, 1 per person, with the reserved sauce and something to soak up all that goodness—a simple side like Polenta (page 47), Basic Risotto (page 50), Roasted Broccoli (page 61), or wild rice. Or complement the richness of the shanks with the bracingly tart Grilled Radicchio with Kumquats (page 103).

PRICE BOX

Lamb shanks: $25 to $30
Carrot: 30¢
Onion: 75¢
Garlic: 75¢
Beer: $1.75
Rosemary and thyme (3 to 4 sprigs each): 25¢

Total price: $28.80 to $33.80; per person: $7.20 to $8.45

ADDED VALUE

Lamb shanks are by no means a cheap cut. Save the bones for making stock (page 35) to help offset the cost.

Using homemade stock and homegrown herbs will also help keep costs down.

INDONESIAN CHICKEN WINGS WITH PEANUT NOODLES AND SPICY SESAME SLAW

This is *such* a fantastic party dish I almost hesitate to share it with you. Not really—that would be selfish—but it's so good, so easy, and so affordable that, if we all started making this, we might start a viral vaguely Asian party food trend. Which actually sounds like a pretty good idea, so let's get on it.

Seriously, this dinner checks all the boxes: affordable (wings, noodles, peanut butter, soy sauce, and cabbage are the main ingredients); easy to make in any quantity; and easy to prep everything ahead.

Serves 6 to 8; doubles easily

WINGS

4 to 5 pounds chicken wings

1 tablespoon olive oil

Salt and freshly ground black pepper

1½ cups soy sauce

½ cup Worcestershire sauce

¼ cup honey

2-inch piece ginger, peeled and minced

4 cloves garlic, minced

3 tablespoons toasted sesame oil

¼ cup rice vinegar

1 to 2 cups Meat Stock (use chicken; page 35) or water

½ cup thinly sliced scallions

SLAW

3 tablespoons soy sauce

¼ cup rice vinegar

3 tablespoons toasted sesame oil

3 tablespoons vegetable or peanut oil

1-inch piece ginger, peeled and minced

3 tablespoons honey

1 tablespoon Cole's Sriracha (see opposite)

4 cups thinly sliced cabbage

½ cup grated carrots

3 tablespoons chopped fresh cilantro

NOODLES

Kosher salt

1 pound linguine

1 recipe Indonesian-Style Peanut Sauce (page 46)

1 cup diagonally sliced sugar snap peas

4 scallions, thinly sliced

¼ cup chopped fresh cilantro (leaves and top 1 inch of stems only)

2 tablespoons toasted sesame seeds

3 tablespoons crushed roasted peanuts

1. Make the wings: Preheat the oven to 325°F.

2. Trim the wings: With a sharp knife or kitchen shears, cut off the tips and save them for making stock. Cut the wings in half through the joint.

3. Heat the olive oil in a roasting pan over 2 burners on medium heat. Season the wings with salt and pepper and sear them in batches, 30 to 60 seconds per side, until browned. Remove to a plate.

COLE'S SRIRACHA

My friend Cole Stryker is an author and a great cook. Early in our friendship he gave me a giant tub of his homemade Sriracha, which he'd made when he wound up with a box of chiles from his CSA. A little goes a long way with this stuff, and it will last practically forever in the fridge. Cole is adamant that you consume your Sriracha in careful quantities; as he says, "What goes into your body must come out eventually."

Here's the recipe.

Makes a little over 1 cup

¼ pound assorted chiles (at least three quarters Fresno,
    Thai cherry, or serrano)
4 cloves garlic, peeled
½ cup rice vinegar
1 tablespoon sugar (Cole prefers to use palm sugar)

1. Wearing latex or rubber gloves, stem and halve the peppers. For a less intense Sriracha, deseed up to half of the chiles.
2. Combine all ingredients in a medium saucepan. Bring to a boil, reduce to a hard simmer, and cook until completely tender, about 8 minutes.
3. Buzz everything in a blender until you can't see any seeds. Let cool, then transfer to an airtight container and refrigerate.

4. In a medium bowl, whisk together the soy sauce, Worcestershire sauce, honey, ginger, garlic, sesame oil, and vinegar. Taste and adjust: It should be salty but not overly so.

5. Pour the excess fat from the roasting pan and arrange the wings in a single layer on the roasting pan. Pour the soy sauce mixture over the wings and add enough stock to completely submerge them. Sprinkle with half the scallions and wrap the pan tightly in aluminum foil.

6. Cook, covered, for at least 2½ but up to 3 hours, carefully pulling back the foil after an hour and a half to give the wings a stir. The sauce should be reducing but the pan should never get dry; add more stock in small increments if necessary. The wings are done when the sauce has reduced greatly and the chicken is dark brown and falling off the bone.

7. Meanwhile, make the slaw: Combine the soy sauce, vinegar, sesame oil, vegetable oil, ginger, honey, and Sriracha in a small saucepan over medium heat, stirring until the honey has dissolved. Remove from the heat. Toss the cabbage and carrots together in a large bowl. Toss in the dressing and let marinate for 1 hour at room temperature or covered in the fridge for up to 4 hours.

8. While the chicken is still in the oven and the slaw is marinating, make the noodles: Bring a large pot of water to a rapid boil. Salt it generously and cook the pasta according to the package's directions. Meanwhile, scoop the peanut sauce into a large, shallow bowl. Add the snap peas and transfer the cooked pasta to the bowl using tongs. Toss together, letting the heat wilt the snap peas and coating the pasta in the peanut sauce. Add a little pasta water to thin the sauce if necessary. Mix in the scallions, cilantro, sesame seeds, and crushed peanuts. You can serve the noodles hot or at room temperature.

PRICE BOX

Chicken wings: $8 to $10
Soy sauce: $3.25
Worcestershire sauce: $1.50
Honey: 75¢
Ginger: 50¢
Garlic: $1
Sesame oil: 75¢
Rice vinegar: $1
Scallions: $2
Cabbage: $1.25
Carrots: 50¢
Cilantro: 75¢; free if homegrown
Linguine: $2 to $2.50
Indonesian-Style Peanut Sauce: $4.50
Sugar snap peas: $2

Total price: $29 to $32.25; per person: $3.63 to $5.37

9. When the wings are done, transfer them to a plate or shallow bowl. Strain the sauce into a bowl through a fine-mesh strainer, skim off the excess fat, and drizzle over the wings. Sprinkle with the remaining scallions and serve with the noodles and slaw.

GOLABKI
(POLISH-STYLE STUFFED CABBAGE)

I don't know about you, but I *always* seem to have at least one carton of plain takeout rice in my refrigerator. And rarely do I feel inspired enough to do much with it; too often it ends up in the compost (the rice, not the carton), an upsetting fate for any food left uneaten.

Considering I'm of entirely Eastern European heritage, it took that inspiration lightbulb a shamefully long time to pop over my head: All that untouched rice was perfect for stuffed cabbage.

If you've ever had golabki before—or holubky or sarma, depending on where on the map of Eastern Europe you land—you know how sweet and silky braised cabbage can be. If you haven't had the pleasure, you are probably wrinkling your nose at the thought of this dish. My friend, you are making a very silly mistake.

As I said above, leftover plain rice is the perfect base for the stuffing. But quinoa, kasha, and barley are all excellent (and more healthful) substitutes.

Likewise, the filling can be tailored to what you have on hand. I like to add mushrooms for earthiness and a parsnip, which is not strictly traditional, for sweetness.

Leftovers keep well, and can be frozen in the sauce for up to two months. I confess that I find golabki addictively delicious cold, right out of the Tupperware, the next day.

Serves 8

1½ to 2½ quarts water

One 2- to 3-pound green cabbage

2 tablespoons olive oil

2 carrots, chopped

1 parsnip, peeled and chopped

1 heaping cup diced button mushrooms

1 large onion, chopped

2 cloves garlic, minced

2 cups cooked rice

½ pound ground beef

½ pound ground pork

Kosher salt and cracked black pepper

1 quart Basic Tomato Sauce (page 37), pureed

1 cup Basic Vegetable Stock (page 34) or Meat Stock (use chicken; page 35)

½ cup sour cream or thick plain yogurt

1. Bring the water to a rolling boil in a large Dutch oven. Core the cabbage, leaving a hollow cylinder in the bottom. Submerge the cabbage in the water, hollowed-core end up. Cover the pot with a tight-fitting lid and remove it from the heat; let the cabbage stew in the water for 10 to 15 minutes.

2. In a large skillet, heat the oil over medium heat. Add the carrots and cook for 2 minutes; add the parsnip and cook for 2 minutes; add the mushrooms and cook for 5 minutes; add the onion and cook for 2 minutes; last, add the garlic and cook for 1 to 2 minutes, until fragrant and the carrots are just knife tender. Remove from the heat and let cool.

3. Remove the cabbage from the water and bring the water back to a boil. Peel off the leaves, working from both ends to keep the leaves from tearing. You'll need 12 to 14 total, not counting the tough outer leaves, which you should set aside for now. When the leaves start to tear, put the cabbage back in the boiling water, cover, and kill the heat. Let sit for another 10 minutes while you devein your stack of leaves: Holding a paring knife parallel to the work surface, peel off the thick ridge of a vein running down the back of each leaf, as if it were a peel or rind. You want the leaves to be moldable, so you need to flatten out the vein. Set the leaves aside in a pile as you go.

4. Remove the cabbage from the water (don't discard the water, though) and resume peeling off the leaves and paring down the veins as needed until you've got 12 to 14 leaves.

5. In a large bowl, combine the rice, cooled sautéed vegetables, and meat. Season heavily with salt and pepper—about twice as much as instinct tells you. The cabbage sucks it up.

6. Make a loose "meatball" of about ⅓ cup of the rice-meat-vegetable filling and place it in the center of a cabbage leaf. Fold the sides over the filling and roll the cabbage up, starting at the stem end. Repeat until all the leaves are filled and rolled.

PRICE BOX

Cabbage: $3
Carrots: 50¢
Parsnip: 50¢
Mushrooms: $1.50
Onion: $1
Rice: 30¢
Ground beef: $4
Ground pork: $3
Basic Tomato Sauce: $3.80 to $7.30
Sour cream or yogurt: 63¢ to 93¢

Total price: $18.23 to $22.03; per person: $2.28 to $2.75

7. Now take the bowl you made the stuffing in and pour the tomato sauce into it. Stir in the stock and 1 cup of the reserved cabbage water. Discard the rest.

8. Line the bottom of the Dutch oven with the reserved outer cabbage leaves. Nestle the stuffed cabbage rolls into the Dutch oven in a single layer. If you need to make multiple layers, separate them with tomato sauce. Pour the tomato sauce over the cabbage rolls; the top cabbage rolls should just peek out from the sauce like little bald heads. Bring to a boil and immediately reduce the heat to low, cover, and cook at a simmer for about 1 hour, until the cabbage is very tender. Check on the rolls frequently and add more tomato sauce if needed.

9. When the golabki are done cooking, remove from the heat and temper about ¾ cup of the hot tomato sauce into the sour cream, whisking to incorporate. Using tongs or a slotted spoon, gently transfer the cabbage rolls to a serving

dish and whisk the tempered sour cream into the rest of the tomato sauce. Ladle the sauce over the cabbage rolls and serve.

VEGETARIAN STUFFED CABBAGE

A cheaper and healthier version of the traditional golabki: Double the mushrooms, carrots, and parsnips (you'll need another tablespoon of oil) and substitute celery, sauerkraut, and/or cooked kidney beans for the meat.

BRENDAN'S MOROCCAN-SPICED LAMB MEATBALLS

For me, the perfumey earthiness of lamb was meant for winter and winter alone. Lamb dishes tend to be oversize-sweater-and-cushy-slippers food, the kind you want to cozy up to. These meatballs are no exception, and making them is a great way to spend a cold, wintry Sunday afternoon.

Chef Brendan McDermott came up with this dish after cooking in a few Mediterranean-influenced restaurants where he learned to really appreciate the seasonings and flavors. After he taught me how to make it, I turned around and made it three more times in as many weeks. Not for myself! Once for friends, once for family, and once for a friend's wedding. It was a hit every time, and it is now my go-to winter recipe for any occasion where I want to make a really good impression.

Serves 6 as a main or 14 or 15 as an appetizer

LAMB

2 tablespoons olive oil

1 large shallot, minced

2 cloves garlic, minced

2 teaspoons paprika

½ teaspoon ground cinnamon

Salt and freshly ground black pepper or grains of paradise (see page 191)

1½ pounds ground lamb

1 large egg

4 tablespoons fresh mint, julienned

½ cup panko or regular breadcrumbs

SAUCE

1 leek, white and light green parts only, rinsed and finely chopped

3 plum or vine tomatoes, cored and chopped

Salt and freshly ground black pepper

Basic Vegetable Stock (page 34), Meat Stock (page 35), water, or wine if needed

GREEK RAITA

8 ounces thick plain yogurt, preferably Greek

⅓ cup peeled, seeded, and finely diced cucumber

⅓ finely diced red onion

1½ tablespoons julienned fresh mint

Zest and juice of ½ lemon

Salt and freshly ground black pepper or grains of paradise (see page 191) to taste

1. Make the lamb: Heat 1 tablespoon of the oil in a large skillet or sauté pan over medium heat. Add the shallot and garlic and sweat for 2 to 3 minutes, until just translucent. Reduce the heat to medium-low and season with the paprika, cinnamon, and salt and pepper. Stir and let cook down until the

onions and garlic are completely soft and brown and sticky, 10 to 12 minutes. If the pan gets too dry, add a few drops of water, just enough to keep the shallots and garlic from burning. Remove from the heat and let cool.

2. In a large bowl, gently mix together the lamb and egg with your fingers; do not mush the lamb. Fold in the shallot-garlic mixture, 2 tablespoons of the mint, the panko, and salt and pepper or grains of paradise to taste until just combined. Cover the bowl and refrigerate for about 15 minutes to let the lamb cool off from all the handling.

3. Get out 2 rimmed baking sheets and take the lamb out of the refrigerator. Pinch off pieces of the lamb and gently roll them into balls no bigger than a golf ball. Line them up on the baking sheets.

4. When all the meatballs are assembled, heat the remaining tablespoon of oil in the skillet you cooked the shallot-garlic mixture in. If that pan's going to be way too small for all the meatballs, you can do the rest of the recipe in a large Dutch oven or heavy-bottomed stockpot.

5. Sear 1 meatball for about 60 seconds per side. This is your tester. Let it cool, then taste it (it's okay if it's pink in the middle—this is lamb) for seasoning. If it's a little bland, season the rest of the meatballs with a little more salt and pepper. Sear the rest of the meatballs, adding just a few to the pan at a time, for about 30 seconds per side until they're all lightly browned. Don't crowd the pan. Remove the browned meatballs to a bowl until they're all browned, reserving the fat in the pan.

6. Make the sauce: Reheat the fat in the pan. Lightly fry the leeks in the fat for 3 to 4 minutes, until softened. Add the tomatoes, season with salt and pepper, and cook down until the tomatoes have released their juices and formed a sauce, 10 to 15 minutes.

7. Nestle the meatballs into the sauce. It's okay if it's a tight fit, but if you absolutely cannot fit all the meatballs in your pan, layer the sauce and meatballs in

a larger Dutch oven or heavy-bottomed stockpot: first a layer of sauce, then a layer of meatballs; sauce, meatballs, and so on. In either vessel, bring the sauce to a simmer. Cook, uncovered, for 25 minutes, or cover and turn the heat down to low and cook for up to 2 hours. Give the pan a gentle shake or stir every now and then to keep the meatballs from sticking, but be careful not to break them up. If the pan gets too dry during the braise, add stock, water, or wine in ¼-cup increments.

8. While the lamb is braising, make the Greek raita: Stir all the raita ingredients together in a bowl. Taste and adjust the seasoning, then cover and refrigerate until ready to use.

9. When the meatballs are done, garnish with the remaining 2 tablespoons mint.

10. Serve the meatballs, 5 to 8 per person as a main, with wild rice, mashed potatoes, or Polenta (page 47) alongside. Spoon some tomato sauce over each plate and top with the raita.

PRICE BOX

Shallot: 50¢

Lamb: $12

Mint: 75¢; free if homegrown

Panko/breadcrumbs: 50¢; free if homemade

Leek: 50¢

Tomatoes: $2

Yogurt: $2

Cucumber: 50¢

Red onion: 25¢

Lemon: 70¢

Total price: $18.45 to $19.70; per person: $1.23 (appetizer), $3.28 (main)

ADD A LITTLE PARADISE

Grains of paradise are seeds with a peppery, lemony flavor. They're originally from West Africa and are related to ginger. They're not cheap, but they stretch very well.

TZIMMES (SHORT RIBS AND FRUIT)

Oh, short ribs. You sweet little bundles of meat and fat and bone, so friendly and free, ready to mingle with the spiciest dry rub, the most sultry red wine, the sweetest fruits. Like so many red meat dishes, my family reserved this mostly for Jewish holidays, most memorably Purim, which falls in early spring—a perfect time for unctuous short ribs braised with sticky-sweet dried fruit. Never an overly strict vegetarian, I would pluck out the apricots and prunes plump and tender with the fatty ribs' juice from the serving dish, enjoying the meat's robust flavor without completely abandoning my meatless pretenses.

Now I am older and wiser and slide the spoon-tender ribs onto my plate along with their not-at-all-vegetarian-anyway sidekicks.

You can use flanken, which are cut thinner, or full beef short ribs; either way, make sure to buy ribs on the bone for better flavor and texture. Calculate ½ to ¾ pound of short ribs per person, or about two 2-inch ribs. If that's beyond your budget, bulk up the rest of the tzimmes with Yukon gold or new potatoes, onions or shallots, and parsnips.

Serves 8

4 to 6 pounds short ribs

Salt and freshly ground black pepper

4 medium sweet potatoes, peeled

½ pound dried apricots

½ pound prunes

4 tablespoons (½ stick) unsalted butter

1 cup lightly packed dark brown sugar

½ teaspoon ground ginger

¾ teaspoon ground cinnamon

½ teaspoon ground allspice

1 tablespoon orange juice

2 teaspoons orange zest

1 tablespoon honey

Olive oil as needed

2 carrots, diced

1. Preheat the oven to 350°F.

2. Rinse the short ribs and pat them dry. Season all over with salt and pepper and bring to room temperature on a plate.

3. Bring a large pot of water to a boil. While it comes up, cut the sweet potatoes into ½-inch cubes. Add them to the water, reduce the heat, and simmer until they slide off the tip of a knife, 10 to 15 minutes. Drain, reserving the water.

4. Put the apricots and prunes in a large bowl and cover by an inch with the boiled sweet potato water. Cover with a lid or plate and let plump for 15 minutes, then drain over a bowl, reserving the liquid.

5. In a small saucepan, melt the butter over low heat. Whisk in the brown sugar, ginger, cinnamon, allspice, orange juice and zest, and honey until dissolved. Taste and adjust: It should be sweet and deep. Remove from the heat and set aside.

6. Heat a glug of oil in a large Dutch oven over medium-high heat. Working in batches, brown the short ribs on all sides, about 1 minute per side. Remove the browned ribs to a plate. Remove the Dutch oven from the heat and add the sweet potatoes and carrots to the Dutch oven. Toss lightly to coat with the fat. Cover with the rehydrated fruit and arrange the short ribs in a single layer over the fruit; it's okay if it's a tight fit. Pour the melted butter mixture over everything and add just enough of the fruit-soaking liquid to come up to the bottom of the short ribs.

7. Cover and braise in the oven for 2 to 3 hours, checking occasionally to make sure there's enough liquid. The sweet potatoes will break

PRICE BOX

Short ribs: $20 to $45
Sweet potatoes: $4
Carrots: 50¢
Dried apricots: $4.50
Prunes: $3
Butter: 85¢ to $1.18
Brown sugar: $1.50
Orange: 90¢

Total price: $35.25 to $60.58; per person: $4.41 to $7.57

down; that's perfectly okay. The tzimmes is done when the meat is fork-tender.

8. To serve, put the Dutch oven in the middle of the table on a trivet or two folded dishcloths and let everyone dig in. (Or when the Dutch oven is cool to the touch, you can slide it right into the refrigerator; reheat over medium-low heat.)

THE BEST BEEF SANDWICH EVER

BRAISED SHORT RIBS WITH CARAMELIZED ONIONS ON CHALLAH

Pulled beef, sweetly caramelized onions, melted cheese, soft, eggy bread: This sandwich will make you forget about Philly cheesesteaks. And best of all, you can put a couple of different leftovers to use: strip leftover meat from the short ribs and top with extra Gruyère from the French Onion Soup (page 120).

Serves 2

6 tablespoons unsalted butter, plus more for buttering the top
½ medium onion, finely diced
1 shallot, minced
1 clove garlic, minced
Dash of ground cinnamon
Salt and freshly ground black pepper
4 thick slices challah
½ cup shredded cheddar or Gruyère cheese
1 cup shredded braised short ribs (from Tzimmes, page 192)

1. Melt 2 tablespoons of the butter in a large cast-iron skillet or sauté pan over medium-high heat. Reduce the heat to medium and add the onion, shallot, garlic, cinnamon, and salt and pepper to taste and cook, stirring occasionally, until the onion is a soft, sludgy pile, about 20 minutes. If the pan gets too dry, stir in a scant tablespoon of water here and there. Remove to a bowl.
2. Wipe the pan dry and melt another 2 tablespoons butter in it over medium-high heat.
3. Arrange the sandwiches: Take 2 slices of bread and butter each using 1 tablespoon of butter. Cover one slice with some of the cheese, ½ cup of the shredded short ribs, 2 to 3 tablespoons of the caramelized onions, and more cheese. Top with the second slice of bread, buttered-side-down. Butter the top of the bread and set aside. Repeat with the remaining bread, cheese, short ribs, and onions and slide the sandwiches into the skillet.
4. Weigh the sandwiches down with a small sauté pan or full kettle. After 1 minute, flip the sandwiches and return the press. Cook for another 2 minutes, flip again, and cook on the first side for another minute. Slide each sandwich onto a plate, slice in half, and serve.

OUR MOM'S BRISKET

Although this is remarkably easy to make, it was a "special occasions" dish in our house, something my mom made almost exclusively for Jewish holidays in the colder months. As it cooks, it fills the house with the softest meat aroma, tempered and sweetened by the glaze and bolstered by earthy onions, carrots, and potatoes.

Brisket is not a cheap cut, and it shrinks almost comically in the braise. Don't panic; the rich meat will go a lot further than you think.

I always serve it like my mom does, with homemade applesauce spiked with horseradish. I know you just wrinkled your nose, but trust me on this—

the fiery horseradish and the sweet apples melt into the meat, making each bite a roundly pleasurable experience.

A 3- to 5-pound brisket will feed 4 to 6 people; a 5- to 7-pound slab of meat will serve up to 8. My mom and I both recommend you buy a double, or first-cut, brisket. This cut has a big "bump" of fat on top, which makes for a richer, softer meal. But double briskets can be difficult to find and sometimes are exorbitantly expensive. You can and should still make this with a single, or second-cut, brisket; just check the pot every 45 minutes or so to make sure there's enough liquid around the brisket to keep it from drying out and up the amount of glaze you slather onto the meat, especially the top. As long as there's enough liquid in your braise, you almost can't overcook a brisket.

Serves 6 to 8, depending on the size of your brisket

1 brisket, preferably double or first-cut

Kosher salt and cracked black pepper

¼ cup Ketchup (page 42), or to taste

2 tablespoons barbecue sauce, or to taste

1 teaspoon Worcestershire sauce, or to taste

1 medium onion

1 tablespoon olive oil

2 to 3 cups beer, Meat Stock (page 35), or water, or a combination

1 tablespoon grainy mustard

1½ teaspoons brown sugar

1 carrot, cut into ½-inch chunks

4 to 8 baseball-size waxy potatoes, quartered

About 1 cup Homemade Applesauce (see opposite)

Horseradish

1. Preheat a Dutch oven or roasting pan large enough to fit the brisket in a 350°F oven.

2. Rinse the brisket and pat it dry. Do not trim off the fat. Season generously on all sides with salt and pepper and set aside to come to room temperature.

HOMEMADE APPLESAUCE

Makes about 2 cups

> 2 pounds apples (any type or mix)
> ¼ to ½ cup water
> ½ tablespoon honey
> 1 cinnamon stick or 1 tablespoon ground cinnamon

1. Peel and core the apples, then chop them roughly. Put them in a large nonreactive saucepan and add just enough water to cover. Place over medium-high heat and stir in the honey and cinnamon. Bring to a boil, then reduce the heat and simmer, stirring occasionally, for 25 minutes, or until the apples have cooked down.
2. With a potato masher or the back of your spoon, mash the apples to break up any too-large chunks or remove the cinnamon stick and blend with an immersion blender for a smoother applesauce.
3. Serve hot or cool completely and store in an airtight container in the fridge for up to a week.

PRICE BOX

Apples: $3

Total price: $3

3. In a small bowl, combine the ketchup, barbecue sauce, and Worcestershire sauce. Mix, taste, and adjust: more ketchup for body, more barbecue sauce for sweetness, more Worcestershire sauce for more salty, smoky umami. Make enough to slather over your entire brisket.

4. Slice the onion in half from stem to base. Lay each half flat-side down on your cutting board and slice thinly into half-moons.

5. Glug the oil into the preheated Dutch oven. Add the onion and season with salt and pepper. Toss the onion in the oil to coat.

6. Slather the ketchup mixture onto the brisket and nestle it onto the onion, fat side up. Slather the top of the brisket with any extra ketchup mixture. Pour in just enough beer to just submerge the onion, coming just past the bottom of the brisket. Slap a tight-fitting lid on the Dutch oven or cover the roasting pan tightly with aluminum foil and seal shut.

7. Braise the brisket for 30 minutes per pound—so at least 1½ hours for a 3-pound brisket and at least 3½ hours for a 7-pounder. Check the liquid level every 45 minutes or so to make sure the braise isn't evaporating too quickly; add more beer, stock, or water as needed.

8. While the brisket braises, make the finishing glaze: In a small bowl (it can be the same one you used to make the ketchup glaze), combine the mustard and brown sugar. Stir together to dissolve the sugar; taste and adjust. It should be sweet but slightly mustardy. (Increase the amount of mustard and brown sugar in a 2 to 1 ratio if you need more for a larger brisket.) Set aside.

9. Arrange the carrot and potatoes around the brisket for the last hour of cooking.

10. The brisket is done when it's fork-tender; remember, as long as there's enough liquid, you can cook it almost indefinitely.

11. Remove the brisket to a plate to rest. Pile the onion, carrot, and potatoes in a bowl. Put the Dutch oven on the stovetop (or the roasting pan over two burners) over medium heat. Bring the braising liquid to a simmer and let simmer, stirring occasionally, for 10 minutes, or until reduced by half. Strain into a gravy boat or cup with a pouring lip.

12. Slather the mustard-sugar glaze over the top and sides of your brisket. Wrap the brisket loosely in foil (you can use the same sheet you used to cover your roasting pan if it's still intact) and roast for 15 minutes, or until the glaze is

sticky and set into the top of the brisket. Remove to a cutting board or plate (if not serving immediately) and let rest, uncovered, for 10 to 15 minutes.

PRICE BOX

Brisket: $30 to $55
Onion: $1
Beer: $1.75
Carrot: 30¢
Potatoes: $2 to $3.75
Homemade
Applesauce: $1.50

Total price: $36.55 to $63.30; per person: $4.57 to $10.55

13. In a medium bowl, mix together the applesauce and horseradish—about 1 teaspoon horseradish to every ½ cup applesauce (you may need more applesauce if your brisket is large). Taste and adjust: It should be sweet at the front and bracingly sinus clearing at the back.

14. To serve, slice the brisket against the grain as thick or thinly as you like. Serve with the braised vegetables, reduced "gravy," and horseradish-spiked applesauce.

15. Store leftover brisket in the gravy. Reheat on the stovetop in a medium pan over medium-low heat, keeping the brisket submerged in the gravy to prevent it from drying out. Hot or cold, the brisket makes excellent sandwiches on good, crusty bread with a slather of spicy mustard and some of the braised onion.

MAPLE-MUSTARD ROASTED PORK

A good grainy mustard and maple syrup make an excellent spicy-sweet glaze for a pork shoulder that's milder than a ham and lets the flavor of the pork come through. Its leftovers make for excellent sandwiches and tacos, too (see page 201).

Like farmers' market beef, locally and sustainably raised pork can be shockingly more expensive than conventional supermarket cuts. As discussed on page 11, there are good reasons for this. And for the conscientious home cook, it means thinking strategically about meat: Save big cuts for special occasions, stretch the meat further in a meal by serving lots of sides, make good use of leftovers, and save the bones for making stock.

Serves 10

One 7- to 8-pound untrimmed pork shoulder

Kosher salt

½ cup grainy mustard

2 cups Meat Stock (use chicken; page 35), Basic Vegetable Stock (page 34), or water

2 tablespoons Dijon mustard

¼ cup maple syrup

1 tablespoon chopped fresh rosemary

2 tablespoons all-purpose flour

1. Preheat the oven to 400°F. Let the pork shoulder come to room temperature while the oven preheats.

2. Place the pork skin side up on a roasting rack placed in a roasting pan. Score the skin and fat in a diamond pattern and rub salt into the score lines. Smear ¼ cup of the grainy mustard all over the shoulder—skin, fat, and meat. Pour about ¼ cup of stock into the bottom of the pan, just enough to make a thin layer of liquid.

3. Roast for 20 minutes, then reduce the oven temperature to 350°F and cook for another 3 to 4 hours. Check in on the shoulder every hour or so to flip it over and add more stock or water to the pan if it gets too dry.

4. Meanwhile, in a small bowl, whisk together the remaining ¼ cup grainy mustard, the Dijon mustard, and maple syrup. Once an hour, brush generously on all sides with the glaze. Continue cooking until the glaze is brown and sticky and the shoulder's internal temperature is 165 to 180°F.

5. Let the pork rest on a cutting board for 30 minutes. Meanwhile, pour the pan juices into a cup and skim off as much of the excess fat as possible. Place the roasting pan over two burners over medium-high heat and deglaze with the remaining stock, scraping up any browned bits on the bottom. Add the rosemary and the skimmed pan drippings and whisk in the flour until a smooth gravy forms. Taste and adjust the seasoning.

PRICE BOX

Pork shoulder: $45 to $70
Grainy mustard: 75¢
Maple syrup: $2

Total price: $47.75 to $72.75; per person: $4.78 to $7.28

6. To serve the pork, remove the skin and chop it into pieces. Thinly slice the meat away from the bone, trimming away excess fat. Serve with the gravy.

MAPLE-MUSTARD ROASTED PORK TACOS

Ideally you would have at least 1 cup of shredded pork leftover per person, but you can stretch your portions with Basic Tomato Sauce (page 37) and dried black or pinto beans cooked in stock made from your pork shoulder's bone.

Serves 4

4 cups leftover pork shoulder
¼ cup pork shoulder pan juices
12 corn tortillas
1 tablespoon olive oil
3 plum tomatoes, chopped
½ cup Meat Stock (use your pork shoulder bone; page 35)
One 12-ounce bottle of brown ale
Salt and freshly ground black pepper

1 jalapeño chile, cut into rings

1 avocado, peeled, pitted, and thinly sliced

1 cup sour cream

2 radishes, very thinly sliced

¼ cup chopped fresh cilantro

2 limes, quartered

1. Preheat the oven to 200°F. Let the pork and juices come to room temperature while the oven preheats.

2. Pour ½ inch of water into the bottom of a big pot or steamer. Line the steamer insert with a clean dishcloth and nestle the stack of tortillas in the cloth. Fold the cloth around the tortillas to cover them, cover with a tight-fitting lid, and bring the water to a boil. Boil for 1 minute, then turn off the heat and transfer the whole thing to the oven to keep warm.

3. Shred the pork with tongs or two forks, discarding excess fat. In a large skillet or Dutch oven, heat the oil over medium heat. Add the shredded pork and cook for 5 to 7 minutes, until browned. Add the pan juices and tomatoes and cook for another 10 minutes, or until the tomatoes have released their juices. Stir in the stock and ale, bring to a simmer, and cook for 15 to 20 minutes, until the pork has absorbed the juices and is more wet than soupy. Season with salt and pepper.

4. Serve the pork on a large platter, with the stack of warm tortillas and the toppings. I like to assemble my taco thusly: corn tortilla; scoop of pulled pork; a few jalapeño rings; a slice or two of avocado; a dollop of sour cream; a sprinkling of radishes and cilantro; and a squeeze of lime.

PRICE BOX

Leftover pork shoulder: $10 to $15

Tortillas: $2

Tomatoes: $2

Ale: $1.75

Jalapeño: 30¢

Avocado: $2.50

Sour cream: $1.85

Radishes: 50¢

Cilantro: 75¢; free if homegrown

Limes: $1.20

Total price: $22.10 to $27.85; per person: $5.52 to $6.96

SPICE-RUBBED PORK TENDERLOIN

You know how sometimes you owe someone big time? After offering profuse thanks and/or apologies, depending on what the situation calls for, make this for your very good friend. It is the perfect midpoint between comfort food and highbrow cooking. He or she will feel impressed and appreciated.

A boned tenderloin from a good butcher or your farmers' market should cost between $7 and $12 per pound and weigh about 1 pound. You can buy it trimmed or untrimmed; remove any silver skin and excess fat from an untrimmed tenderloin with a sharp paring knife before seasoning.

Serves 2 or 3; doubles easily

1 whole pork tenderloin (about 1 pound)

1½ teaspoons fine salt

1½ teaspoons granulated sugar or light brown sugar

1 teaspoon ground cumin, coriander, garlic powder, chili powder, or cayenne powder

Freshly ground black pepper

Olive oil as needed

1 cup white or red wine or beer

¼ cup Meat Stock (use chicken or pork; page 35), Basic Vegetable Stock (page 34), or water

1 teaspoon unsalted butter

1. Preheat the oven to 400°F.

2. Trim excess fat and silver skin (tough, glossy, plasticlike tissue) from the tenderloin. Combine the salt, sugar, cumin, and pepper to taste and rub all over the tenderloin.

3. Heat a film of oil in an ovenproof skillet or sauté pan over medium-high heat. Sear the tenderloin on all sides, 60 to 90 seconds a side, without burning the spice rub. Transfer the skillet to the oven and roast for 20 to 25 minutes for

medium-rare/medium, 25 to 30 minutes for well-done.

4. Transfer the tenderloin to a cutting board and let rest for 15 to 30 minutes.

5. Put the skillet back over medium heat and deglaze with the wine and stock, scraping up all the browned bits. When the liquid has reduced by at least half, stir in the butter to give it a nice sheen. Remove from the heat.

6. Slice the tenderloin into ½-inch-thick medallions and serve, drizzled with the pan juice.

PRICE BOX

Pork tenderloin: $7 to $12
Wine/beer: 75¢ to $1.50

Total price: $7.75 to $13.50; per person: $2.58 to $6.75

CIDER-BRINED PORK CHOPS

Brining the pork chops leaves them tender and succulent; the apple cider gives a faintly sweet fall note.

Double- or center-cut pork chops should be at least 1 inch thick. In my experience, the price of pork chops can fluctuate wildly and unpredictably from market to market and farmer to farmer; these chops might come in well under $8 per person or they might cost more. I've included this recipe because, even when they do go over $8 per person, they are a great source of lean protein and a filling, easy-to-make main dish. A good salad and some hearty potatoes, rice, or pasta, can easily stretch the chops to feed two people each. The bones should be saved for making pork stock.

Serves 2; doubles easily

2 bone-in, double- or center-cut pork chops (at least 1 inch thick)

¼ cup kosher salt

¼ cup maple syrup

2 cups apple cider

Fresh cracked black pepper to taste

2 tablespoons olive oil

1 tablespoon unsalted butter

2 cloves whole, unpeeled garlic

2 teaspoons chopped fresh rosemary

Grainy mustard, for serving

1. Let the pork chops come to room temperature. Whisk together the salt, maple syrup, and cider until the salt and syrup are dissolved. Put the pork chops in a gallon-size zip-top bag and pour the brine over them; add enough water to cover the chops. Seal the bag and brine, refrigerated, for at least 4 hours or as long as overnight.

2. Remove the pork chops from the brine, rinse, and pat dry. Season on both sides with salt and pepper.

3. Heat the oil in a large, heavy skillet over medium heat. Add the pork chops and sear until browned, 3 to 4 minutes. Flip and sear the other side, 3 to 4 minutes.

4. Add the butter, garlic, and rosemary and cook for another 6 to 8 minutes, until a meat thermometer inserted in the center of one chop reads 145°F.

5. Move the pork chops and garlic cloves to a cutting board and let cool, at least 5 minutes. Serve with the mustard.

PRICE BOX

Pork chops: $10 to $24

Kosher salt: 25¢

Maple syrup: $1

Apple cider: $2

Garlic: 25¢

Rosemary: 25¢; free if homegrown

Total price: $13.50 to $27.75; per person: $6.75 to $13.88

ROAST CHICKEN AND VEGETABLES WITH MUSTARD JUS

Roast chicken isn't a recipe. It's a method.

What can I say? This dish does have the power to convert. Think you don't like chicken? Try this roast. Never tried cooking a whole chicken before because you were afraid it'd be raw inside? Make this. Right now.

Filling the bottom of your roasting pan with a layer of root vegetables makes this a one-dish meal: The vegetables soak up the chicken's drippings while providing support for the chicken itself so you won't spend an hour after dinner scraping bits of hardened chicken skin and solidified schmaltz off the wires of your roasting rack. Fat-infused roasted vegetables and minimal cleanup? Why are you not making this already?

Serves 4

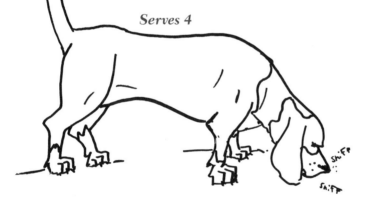

CHICKEN

One 3- to 5-pound pastured chicken

2 big handfuls of small potatoes, like fingerlings or baby new potatoes, or 2 medium Yukon gold potatoes, cut into 1-inch chunks (or a mix of any root vegetables you like)

8 or 9 whole cloves garlic

1 medium red or yellow onion, halved and sliced

1 medium carrot, chopped

1 medium parsnip, peeled and chopped

Kosher salt and freshly ground black pepper

1 lemon, quartered

½ bunch fresh thyme

MUSTARD JUS

½ cup Meat Stock (use chicken; page 35), white wine, beer, or water

2 tablespoons grainy mustard

2 teaspoons fresh thyme leaves

Salt and freshly ground black pepper

1. Make the chicken: Preheat a roasting pan in a 400°F oven. Let the chicken come to room temperature while the oven preheats. Make sure the cavity of the chicken is empty; reserve any bits and pieces inside for making stock later.

2. Put the potatoes, 6 cloves of the garlic, the onion, carrot, and parsnip in the roasting pan. Season with salt and pepper.

3. Rinse the chicken thoroughly, inside and out, then pat it dry inside and out. Rub 1 tablespoon of salt and a few grinds of black pepper in the chicken's

cavity. Shove the lemon, 2 or 3 cloves garlic, and a few whole sprigs of thyme into the cavity.

4. Truss the chicken by bringing a length of kitchen twine from behind the chicken's back, then cross it in a figure eight around the ends of the drumsticks. Pull the twine ends together to bring the drumsticks over the top of the cavity and cross the chicken's ankles. Tie the twine tightly to hold the legs in place.

"Trussing" means to tie up. Kinky!

5. Rub 1 to 2 tablespoons more salt onto the chicken's skin—front and back, and be sure to get in the crevices at the hips and under the wings. Grind pepper all over the bird and sprinkle it with some thyme leaves. Tuck the chicken's wingtips under its shoulders, as if it had its "hands" behind its head.

6. Lay the chicken breast-up on the vegetables. Roast for 15 minutes, then reduce the oven temperature to 350°F and roast for another 15 minutes. Flip the bird over and roast for 20 minutes to cook the underside, then flip back to breast side up and roast for another 20 minutes, or until the juices run clear. Give the pan a toss every time you flip the bird to keep the vegetables from sticking.

7. When the juices run clear, move the chicken to a cutting board and scoop the vegetables into a large serving bowl. Let the chicken rest, uncovered, while you make the jus.

8. The vegetables will have soaked up most of the chicken's drippings, so set the roasting pan over two burners over medium-low heat. Pour in ½ cup stock and deglaze the pan by scraping up any bits stuck to the bottom. Stir in the mustard and thyme. Taste, adjust the seasonings, and remove from the heat.

9. Carve the chicken: First, remove the trussing twine and separate the thighs and drumsticks from the body at the hip by carving smoothly through the hip joint. Then carve down either side of the breastbone, all the way to the rib cage. Carve along the arc of the rib cage and cut through the shoulder joint to detach the breasts.

10. Now take a minute for yourself. Flip the chicken over and pop the "oysters" out of the chicken's back and eat them right away. The gamey, sweet, meta-chickeny oysters, by the way, are little meat globes positioned about where kidneys would be on a human on the chicken's lower back, about parallel to the thigh joints. They will yield to your fingertip. After you've savored the oysters, follow suit with the pope's nose, a lovely bit of mostly fat at the tail stump that should be one or two bites of perfectly salty crispy chicken-ness.

11. Serve each person a quarter of the chicken with a healthy dose of the mustard jus, a good heap of the chicken-roasted vegetables, and a side salad to make you feel virtuous.

PRICE BOX

Chicken: $8 to $12

Potatoes: $1

Lemon: 50¢

Garlic: $1

Onion: $1

Carrot: 30¢

Parsnip: 50¢

Thyme: $1.50

Wine/beer (optional): 50¢

Total price: $13.80 to $18.30; per person: $3.45 to $4.58

WHOLE ROASTED TROUT WITH POTATOES, TOMATOES, AND LEMON

This is a quick, healthy, and hearty meal for two, but you must use the freshest trout possible, preferably one you bought that morning from a local fisherman (if your farmers' market has one) or a fantastic fishmonger.

Serves 2

1 2-pound fresh trout, cleaned

Kosher salt and freshly ground black pepper

½ pound fingerling or baby new potatoes

½ pint cherry or grape tomatoes

1½ lemons

6 whole cloves garlic

1 bunch fresh thyme

2 tablespoons olive oil plus ¼ cup

2 tablespoons pine nuts (optional)

Pinch of crushed red pepper flakes

¼ cup grated Parmesan or pecorino cheese (optional)

2 to 3 good handfuls of salad greens

1. Preheat the oven to 400°F. Rinse the trout and pat dry inside and out. Season the cavity with salt and pepper.

2. Rinse the potatoes and tomatoes and pat dry in a clean dishcloth. Slice 1 lemon into thin rounds. In a roasting dish or Dutch oven, toss the tomatoes, potatoes, 5 cloves of the garlic, half of the lemon slices, half of the thyme, and 2 tablespoons of the oil; season with salt and pepper.

3. Stuff the trout's cavity with the remaining lemon slices and thyme, reserving 1 tablespoon of the thyme leaves. Season the trout's skin with salt and pepper and lay on the bed of potatoes and tomatoes.

4. Roast the fish for about 15 minutes, then flip and roast for another 7 to 9 minutes. Flip back again and roast until the skin is bubbly and just starting to brown, 5 to 6 more minutes.

5. Remove the fish from the oven and let rest for a few minutes while you make the dressing.

6. Heat a small skillet over medium heat. Toast the pine nuts, if using, for 6 to 7 minutes or until fragrant. Remove from the heat.

7. Roughly chop the remaining clove of garlic and crush it in a mortar and pestle with some salt and the reserved 1 tablespoon thyme leaves. Strain in the juice of the remaining ½ lemon and whisk together. While whisking, slowly pour in the remaining ¼ cup oil in a thin, steady stream. Whisk until blended; taste and adjust, whisking in some black pepper, the red pepper flakes, and pine nuts while they're still hot. For a thicker dressing, whisk in the grated cheese; the pine nuts will melt the cheese slightly, further thickening the dressing.

PRICE BOX

Trout: $4 to $7
Potatoes: 75¢
Tomatoes: $2.50
Lemons: $1.40
Thyme: $1; free if homegrown
Pine nuts (optional): 75¢
Garlic: 75¢
Parmesan (optional): 75¢
Salad greens: $1

Total price: $11.15 to $15.90; per person: $5.58 to $7.95

8. Remove the lemons and thyme from the fish's cavity. Lay the fish flat and remove the spine, working carefully to extract as many small bones as possible and keep the fillets intact. You can pry the spine up with the edge of a paring knife or the tines of a fork, then lift it out with your fingers.

9. In a serving bowl, toss together the greens with some of the salad dressing, just enough to coat.

10. Serve each fillet with some of the simple salad, a generous portion of potatoes and tomatoes, and a healthy drizzle of the dressing over the fish and vegetables.

MUSSELS WITH ALE AND GARLIC

In a lot of ways, mussels are a "wonder food": affordable and versatile, high in protein, low in fat, and easy to grow naturally in salt and fresh water. Mussels can be smoked, grilled, or battered and fried, but I prefer them steamed in broth. I've had mussels in coconut broth with lemongrass and chiles; with curry, mango, and anise; even with sake, ginger, and scallions. And then there's Belgian-style: a broth of butter, beer, and garlic. Use a beer you love and don't skimp on the butter.

Mussels are fantastically unfussy, too. Keep them in your fridge under a damp cloth for up to 2 days before cooking them. For a casual brunch or dinner party, plop your pot of mussels in the middle of the table with a heap of crusty baguettes (or even better, a tangle of fresh french fries) and encourage everyone to dig in. Then immediately start thinking of what kind of broth you'll steam your mussels in next time.

This recipe can be halved or doubled easily; figure on ½ pound of mussels per person and adjust accordingly.

Serves 4

2 pounds mussels	**16 ounces beer**
4 tablespoons (½ stick) unsalted butter	**A loaf of good crusty bread for serving**
6 cloves garlic, minced	**2 lemons, quartered, for serving**
Salt and freshly ground black pepper	

1. Clean the mussels: Scrub them under cold water and pull off the beards, the ropy "strings" running along the shell hinges. Not every mussel will have a beard, so don't make yourself crazy trying to find them all.

2. Melt the butter in a Dutch oven over medium-low heat. Add the garlic and cook about 2 minutes. Add the mussels and season lightly with a small pinch (⅛ teaspoon) of salt and pepper; immediately pour the beer over the mussels and cover the pot. Leave covered and cook for about 10 minutes, shaking once halfway through. After 10 minutes, remove the cover; the mussels should have opened. If none are opened, cover and let cook for another 2 minutes, then check again.

3. Once all or most of the mussels have opened (discard any that don't open), serve in shallow bowls with some of the pan juice, accompanied with big hunks of baguette and the lemon quarters.

PRICE BOX

Mussels: $6
Butter: 85¢ to $1.18
Garlic: 75¢
Beer: $2
Bread: $3.50
Lemons: $1.40

Total price: $14.50 to $14.83; per person: $3.63 to $3.71

SPICE-RUBBED SALMON

I'll spare you the spiel about how healthy salmon is for you; undoubtedly you have heard it all before, probably more than once, from a well-meaning health-obsessed friend or relative.

Like most fish, though, salmon isn't necessarily cheap—we're not talking canned tuna here—but it can be affordable. Expect to spend about $6 to $8 per 8-ounce fillet, a perfectly fine serving for one.

As overfishing takes its toll on the fish, the oceans, and, in turn, the fishing industry, "good" fish is harder to find at reasonable prices; hopefully this eventually will balance out, as it's in everyone's best interests in the long run to take better care of our oceans and the tasty things that swim in them. In the meantime, my best advice is to approach most fish like a treat: to be eaten infrequently, but, when you do, get the best fish you can, cook it gently, and keep the seasoning light so you may really taste it. Wild Alaskan salmon and

MSC-certified farmed U.S. salmon are the most ecologically and environmentally friendly options and, frankly, taste the best too.

Serves 4

Two 1-pound salmon fillets, halved

Olive oil as needed

½ teaspoon fine sea salt

1 teaspoon brown sugar

1½ teaspoons paprika

Pinch of cayenne pepper

¼ cup thick plain yogurt

1 tablespoon Dijon mustard

½ tablespoon honey

2 tablespoons snipped fresh chives

Salt and freshly ground black pepper

1. Preheat the oven to 350°F.

2. In a small bowl, combine the sea salt, brown sugar, ½ teaspoon of the paprika, and the cayenne pepper. Rub the spice mix over both sides of each salmon fillet.

3. Heat a glug of oil in a cast-iron skillet or ovenproof pan over medium-high heat. Sear the salmon, skin-side-down, for 2 minutes; flip and sear the top side for 1 minute. Flip back over and transfer the skillet to the oven.

4. Bake for about 15 minutes, until easily flaked with a fork. Let rest for 10 minutes while you make the sauce.

5. In a small bowl, combine the yogurt, mustard, honey, remaining paprika, and chives; season with salt and black pepper. Taste and adjust. Serve alongside the salmon.

PRICE BOX

Salmon: roughly $26
Yogurt: 75¢
Chives: 25¢; free if homegrown

Total price: roughly $27; per person: roughly $7

CHINESE-STYLE LEEK AND PORK DUMPLINGS (*JIAOZI*)

These were inspired by my tour through the restaurants of Flushing, Queens, with Adam Roberts, aka the Amateur Gourmet. We hit at least five or six different places, each offering dishes neither of us had heard of, let alone tried, before. But we agreed that the standout dish was the dumplings of White Bear, a former ice-cream-parlor-turned-unassuming-dumpling mecca. We enjoyed them so much that Adam and I did our best to re-create those dumplings. The recipe came out surprisingly well, and it has become a favorite at home for Kit and me.

Makes 30 to 40 dumplings, or 5 to 10 servings

WRAPPERS

1¾ cups all-purpose flour

½ cup water

DIPPING SAUCE

1-inch piece fresh ginger, peeled and minced

1 scallion, thinly sliced

2 tablespoons soy sauce

2 tablespoons rice vinegar

FILLING

1 leek

1 pound ground pork

2 to 3 scallions, thinly sliced

1-inch piece fresh ginger, peeled and minced

1 clove garlic, minced

1 teaspoon soy sauce

1 teaspoon rice vinegar

1 egg, lightly beaten, for the egg wash (optional)

1. Make the wrappers: Combine the flour and water in a large bowl and mix until you have one large sticky ball of dough. Place the dough on a lightly floured surface and knead for a few minutes to develop the gluten; the dough should be springy and shiny. Form the dough into a ball and wrap it tightly in plastic wrap. Let sit for 10 minutes or so while you make the dipping sauce and filling.

2. Make the dipping sauce: Whisk all the dipping sauce ingredients together in a small bowl. Taste and adjust. Cover and place in the fridge until you are ready to serve.

3. Make the filling: Remove the root and leathery part of the dark green end of the leek. Halve lengthwise and thinly slice, then rinse the leek in a mesh strainer, rubbing running water through the segments and separating them with your fingers. Pat the leek dry in a clean dishcloth and put it in a large bowl. Add the pork, scallions, ginger, garlic, soy sauce, and vinegar. Mix together gently with your hands and put the bowl in the refrigerator to rest while you form the wrappers.

4. Form the wrappers: Lightly flour a work surface. Quarter the dough and roll the quarters out into 1-inch-thick logs. Divide the logs into 1-inch-square segments. Roll the segments into balls and flatten them as thin as possible with a rolling pin.

5. Start filling the wrappers with the chilled filling: Cup a wrapper in your palm and paint the rim of the wrapper with a little beaten egg or water to help seal. Place about 1 tablespoon of the filling in the center. Don't place too much filling into your wrappers or they will explode when you cook them.

6. Pinch in the far edge of the wrapper and repeat 2 or 3 times around the far side of the wrapper. Then fold the near side of the wrapper over the filling and pinch the dumpling closed. This can take some practice, so feel free

to seal your dumplings the best you can until you get the hang of it. Even if they look lumpy and misshapen, they'll taste delicious. Set the finished dumplings on a lightly floured baking sheet.

7. If you are boiling the dumplings, bring a large pot of water to a rolling boil. Place 8 to 10 dumplings in the pot and stir to keep them from sticking. Boil for 6 to 8 minutes, until the dumplings float to the top of the pot. Remove using a skimmer or slotted spoon.

8. If you are pan-frying the dumplings, heat 1 to 2 tablespoons oil in a large skillet over high heat. Nestle the dumplings in the pan, crimped top facing up. The pan should be crowded, but the dumplings should not be smashed in or they will stick together and rip when you try to remove them. Sear the bottoms of the dumplings until golden brown, 1 to 2 minutes. Pour about ½ cup of water into the pan—just enough to come about one third of the way up the sides of the dumplings. Cover with a tight-fitting lid and let the dumplings steam for 3 to 4 minutes. Uncover and let the water evaporate. Using tongs or a spatula, carefully transfer the dumplings to a platter.

9. Serve the boiled or fried dumplings with the dipping sauce.

PRICE BOX

Flour: 50¢
Ginger: $1
Scallions: 50¢
Leek: 50¢
Ground pork: $8

Total price: $10.50; per person: $1.05 to $2.10

BETWEEN CRUSTS

VEGGIE BURGERS

It's a little embarrassing to admit this: For more than ten years, I was a vegetarian, and I never even *considered* making my own veggie burgers. But who could blame me, when most of the prepared offerings ranged from freezer aisle meat substitutes to one horrifically unhealthy restaurant concoction that involved a cup of mayonnaise *and* deep-frying.

Luckily, I have Chef Brendan, and although he's never been a vegetarian himself, his veggie burger recipe is hands-down *the best veggie burger I've ever eaten*. His secret: fresh roasted vegetables. Seriously, that's it. No fake veggie protein, no weird filler, and absolutely no cup of mayo.

These delicate veggie burgers can be grilled, but I recommend grilling them on a grill pan to prevent them from falling apart.

Makes 8 to 10 burgers

4 carrots, finely diced

Olive oil

Kosher salt

2 shallots

1 leek, white and light green parts only, cleaned and dried

1 jalapeño chile

2 ears corn, husked and silks removed

1 cup diced mushrooms

1 tablespoon chopped fresh rosemary

1 tablespoon chopped fresh thyme

1 cup cooked black beans

½ cup cooked brown rice (you can use leftover takeout rice)

1 to 2 tablespoons mustard

¼ cup Ketchup (page 42)

¼ to ⅓ cup panko or regular breadcrumbs

1 large egg (optional, if needed)

Cheddar, American, Swiss, or your favorite cheese for topping (optional)

8 to 10 hamburger buns

Condiments of your choice

Sliced tomatoes and onions for serving

Lettuce for serving

Cooked bacon (optional)

1. Preheat a rimmed baking sheet in a 400°F oven.

2. In a large bowl (you can use the same bowl for all the elements of the burgers), toss the carrots with 1 tablespoon oil and 2 generous pinches of salt and arrange in an even layer on the baking sheet and roast, 5 to 6 minutes, while you prepare the next step.

3. While the carrots roast, mince the shallots and leek. Remove the stem end from the jalapeño and run a butter or table knife between the flesh and pith. The pith and seeds should slide right out. Then halve, julienne, and dice it. In the bowl that you tossed the carrot in, toss the shallot, leek, and julienned jalapeño with 1 tablespoon oil and a good pinch of salt and add to the baking sheet with the carrot, tossing to combine. Put back in the oven for 5 to 6 minutes, while you prepare the next step.

4. Shave the kernels off the corn cobs: Hold each ear of corn upright in the bowl and shave down the sides with a sharp chef's knife. Then run the back of the blade against the bare cob to extract the sweet, starchy pulp and juices. In the same bowl, toss the corn, mushrooms, rosemary, and thyme together with a final tablespoon of oil and generous pinch of salt. Dump the mixture onto the baking sheet and toss or fold into the rest of the vegetables. Cook until evenly softened, 10 to 15 minutes.

5. Meanwhile, pour the beans and rice into the bowl and mush them together with your hands. When the roasted vegetables are cool enough to handle, fold them into the beans and rice with your hands along with the mustard, ketchup, and panko.

6. Scoop up a handful of the mixture and form it into a patty—it should be just bigger than the cup of your palm. If the mixture won't hold, and you're not serving the burgers to vegans, mix in the egg as a binder. (If you are serving to vegans, add a dash or two of water for bonding.) Repeat making patties with the remaining mixture.

7. Heat 1 to 2 tablespoons oil in a large skillet or on a griddle over medium heat. When the oil's hot, add veggie burgers one at a time and cook for 5 to 6 minutes, until browned. Then flip them over to brown on the other side and heat through, 5 to 6 minutes. If you're topping with cheese, top each burger with a slice of cheese after flipping over.

8. Serve on hamburger buns and with an array of condiments, sliced tomatoes and onions, lettuce, and bacon, if you like.

PRICE BOX

Carrots: $1
Shallots: $1
Leek: 50¢
Jalapeño: 30¢
Corn: $1
Mushrooms: $3
Black beans: $1
Rice: 50¢
Homemade Ketchup: 30¢

Total price: $8.60; per person: 86¢ to $1.08

SWEET POTATO AND CORN EMPANADAS WITH CHIPOTLE DIPPING SAUCE

I like to make this when I can get my hands on good, peak-season fresh corn. I keep the seasoning inside the empanadas to a minimum: I like the gentle sweetness of both potato and corn to shine brightly. A decent amount of sea salt and a bit of cinnamon and nutmeg are enough to enhance the vegetables' flavors without overshadowing them. The chipotle yogurt is an assertive contrast to the silky sweet potato in the empanada filling.

When corn is out of season or my market's run out, I replace the corn with cooked black beans. Leftover roasted pulled pork or chicken or even just some sautéed leeks make a nice replacement or addition too.

Makes about 12 empanadas, or 4 to 6 servings

DOUGH

2¼ cups unbleached all-purpose flour

1 teaspoon fine salt

½ cup (1 stick) cold salted butter, cut into ½-inch cubes

1 large egg

½ cup ice-cold water

1 tablespoon apple cider vinegar

1 large egg white, beaten, for the egg wash

FILLING

1 large sweet potato (about 1½ pounds)

A few good pinches of fine sea salt, plus more to taste

1 tablespoon unsalted butter

1 large egg, lightly beaten

1 cup roasted corn kernels (or cooked black beans, sautéed mushrooms and/or leeks, and/or shredded roasted meat)

Freshly ground black pepper

½ teaspoon freshly grated nutmeg

½ teaspoon ground cinnamon

CHIPOTLE DIPPING SAUCE

1 cup thick plain yogurt

1 teaspoon olive oil

1 canned chipotle chile in adobo sauce, seeded and chopped, plus 2 teaspoons of the adobo sauce or chipotle hot sauce

1. Preheat the oven to 400°F.

2. Make the empanada dough: In the bowl of a food processor or in a large bowl, combine the flour and salt. Pulse in the butter or massage it in with your fingers until the mixture resembles coarse crumbs. In a second, smaller bowl,

beat the egg, then beat in the water and vinegar. Pulse or mix the egg mixture into the flour-butter mixture until a shaggy dough forms.

PRICE BOX

Flour: 50¢
Butter: $1.70 to $2.32
Eggs: $1.15
Sweet potato: $1
Roasted corn: $1
Yogurt: $2
Chipotle and adobo: 35¢

Total price: $7.70 to $8.32; per person: $1.28 to $2.08

3. Turn the dough out onto a clean, floured surface and gently knead it just until it becomes a coherent dough, but no more. Shape it into a ball and wrap it in plastic wrap. Refrigerate for 1 hour, which, as luck would have it, is about as long as it'll take for you to get the filling together.

4. Make the filling: Stab the sweet potato all over with a fork. Put the whole sweet potato on a piece of aluminum foil, sprinkle it with salt, and close the foil tight around it. Bake until a sharp knife slides easily into it, about 45 minutes. Remove from the oven and let it rest, still wrapped in the foil, until it's cool enough to handle. The skin should come right off in great big peels. Save the skin for making stock. Turn the sweet potato flesh into a large bowl, add the butter, and mash it down with a fork. Stir in the beaten egg, the corn, pepper to taste, and the nutmeg and cinnamon. Mix until well combined.

5. Remove the dough from the fridge and let it come up to room temperature, about 15 minutes. Flour your clean work surface again and roll the dough out to about ⅛ inch thick. Use a clean water glass, jam jar, or can to stamp out circles 3 to 5 inches in diameter.

6. Arrange the dough circles on baking sheets with about 1½ inches between each round. Scoop 1 tablespoon of filling into the center of each round, leaving about a ½-inch edge clean of filling. Lightly brush the dough edge with the egg wash and fold the dough over into half-moons. Press the edges together gently with the tines of a fork, then use the fork to make air vents in the top of each empanada. Brush each empanada with the egg wash for a nice shiny finish and bake for 15 to 17 minutes, until lightly browned.

7. While the empanadas bake, make the chipotle dipping sauce by combining all the ingredients in a small bowl. Refrigerate until you are ready to serve the empanadas.

THE SANDWICH THAT TASTES LIKE SUMMER

You can toast the bread first, if you like, but I prefer this sandwich with thick, soft fresh bread to soak up the bacon fat and tomato juices.

Serves 1

½ large heirloom tomato

Salt and freshly ground black pepper

2 teaspoons Cole's Sriracha (page 183)

1½ tablespoons Mayonnaise (page 43)

2 slices fresh Basic Whole Wheat/ White Blend Bread (page 54)

3 slices good bacon

1. Thickly slice the tomato and season with salt and pepper. Set aside.

2. In a small bowl, stir together the Sriracha and mayonnaise. Taste and adjust: more Sriracha for heat, more mayonnaise for mildness, and a little salt and pepper if needed. Spread the Sriracha mayo thickly over both slices of bread.

3. Heat a large skillet or sauté pan over medium-high heat. Add the bacon, turn the heat down to medium, and cook for 3 to 4 minutes per side, until browned and crisp. Break or slice each bacon strip in half and press 3 half slices onto the bottom slice of bread.

4. Pile the tomato onto the bottom slice of bread. Top with the remaining bacon and slice of bread and press together.

PRICE BOX

Bacon: $1.70

Tomato: $1.50

Total price: $3.20

APPLE, GOUDA, AND SPINACH QUESADILLA

You can make the tortillas for yourself—it's exceedingly easy to do—or use store-bought white or whole wheat tortillas. Just be aware that the majority of supermarket-brand flour tortillas are chock-full of polysyllabic preservatives, if that ain't your thing.

Traditionally flour tortillas are made with lard. You are not supposed to substitute vegetable oil or vegetable shortening, but as someone who generally doesn't keep lard around—and I imagine you don't either—I have only ever made them with vegetable oil, and they taste perfectly good to me.

I like to add a bit of buckwheat flour to the tortilla dough. Buckwheat's subtle toastiness complements the tart apple, nutty cheese, and mild spinach.

Serves 4

TORTILLAS

1 cup all-purpose flour, plus more for kneading

⅓ cup buckwheat or whole wheat flour

¼ teaspoon fine salt

¾ teaspoon baking powder

1 tablespoon vegetable oil

⅓ cup plus 2 tablespoons cold water

FILLING

Olive oil as needed

2 bunches fresh spinach, cleaned and stemmed, or 1½ cups cooked greens

Salt and freshly ground black pepper

1 heaping cup grated Gouda cheese

1 large, tart apple, cored and thinly sliced

1. Make the tortillas: Preheat the oven to 200°F.

2. Whisk the flours, salt, and baking powder together in a large bowl. Mix the vegetable oil in with your fingers until the dough forms coarse crumbs, then mix in the water until the dough comes together. Add more flour or water as needed, until the dough comes together into a manageable ball.

3. On a lightly floured surface, knead the dough until smooth and elastic, 5 to 8 minutes. Divide the dough into 8 equal pieces and roll each into a ball. Cover the rolled balls with a damp paper towel while you roll the rest.

4. Roll out the tortillas: Flour a clean work surface, your rolling pin, and your hands. Roll each round out into a very flat circle, rolling with one hand and rotating the dough with the other hand. Dust the tortillas with more flour and stack them as you go under your damp paper towel.

5. Heat a large skillet or sauté pan over medium-high heat. Cook a tortilla on one side until dry and just golden, 2 to 3 minutes; flip and repeat. Transfer the tortillas to a baking sheet in the oven to keep warm. Cover with a damp paper towel to keep from drying out.

6. Make the filling. For fresh spinach: Heat the oil in a large skillet or sauté pan over medium-low heat. Add the spinach, season with salt and pepper, and sauté until wilted. Remove to a colander to drain off excess liquid and let cool slightly.

7. Dry the skillet with a paper towel and reheat over medium heat. Lay a tortilla in the hot pan. Sprinkle with some cheese and cover with a layer of apple slices, then a layer of the cooked greens. Cover with more cheese and a second

PRICE BOX

Buckwheat flour: 25¢
Spinach: $4; free if using leftovers
Gouda: $3; free if using leftovers
Apple: 85¢

Total price: $1.10 to $8.10; per person: 28¢ to $2.03

tortilla. Press down gently and cook for 2 to 3 minutes, until the cheese on the bottom side is melted and the bottom tortilla is chestnut brown in spots. Flip with a large, flat spatula and cook on the other side for 2 to 3 minutes. Transfer to a plate to cool for a few minutes, then cut into quarters and serve. Repeat with the remaining tortillas and filling. (You can transfer the cooked quesadillas to the 200°F oven to keep warm while you prepare the rest.) Serve when all the quesadillas are cooked.

BUTTERNUT SQUASH AND MUSHROOM TART

I first made this when a friend hired me to cater her wedding. The bride was a vegetarian, and I knew from my own experiences at catered, sit-down events how dismal the vegetarian options usually are. I wanted her meal to be as filling and appetizing as everyone else's, and that's how I came up with this tart.

Serves 4 as a main or 8 to 10 as an appetizer

1 small butternut squash

Olive oil as needed

Kosher salt and freshly ground black pepper

4 cups thinly sliced mushrooms

4 cloves garlic, minced

2 tablespoons chopped fresh rosemary

Up to ½ cup white wine

2 tablespoons fresh thyme leaves

2 to 3 tablespoons heavy cream

¼ teaspoon freshly grated nutmeg

Pinch of ground cinnamon

1 large egg, separated

1 sheet of puff pastry

½ cup chèvre or other soft goat cheese, softened

¼ cup grated pecorino cheese

1 tablespoon water

RAID THE FRIDGE

Put your leftovers to work! Use extra Gouda from the French Onion Soup (page 120) (you can combine it with other cheeses you have around) and leftovers from Tzimmes (page 192), Our Mom's Brisket (page 195), or Maple-Mustard Roasted Pork (page 199) for a meaty addition.

1. Preheat a rimmed baking sheet in a 425°F oven.

2. Halve the squash lengthwise and scrape out the seeds. Rub the flesh and skins with oil and season the flesh with salt and pepper. Lay the squash flesh side down on the preheated baking sheet and roast for 20 to 25 minutes, until the skin is browned and wrinkled and a knife slides easily into the flesh. Remove from the oven and let cool; turn the oven temperature down to 400°F.

3. Meanwhile, heat a good glug of oil in a large skillet, preferably cast-iron, over medium heat. Add the mushrooms, season with salt and pepper, and cook for 5 to 8 minutes, until the mushrooms have released and reabsorbed some of their juices. Add the garlic and rosemary and toss together. Turn the heat to medium-low and keep cooking; if the pan starts to get too dry, douse it with a splash of wine. Scrape to deglaze and keep cooking until the mushrooms have shrunk by about half and are soft, about 10 minutes. At the last minute, fold in the thyme and remove from the heat. Let the mushrooms rest while you prepare the squash.

4. As soon as the squash is cool enough to handle, peel the skin off. Transfer the flesh to a large bowl and mash it with the back of a fork. Mash in the cream, starting with 2 tablespoons, the nutmeg, and cinnamon. When the mixture is cooled completely, whisk in the egg yolk. Season with salt and pepper.

5. Lightly flour a work surface and a rolling pin. Unfold the puff pastry and roll it out to the size of whatever pan you're going to use—either a 9-inch pie pan or a 9 x 13-inch baking dish. Drape the puff pastry into the pan and push it in gently. Let the excess dough hang over the edges for now.

6. Prick the bottom of the pastry all over with a fork. Spread the butternut squash about ½ inch thick over the bottom of the pastry; it should come about halfway up the tart's sides. Cover with an even layer of the mushrooms. Dot evenly with the chèvre and cover in an even dusting of pecorino.

7. In a small bowl, beat the egg white with the water into an egg wash. Brush over the exposed puff pastry; trim off any bits of dough that hang low down the outside of the baking dish.

8. Bake the tart for 15 to 20 minutes, until the cheese is melted and the crust is golden brown. Remove from the oven, let cool for 5 minutes, then slice into wedges or squares and serve.

PRICE BOX

Butternut squash: $3

Mushrooms: $4

Garlic: 50¢

Herbs: 50¢; free if homegrown

Wine: 75¢

Heavy cream: 25¢

Puff pastry: $3

Goat cheese: $3.50

Pecorino: 75¢

Total price: $15.75 to $16.25; per person: $1.58 (appetizer), $4.07 (main)

MUSTARD GREENS, APPLE, AND CHEDDAR QUICHE

This quiche only calls for four eggs but will easily feed eight people with a nice salad on the side. What I love about this recipe is how bold every ingredient is: There's a lovely tug of war going on between the spicy mustard greens and the sweet-tart apple, the mild eggs, and the sharp cheddar. Balancing it all is the nutty, almost sourdough-like buckwheat crust.

You could make the crust and the filling for this quiche on a Sunday and combine the two while the oven preheats on Monday; about 45 minutes later, you'll be sitting down to a hot, delicious dinner, with leftovers for lunch or a second dinner later in the week (unless your family numbers eight, in which case, just double the recipe and make it in a lasagna pan for leftovers).

While this quiche is fantastic hot, it's actually even better cold the next day.

Makes one 9-inch pie, or 8 servings

½ recipe Pâte Brisée (page 56), made with half all-purpose flour and half buckwheat flour

Olive oil

½ yellow onion, diced

2 cloves garlic, diced

1½ tart apples, cored and diced

Salt and freshly ground black pepper

1 bunch mustard greens, stemmed and torn or cut into bite-size pieces

4 large eggs

½ cup sharp cheddar cheese

½ cup smoked cheddar cheese

⅓ cup thick plain yogurt

1. Preheat the oven to 350°F.

2. Roll the dough ⅛ inch thick and drape it over a pie dish. Gently and very lightly press the crust into the dish and trim the overhang. Cover the crust with plastic wrap and put it in the fridge while you prepare the filling.

3. Heat a glug of oil in a high-sided sauté pan over medium heat. Add the onion and garlic and cook until caramelized, about 6 minutes. Add the apples and season with salt and pepper. Add the mustard greens and cook, stirring, for about 5 minutes, until the greens have wilted and everything is combined. Remove from the heat, strain, and let cool.

BUYING MUSTARD GREENS

When buying mustard greens at the farmers' market, look for big, broad leaves with crisp curls and strong, thick stems. Tear off a tiny corner of a leaf and give the greens a sniff: They should smell green but spicy, like strong mustard.

If your market doesn't have mustard greens or you find them too strong, substitute a bunch of chard or kale and mix a tablespoon of your favorite mustard (but not honey mustard) in with the cheese.

A NOTE ON THE CHEESE

I like to do a 50-50 blend of sharp cheddar and smoked cheddar, but 50-50 sharp and mild or all sharp or all smoked would work nicely too. Try not to use only mild cheddar; you want a cheese that will stand up to the strong greens. Gruyère, Gouda, a strong Swiss, or a sharp goat cheese would play nicely with the mustard greens too.

4. Beat the eggs in a small bowl. Combine the two cheeses in another small bowl. In a larger bowl, combine ¾ cup of the cheese mixture and the yogurt. Fold in the cooled greens and apples, then mix in the beaten eggs.

5. Pour the filling into the pie crust. Sprinkle the remaining ¼ cup cheese on top and bake until the crust has darkened slightly and the cheese is a bubbling golden brown, about 45 minutes. Cool, then slice and serve, or let cool to room temperature, refrigerate, and serve cold.

PRICE BOX

Pâte Brisée : $1.83 to $2.85
Onion: 50¢
Apples: $1
Mustard greens: $2.50
Eggs: $1.50
Cheddar cheese: $4.50
Yogurt: 65¢

Total price: $12.48 to $13.50; per person: $1.56 to $1.69

THANKSGIVING LEFTOVER POT PIES

I am a huge fan of repurposing leftovers, especially after a gluttonous feast like Thanksgiving. Even if it's the one time of year when everyone's stomachs actually are as big as their eyes, we always have a ton of leftovers. Happy though I am to scarf down cold roasted root vegetables right out of the container, this gets old after a few days. Something must be done with all the food. Preferably something all at once, that dirties very few dishes, and that I can, ideally, even freeze and save for much later.

The answer: pot pies.

In theory, all of your leftovers can go into these pot pies (with the exception of from-the-can jellied cranberry sauce). Be inventive. Do you have leftover sweet potatoes, the kind with the burnished marshmallow crust? Remove the marshmallows and stir your sweet potatoes into your base. Leftover green bean casserole? Great! Chop the beans up a bit and toss them in. Leftover creamed spinach? Perfect.

If you've got too many pot pies or just can't take another bite of turkey, you can wrap these pot pies tightly in aluminum foil and store them in a container in the freezer for a couple of months, then reheat, covered, at 350°F for 20 minutes.

The ingredients below are meant to be a sample of what you can put in your pot pies; add as much or as little of each as you want, bearing in mind how much space you have available for the filling (you can always double the pie crust recipe if you have extra filling ingredients).

Makes one 9-inch pie, three 5-inch pies, or 8 to 12 muffin pan pies

1 recipe Pâte Brisée (page 56)

Mashed potatoes

Basic Vegetable Stock (page 34) or Meat Stock (use turkey or chicken; page 35) and/or gravy

Salt and freshly ground black pepper

1 to 2 tablespoons unsalted butter, as needed

All-purpose flour for rolling the dough

1 egg, for the egg wash

ANY OR ALL OF THE FOLLOWING

Turkey, shredded or cut into ½-inch cubes

Sweet potatoes

Brussels sprouts with or without bacon

Roasted vegetables and/or potatoes, cut into ½-inch dice

Creamed spinach

Green bean casserole, cut into ½-inch dice

1. Preheat a rimmed baking sheet in a 350°F. oven.

2. Divide the dough into as many pieces as needed: 2 for a 9-inch pie, 6 for three 5-inch pies, or 16 to 24 for muffin pan pies, depending on the size of the pan. Roll each portion of dough into a ball.

3. Lightly flour a work surface and roll out each round of dough ⅛ inch thick to the desired size. Roll the dough over the rolling pin to transfer to the pie

or muffin pan. Gently push it down into the pan and trim off the excess, allowing ½ inch to hang over the sides of the pie pans or ¼ inch extra dough for muffin pans. Repeat as necessary until half your dough is rolled and put into pans. Set aside.

4. In a medium saucepan, whisk together the mashed potatoes and about half as much stock and/or gravy over low heat until creamy and smooth. Add any other ingredients on the list or that you have in the fridge and heat for 5 to 10 minutes, until warmed through, adding more stock as needed. Season with salt and pepper and melt in the butter to keep the filling moist in the pies.

5. Heap enough filling into each pie crust to create a mound that just peaks above the pan in the center.

6. Roll out the remaining dough balls on your floured surface ⅛ inch thick for the pot pie tops. Drape each top over a filled pie, trim off any excess dough, and crimp the edges closed: Crimping not only looks pretty; it's also functional, as it seals the filling in. To crimp, pinch one side of the dough with two fingers and pinch from the other side with the other finger, creating little "U"s along the rim of the pie. Cut 2 or 3 vents in the top of each pie to allow air to escape during baking.

7. Beat the egg in a ramekin and brush it over the crust. Place the pies or muffin pan on the preheated baking sheet and bake for 30 minutes, or until the crusts are golden brown.

8. Let rest for 10 minutes, then serve. Alternatively, let the pies cool to room temperature, wrap tightly in aluminum foil, and freeze for up to 2 months.

PRICE BOX

Since you'll use leftovers almost exclusively in this recipe, the only thing you need to make from scratch is, possibly, the pie dough.

Pâte Brisée: $3.65 to $5.70

Total price: $3.65 to $5.70; per slice: 46¢ to 71¢

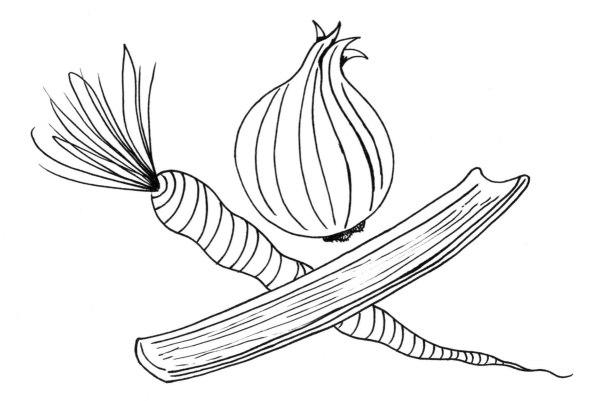

Chapter Nine

Desserts

Some people consider themselves cooks but not bakers; others, the exact opposite. To those who avoid baking because of the rigidity of science, I say, as kindly as possible: relax. It's all in your head.

Baking, as those who love to bake know, is actually not so different from cooking. Yes, it's more important to follow written instructions in baking than to go by feel or senses alone, but that's not to say it's all as mechanical as lab work. When you know what effect an egg yolk as opposed to an egg white will have on a cookie dough, there's a little room to experiment. When a cake is done baking, your nose may tell you before your timer. And just because a recipe calls for a pinch of cinnamon doesn't necessarily mean you can't omit it entirely or double it, based on your preferences.

The nice thing about baking is that, for the most part, the ingredients generally are inexpensive pantry items: an egg or two, some flour and sugar, a stick of butter or some vegetable oil. Use this as a reason to experiment. Not a lot, necessarily, but enough to get you to the point where you feel comfortable using your oven to make cakes and cookies as well as roasts and stews. And if you never do find that comfort spot, there's always poached fruit and beeramisu waiting for you on the non-oven side of the baking world.

PUMPKIN WHOOPIE PIES

I have no problem with pumpkin pie; in fact, I love pumpkin pie. But that doesn't mean you can't mix up your holiday desserts every now and then—especially if your family's anything like mine and half the guests bring a pumpkin pie to Thanksgiving dinner. These whoopie pies are especially great for a big Halloween or Thanksgiving party where one or even two pumpkin pies aren't enough. This recipe is adapted from one by *Baked*'s Matt Lewis and Renato Poliafito.

Makes 6; doubles or quadruples easily

CAKES

½ cup (1 stick) unsalted butter, melted, plus 1 tablespoon butter for the baking sheet (not necessary if using a silicone mat)

1½ cups all-purpose flour

½ teaspoon kosher salt

½ teaspoon baking powder

½ teaspoon baking soda

2 tablespoons ground cinnamon

1½ teaspoons ground ginger

1½ teaspoons ground cloves

1 teaspoon ground star anise

1 cup firmly packed light brown sugar

1½ cups pure pumpkin puree (not pumpkin pie filling), chilled

1 large egg, lightly beaten

1½ teaspoons vanilla extract

CREAM CHEESE FROSTING FILLING

1½ cups powdered sugar, or to taste

4 to 6 ounces softened cream cheese

1½ teaspoons vanilla extract, or to taste

1. Make the cakes: Preheat the oven to 350°F. Butter a rimmed baking sheet or line it with a silicone mat.

2. Combine the flour, salt, baking powder, baking soda, cinnamon, ginger, cloves, and star anise in a large bowl.

3. In a second large bowl, whisk together the brown sugar and melted butter. Whisk in the chilled pumpkin puree, egg, and vanilla.

4. Gently fold the dry ingredients into the wet ingredients and mix until just combined.

5. Using a large spoon or ice cream scoop, scoop the mixture one spoonful at a time onto the prepared baking sheet. Be sure to space the cookies at least 1 inch apart.

PRICE BOX

Butter: $1.70 to $2.35
Flour: 38¢
Cinnamon: 15¢
Brown sugar: $1.75
Pumpkin puree: $2
Vanilla: 75¢
Powdered sugar: 75¢
Cream cheese: $2.65

Total price: $10.13 to $10.78; per person: $1.69 to $1.80

6. Bake until the tops have darkened slightly and have just cracked, about 15 minutes. Remove from the oven onto a cooling rack and cool completely.

7. While the cookies cool, make the filling: Whip together all the frosting ingredients until smooth and uniform. Taste and adjust: You may want it sweeter, tarter, or more flavorful. Whip in more powdered sugar, cream cheese, or vanilla as needed.

8. With a spatula, transfer the frosting to a zip-top bag and mush it all over to one side. Snip off the opposite bottom corner—just about ¼ inch of it—to turn it into a piping bag.

9. Flip the cookies over so their flat bottoms face up. Pipe an even layer of frosting onto the bottom of half the cookies and top with an unfrosted half, making sandwiches.

10. Move the whoopee pies to the refrigerator to set for 30 minutes.

JUMBLE BERRY PIE

I am very honestly in awe of my brother Max's girlfriend, Stephanie Strohm. Stephanie is an extremely talented author and baker. Her adorably named Jumble Berry Pie is one of her best: With a latticed top crust, it's the quintessential summer dessert, especially with a scoop of ice cream on top.

Makes one 9-inch pie; serves 8

All-purpose flour, for rolling the crusts

1 recipe Pâte Brisée (page 56)

1 cup hulled, sliced strawberries

1 cup raspberries

1 cup blackberries

2 cups blueberries

½ cup sugar

¼ cup King Arthur Flour pie thickener, or 3 tablespoons arrowroot powder or cornstarch

1 egg yolk (optional)

1 tablespoon milk or water (optional)

2 tablespoons baker's sugar (optional)

1. Line a rimmed baking sheet with aluminum foil or a silicone mat and place it in the upper third of the oven. Preheat the oven to 375°F.

2. On a lightly floured work surface, divide the dough in half. Roll out one half to about ⅛ inch thick and roll it over your rolling pin. Drape the pie crust into a 9-inch pie plate and gently push the crust into the plate and up the sides.

3. In a large bowl, mix together all the berries, the sugar, and pie thickener. Pile the filling in the pie crust. Set aside.

4. Re-flour your work surface, if necessary, and roll out the second piece of dough. You can roll it ⅛ inch thick and drape it over the filling for a closed pie, or you can roll it a little thicker and make a lattice crust.

5. To make a closed pie, roll the crust over your rolling pin and drape it over the pie filling. Trim off any excess on the top and bottom crusts, leaving about ¼ inch of extra crust all around. Pinch the crusts together by making a wide indentation with two fingers of one hand and pushing into that indentation with one finger of your other hand, making little "U"s all around the edge of the crust. Cut 3 to 5 venting slits in the top of the pie crust.

6. To make a lattice crust, cut the second piece of rolled-out dough into ½-inch- to 1-inch-wide strips with a knife, bench scraper, or pizza cutter. You can then weave the strips over and under each other in a crosshatch and roll the lattice gently over your rolling pin to transfer it to the pie in one piece. You can also just drape the strips over the pie in a diamond pattern—one set going one way, turn the pie 90 degrees and drape the other set in the opposite direction—which will still look impressive. Trim off any overhanging dough to ¼ inch and seal the edges as for the closed pie.

7. For a shiny pie crust, whisk together the egg yolk and milk in a small bowl. Brush over the crust. You can then sprinkle the baker's sugar over the crust for a nice sparkly crunch.

8. Bake the pie on the lined baking sheet to catch any spills, until the crust is golden and the filling is bubbling, about 50 minutes.

9. Let cool for at least 20 minutes before serving.

PRICE BOX

Pâte Brisée: $3.65 to $5.70

Strawberries: $2.50

Raspberries: $2

Blackberries: $2

Blueberries: $2

Sugar: 55¢

Pie thickener: 25¢ to $1.25

Total price: $12.95 to $16; per person: $1.62 to $2

TOASTER PASTRIES

Do you remember how in the beginning of this book I told you that the meal plan choices my freshman year of college were so bad, I often had to rely on Pop-Tarts for basic sustenance?

Well, since those dark, young days filled with so many overfrosted, over-sugared, underfruited "jam"-filled desserts-as-meals, I'm happy to say that I've all but sworn off these anemic cereal aisle staples. And you can too! By making them yourself, at home, from all natural ingredients. They will taste richer than their store-bought brethren, which means you'll savor them and appreciate them more.

These little hand pies can be sweet or savory and are fantastic around the holidays: Fill them with homemade pie filling or jam or leftover cranberry sauce. They freeze well and reheat quickly in the oven or toaster, so they're great to have on hand for friends or family who pop in (get it?) during the holidays.

To give these pastries a grown-up edge, I drizzle them with a maple-bourbon glaze once they've cooled. But a brush of egg wash and a sprinkling of baker's sugar or just some of your favorite frosting would be just as nice.

Below are recipes for pumpkin custard, apple pie, and cranberry sauce toaster pastries. For savory fillings, combine different cheeses with fruits or jams and even thinly sliced cured meats like prosciutto or speck. For example, Brie with honey and prosciutto; goat cheese with fig jam and rosemary; or blue cheese and fig jam with toasted, crushed walnuts are all delicious savory fillings.

Makes about ten 4 x 3-inch pastries

1 recipe Pâte Brisée (page 56)

PUMPKIN CUSTARD FILLING

1½ teaspoons all-purpose flour

⅓ cup packed light brown sugar

¾ cup pure pumpkin puree (not pumpkin pie filling)

¼ teaspoon salt

¼ teaspoon ground nutmeg

¼ teaspoon ground cloves

¼ teaspoon ground ginger

½ teaspoon ground cinnamon

¾ to 1 cup milk

1 large egg

Baker's sugar (optional)

APPLE PIE FILLING

½ cup light brown sugar

1 teaspoon ground cinnamon

½ teaspoon ground ginger

1 tablespoon all-purpose flour

1 apple, peeled, cored, and thinly sliced

LEFTOVER CRANBERRY SAUCE FILLING

1 tablespoon arrowroot powder or cornstarch

1 tablespoon water

1 tablespoon light brown sugar

1 cup leftover homemade cranberry sauce

MAPLE-BOURBON GLAZE (OPTIONAL)

⅓ cup powdered sugar

2 tablespoons maple syrup

½ teaspoon ground cinnamon

½ teaspoon vanilla extract

1 tablespoon bourbon

TOPPINGS

1 large egg, beaten with 2 tablespoons water, for the egg wash

Baker's sugar (optional; if not glazing the pastries)

1. Preheat the oven to 350°F and remove the dough from the fridge so it can come up to room temperature while you assemble the filling.

2. *To make the pumpkin custard filling:* In a small bowl, whisk together the flour, brown sugar, and salt. In a medium saucepan, heat the pumpkin puree with the spices over medium-low heat, stirring frequently to prevent scorching, for about 10 minutes. This "wakes up" the spices while thickening the puree slightly; both good things. Remove from the heat and whisk in the flour mixture. Whisk in the milk and temper in the egg by mixing a little of the pumpkin mixture into the egg until the egg has come up in temperature. When the egg is noticeably warmer, whisk it slowly into the pumpkin mixture. Be careful not to scramble the egg—slowly is the key here. Set the mixture aside to cool and thicken while you roll out your dough.

3. *To make the apple pie filling:* Combine the brown sugar, cinnamon, ginger, and flour in a medium bowl and fold in the apple.

4. *To make the leftover cranberry sauce filling:* Whisk the arrowroot with the

PRICE BOX

Pumpkin Custard Pastries

Pâte Brisée: $3.65 to $5.70
Brown sugar: 60¢
Pumpkin puree: $1.15
Milk: 50¢
Maple-bourbon glaze (optional): 65¢ to $1.20

Total price: $5.90 to $9.15; per person: 59¢ to 92¢

Apple Pie Pastries

Pâte Brisée: $3.65 to $5.70
Brown sugar: 90¢
Apple: 85¢
Maple-bourbon glaze (optional): 65¢ to $1.20

Total price: $5.40 to $8.65; per person: 54¢ to 87¢

Cranberry Sauce Pastries

Pâte Brisée: $3.65 to $5.70
Arrowroot powder/cornstarch: 10¢ to 15¢
Maple-bourbon glaze (optional): 65¢ to $1.20

Total price: $3.75 to $7.05; per person: 38¢ to 71¢

water in a small bowl. In a medium bowl, stir the brown sugar into the cranberry sauce—you want it to be a little sweeter for the pastries than it was as
a Thanksgiving garnish. Stir the arrowroot mixture into the sauce.

5. Roll out the dough: Roll a round of dough out to a 9½ x 12½-inch rectangle.
    Trim any uneven edges with a ruler, then measure out 3 x 4-inch rectangles.

6. Arrange half of the pie rectangles on a rimmed baking sheet lined with
    parchment paper or a silicone mat. Place 1 heaping tablespoon of filling in
    the center of each rectangle and paint the edges with the egg wash. Gently
    seal each pastry shut with the remaining pastry rectangles, using the tines of
    a fork to gently press the edges together. Try to push out any air bubbles. Poke
    the tops of each pastry with the fork to create air vents, then brush the pas-
    tries with more egg wash so they'll develop a nice sheen in the oven. Sprinkle
    with baker's sugar if you aren't going to glaze the baked pastries.

7. Bake for 25 to 30 minutes, until the crusts are golden brown, rotating the
    pan once halfway through baking (bake them for only 15 to 20 minutes if
    you're going to freeze them for reheating later).

8. Cool the pastries on a wire rack for 10 minutes. While the pastries are cooling,
    if you are going to glaze the pastries, combine all the glaze ingredients and
    stir to dissolve the powdered sugar. Then frost and, once the frosting's set,
    serve.

APPLE CAKE

This cake is about as close to perfection as a fall cake can come: grown-up enough to serve for brunch, afternoon tea, or at the end of a sophisticated dinner, but sweet enough to feel like a good and proper dessert and sate your dessert craving. The only butter in the cake is what you spread around the cake pan, and yet the cake forms a sublime, slightly crunchy caramelized crust on the top and bottom. The apples sink and melt into the batter, keeping the cake moist without weighing it down.

You could change the cake entirely by adding ginger to the cinnamon, or perhaps a teaspoon of ground cardamom, or substitute a dash of rum or Calvados for half of the vanilla. Possibilities? Endless.

Makes 1 large Bundt cake

Unsalted butter for the pan

2 or 3 large, tart apples, peeled and cored

2 tablespoons granulated sugar

2 tablespoons ground cinnamon

2 cups all-purpose flour

2 cups firmly packed dark brown sugar

4 teaspoons baking powder

¼ teaspoon salt

4 large eggs

1 cup vegetable oil

2½ teaspoons vanilla extract

Powdered sugar or toasted slivered almonds for topping (optional; if not making the glaze)

¼ cup maple syrup, or as needed (optional; for the glaze)

2 to 3 tablespoons powdered sugar (optional; for the glaze)

1. Preheat the oven to 350°F and lightly butter a 9-inch cake or Bundt pan.

2. Chop the apples into uniform chunks and toss in a bowl with the granulated sugar and cinnamon. Set aside.

3. In a large bowl, combine the flour, brown sugar, baking powder, and salt. Stir in the eggs and oil, then the vanilla.

4. Either gently fold the apples into the batter and pour everything into the cake pan, or pour one third of the batter into the prepared cake pan, then half of the apples, one third of the batter, the second half of the apples, and finish with the remaining third of the batter. There should be quite a bit of extra room at the top of the pan; trust me, you'll need it.

PRICE BOX

Apples: $2

Flour: 50¢

Brown sugar: $3.65

Eggs: $1.50

Vegetable oil: $1.40

Vanilla extract: $1.25

Maple syrup (optional): $2

Total price: $10.30 to $12.30; per person: $1.29 to $1.54

5. Bake for 65 minutes, or until a knife inserted in the center of the cake comes out clean. Cool completely in the pan, then invert onto a plate and flip back over. Sprinkle generously with powdered sugar, toasted slivered almonds, or a maple syrup glaze made by stirring the powdered sugar into the maple syrup to desired thickness.

SOUTHERN FRUIT COBBLER

Double-crust, Dutch oven, Southern-as-Daisy-Dukes peach and berry cobbler: wickedly unhealthy but astoundingly delicious.

It's good with any baking fruit—a mix of berries and cherries, peaches and apricots, apples, pears, and even pineapple—and either crust can be optional, if you find you don't have the time for both (though the entire dish is fairly easy to throw together in a jiffy).

Serves 10 to 14

DROP CRUST

1 cup (2 sticks) cold unsalted butter, cut into ¼-inch chunks, plus 1 teaspoon for buttering the pot

1¼ cups all-purpose flour

½ cup granulated sugar

¼ cup cornmeal or masa harina (fine-ground Mexican-style cornmeal)

2 teaspoons baking powder

½ teaspoon fine sea salt

¾ cup milk

FILLING

About 6 tennis-ball-size ripe peaches

1 pint fresh local berries (any kind)

1 to 2 tablespoons granulated sugar

Juice and zest of ½ lemon

1 teaspoon vanilla extract

1 ounce bourbon (optional)

1 to 2 tablespoons all-purpose flour

CRUMB CRUST

¼ cup broken pecans or rolled oats

¼ cup packed light brown sugar

1 cup all-purpose flour

½ teaspoon fine sea salt

4 tablespoons (½ stick) unsalted butter, melted

Crème fraîche, plain yogurt, or vanilla ice cream for topping

1. Make the drop dough: Preheat the oven to 375°F. Butter the bottom and sides of a 4- to 5-quart Dutch oven or heavy-bottomed 13 x 18-inch baking dish.

2. In the bowl of a food processor, combine the flour, granulated sugar, cornmeal, baking powder, and salt and pulse together. Pulse in the butter in small batches. Don't overpulse; stop when the dough resembles fine, soft crumbs. Pulse in the milk until the dough is slightly wet but still cohesive. Don't overwork—just mix to combine.

3. Drop the dough into the prepared Dutch oven with an ice cream scoop or large spoon. It doesn't matter if there are small gaps in the dough; they'll cook out. Just don't smash the dough down.

4. Bake for 15 to 20 minutes, until golden brown.

5. While the drop crust bakes, prepare the fruit: Pare the peaches: Using a table knife, cut each peach in half lengthwise and slice it into segments around the pit. Peeling the peaches is unnecessary labor: the skins will soften into velvety perfection as they bake. Leave your peach segments as they are or chop them into 1-inch cubes; it's up to you.

6. Put the peaches in a large bowl. Add the berries (hull and slice strawberries first). Macerate the fruit by stirring in the granulated sugar, the lemon juice, and lemon zest. Stir in the vanilla and bourbon, if using. Finally, fold in enough flour to thicken the juices. Set aside.

7. To make the crumb crust topping, combine the pecans, brown sugar, flour, and salt in the food processor. Slowly pulse in the butter until the mixture is coarse and crumbly but easily forms lumps when you press it together.

PRICE BOX

Butter: $4.25 to $5.88

Flour: 60¢

Sugar: 55¢

Cornmeal: 15¢

Milk: 75¢

Peaches: $4.50

Berries: $3

Lemon: 70¢

Bourbon (optional): 75¢ to $1.50

Pecans or oats: 75¢ to $1.25

Brown sugar: 60¢

Total price: $15.85 to $19.48; per person: $1.13 to $1.95

8. Remove the baked bottom crust from the oven. Pour the fruit onto the hot drop crust and sprinkle the pecan crumb crust over it in an even layer. The fruit probably will poke through; that's okay. This crust should be thin to compensate for the thick bottom crust.

9. Bake, uncovered, for 45 to 60 minutes, until the crumb crust is browned and the fruit is bubbling. Let cool for 20 minutes, then serve by scooping out with an ice cream scoop or large spoon. Serve in a bowl with a dollop of crème fraîche, plain yogurt, or vanilla ice cream.

CRANBERRY DARK CHOCOLATE OATMEAL LACE COOKIES

I love the balance of these cookies: not too sweet, not too tart. Like true oatmeal lace cookies, they spread out and get thin as they bake, meaning crisp edges and an almost toffeelike, toasted oat center. But be mindful of the spreading when you bake them, and give them generous space on your baking sheets so they don't glob together into one meta-cookie.

Makes 2 to 3 dozen cookies

½ cup (1 stick) unsalted butter, at room temperature

¾ cup granulated sugar

¼ cup packed light brown sugar

1 teaspoon vanilla extract

1 large egg

1 cup all-purpose flour

1 cup rolled oats

½ teaspoon baking powder

½ teaspoon baking soda

½ teaspoon salt

1½ teaspoons ground cinnamon

1½ teaspoons freshly grated nutmeg

½ cup dried cranberries

½ cup dark chocolate chips or chunks

¼ cup milk, plus more if needed

1. Preheat the oven to 350°F and line two rimmed baking sheets with silicone mats or parchment paper.

2. In a large bowl, beat the butter and sugars together until fluffy. Beat in the vanilla and egg.

3. In a separate bowl, combine the flour, oats, baking powder, baking soda, salt, cinnamon, and nutmeg with a fork or whisk. Fold in the cranberries and chocolate. Add half of the dry ingredients to the dough, beat for a moment, then add the milk. Beat for about 10 seconds, then add the remaining dry ingredients and a little more milk, if necessary, to make a soft dough.

4. Refrigerate the dough for about 15 minutes to chill. Using a measuring spoon or kitchen teaspoon, scoop the dough onto the baking sheets. Be sure to leave plenty of space around each cookie—they will flatten and spread out quite a bit as they bake.

5. Bake for 15 minutes, or until golden brown on top, rotating the pans once halfway through baking. Let cool slightly, then remove to a cooling rack to cool completely.

PRICE BOX

Butter: $1.70 to $2.35
Granulated sugar: 75¢
Brown sugar: 60¢
Flour: 25¢
Oats: $1
Cranberries: $2.50
Chocolate: $2.50

Total price: $9.30 to $9.95;
per cookie: 26¢ to 42¢

HONEY-CORNMEAL COOKIES

This is my take on classic Italian *zaletti,* lightly sweetened cookies with a nutty crunch from coarse-ground cornmeal. Crunchy and crumbly, they're more like biscotti than traditional cookies. I like to flavor these cookie-biscuits with cinnamon, lemon, and vanilla, but dried fruit and almond extract make delicious substitutions.

Coarser cornmeal gives the cookies a hard crunch; for a gentler texture, give your cornmeal a few pulses in a food processor.

Makes 2 to 3 dozen cookies

1¾ cups all-purpose flour

1 cup coarse or fine cornmeal

½ teaspoon salt

½ teaspoon baking soda

1 tablespoon ground cinnamon

1 cup (2 sticks) unsalted butter, softened

½ cup plus 1 tablespoon honey

1 large egg plus 1 egg yolk

Zest of 1 lemon

1 teaspoon vanilla extract

1. Mix the dry ingredients together in a large bowl.

2. In a stand mixer or in a large bowl with a hand mixer, cream together the butter and ½ cup of the honey. Beat in the egg, then the egg yolk. Mix in the lemon zest and vanilla.

3. Gradually beat in the dry ingredients until combined.

4. Dump the dough onto a large piece of plastic wrap, wrap tightly, and refrigerate for 1 hour, or until firm enough to handle.

5. On a lightly floured surface, divide the dough in half lengthwise and roll each half into a cylinder about 3 inches in diameter. Wrap the cylinders in plastic wrap and freeze until ready to bake.

6. Preheat the oven to 350°F. Line two rimmed baking sheets with silicone mats or parchment paper.

7. Slice the dough into ¼-inch rounds and space them evenly on the baking sheets. If the dough crumbles when you cut it, let it warm up for 5 to 8 minutes. Brush the tops of the cookies with the remaining 1 tablespoon honey.

8. Bake the cookies until the tops are golden, 10 to 14 minutes, rotating the sheets about halfway through the baking time. Transfer the cookies to a cooling rack and cool for about 10 minutes before serving.

PRICE BOX

Flour: 50¢
Cornmeal: 60¢
Butter: $2.40 to $4.70
Honey: $2.25
Lemon: 70¢

Total price: $6.45 to $8.75; per cookie: 20¢ to 37¢

SEA SALT–HONEY CARAMELS

This is candy for grown-ups: rich and decadent, sweet tempered by a kiss of salt and the warm scent of honey. Because you're using so much honey, choose one with a defined flavor; the notes of lavender or citrus or clover or wildflower will come through in the candies, making it worth the extra cost of good honey. You will need a candy thermometer for this, but you can get a perfectly good one for under $20.

Makes 20 to 40 caramels, depending on the size

1 tablespoon unsalted butter (for the pan)

1 tablespoon plus ½ teaspoon vanilla extract

1 cup heavy cream

1 cup good honey

1 teaspoon good flaky sea salt

1. Generously butter a 9 x 13-inch baking dish.

2. In a heavy-bottomed, nonreactive saucepan, heat the cream and ½ teaspoon of the salt over medium-high heat. Stir frequently to keep from scalding. When the cream hits a simmer, stir in the vanilla and honey.

3. Bring to a boil, immediately reduce the heat to a simmer, and cook, stirring constantly, to 260°F. Immediately remove from the heat and pour into the prepared baking dish.

4. Refrigerate for 10 to 15 minutes to set the caramel; it should just take the indentation of your finger when firmly pressed.

5. Line a baking sheet with a silicone mat or length of waxed paper. Using a spatula, invert the caramel onto the lined baking sheet. Cool completely, then sprinkle with the remaining ½ teaspoon salt.

6. Cut the caramels into small pieces (I usually do ½ x 2 inches) and wrap each piece in a 3-inch square of parchment paper.

PRICE BOX

Heavy cream: $4
Vanilla extract: $1
Honey: $4.50

Total price: $9.50; per caramel: 16¢ to 32¢

Bibliography

AllAboutAgave.com. "Agave Nectar and the Glycemic Index." Accessed September 2, 2012. http://www.allaboutagave.com/agave-nectar-and-the-glycemic-index.php.

Bittman, Mark. "Eating Food That's Better for You, Organic or Not." *The New York Times*, March 21, 2009. Accessed September 5, 2012. www.nytimes.com/2009/03/22/weekinreview/22bittman.html.

Chait, Jennifer. "11 Frequently Asked Questions About Organic Certification Exemption: Basic Rules for Non-Certified Organic Farms." About.com. Accessed September 5, 2012. http://organic.about.com/od/organiccertification/tp/11-Frequently-Asked-Questions-About-Organic-Certification-Exemption.htm.

Chait, Jennifer. "8 Differences Between Organic Food and Sustainable Food." About.com. Accessed September 5, 2012. http://organic.about.com/od/organicindustrybasics/tp/8-Difference-Between-Organic-Food-And-Sustainable-Food.htm.

Crane, Dan. "Worth One's Salt." Slate.com, Tuesday, April 26, 2005. Accessed September 5, 2012. http://www.slate.com/articles/life/shopping/2005/04/worth_ones_salt.html.

Fisher, M.F.K. *How to Cook a Wolf.* New York: Duell, Sloan & Pearce, 1942.

"Flour, Types of Flour, How to Buy Flour, How to Store Flour." What's Cooking America. Accessed July, 31, 2012. http://whatscookingamerica.net/Bread/FlourTypes.htm.

Foley, Michele. "What's the Difference Between Brown Sugars?" Chow.com, August 8, 2007. Accessed July 31, 2012. http://www.chow.com/food-news/54067/whats-the-difference-between-brown-sugars/.

Freeman, Shanna. "How Salt Works." HowStuffWorks.com. Accessed September 1, 2012. http://science.howstuffworks.com/innovation/edible-innovations/salt2.htm.

Gary Ibsen's Tomato Fest, "Tomatoes and Growing Information." Accessed August 10, 2012. www.tomatofest.com/tomato-growing-zone-map-3.html.

Horsley, Scott. "U.S. Growers Say China's Grip on Garlic Stinks." NPR.com. June 30, 2007. Accessed July 31, 2012. www.npr.org/templates/story/story.php?storyId=11613477.

Johannes, Laura. "Agave Syrup May not Be so Simple." TheWallStreetJournal.com, October 27, 2009. Accessed July 31, 2012. http://online.wsj.com/article/SB10001424052748704335904574497622806733800.html.

Kindy, Kimberley, and Lyndsey Layton. "Purity of Federal 'Organic' Label Is Questioned." *The Washington Post,* July 3, 2009. Accessed September 5, 2012. www.washingtonpost.com/wp-dyn/content/article/2009/07/02/AR2009070203365.html.

Klein, Laura. "17 Tips to Shop for Organic Foods on a Budget," Organic Authority. Accessed July 31, 2012. www.organicauthority.com/organic-food/organic-food-articles/top-tips-for-shopping-for-organic-foods-on-a-budget.html#s.abesqj4habiaa.

Kliff, Sarah. "No, Congress Did not Declare Pizza a Vegetable." *The Washington Post,* November 21, 2011. Accessed September 5, 2012. www.washingtonpost.com/blogs/ezra-klein/post/did-congress-declare-pizza-as-a-vegetable-not-exactly/2011/11/20/gIQABXgmhN_blog.html.

Lazarony, Lucy. "17 Tips for Buying Organic Foods on the Cheap." Bankrate.com. Last modified July 8, 2008. Accessed July 31, 2012. www.bankrate.com/brm/news/cheap/20040901a1.asp.

LocalHarvest. "Farmers Markets / Family Farms / CSAs / Local Food." Accessed August 1, 2012. www.localharvest.org.

LocalHarvest. "Community Supported Agriculture." Accessed August 1, 2012. www.localharvest.org/csa.

Marine Stewardship Council. "Where to Buy." Last modified June 23, 2011. Accessed August 1, 2012. www.msc.org/where-to-buy.

Marine Stewardship Council. "Cook, Eat, Enjoy." Last modified April 26, 2010. Accessed August 1, 2012. www.msc.org/cook-eat-enjoy.

Mayo Clinic. "Grass-Fed Beef: What Are the Heart-Health Benefits?" Last modified January 25, 2012. Accessed August 1, 2012. www.mayoclinic.com/health/grass-fed-beef /AN02053.

Mercola, Joseph. "Another Reason to Ignore the Warnings About This Super Food." Mercola.com, September 2, 2011. Accessed July 31, 2012. http://articles.mercola.com /sites/articles/archive/2011/09/02/why-does-this-commonly-vilified-food-actually-prevent -heart-disease-and-cancer.aspx.

Mazzoncini, M., Belloni, P., Risaliti, R., & Antichi, D. "Organic vs Conventional Winter Wheat Quality and Organoleptic Bread Test." Proceedings of the 3rd International Congress of the European Integrated Project Quality Low Input Food (QLIF), University of Hohenheim, Germany, March 20–23, 2007. Accessed August 1, 2012. Available at: http://orgprints.org/9753/.

Monterey Bay Aquarium. "Fishing Methods." Accessed July 8, 2012. www.monterey bayaquarium.org/cr/cr_seafoodwatch/sfw_gear.aspx.

Monterey Bay Aquarium. "The Super Green List: Connecting Human and Ocean Health." Accessed July 8, 2012. www.montereybayaquarium.org/cr/cr_seafoodwatch /sfw_health.aspx.

Monterey Bay Aquarium. "2012 Culinary Chart of Alternatives." Last modified January, 2012. Accessed July 8, 2012. www.montereybayaquarium.org/cr/cr_seafoodwatch/sfw_alternatives.aspx.

Morris, Michele. "Benefits of Eating What's in Season." Gaiamlife.com. Accessed July 31, 2012. http://life.gaiam.com/article/benefits-eating-what-s-season.

NRDC. "Sustainable Seafood Guide." Accessed September 5, 2012. www.nrdc.org/oceans/seafoodguide.

NRDC. "Mercury Contamination in Fish." Accessed September 5, 2012. www.nrdc.org/health/effects/mercury/tuna.asp.

NRDC. "Eat Local: Find Fresh Food Near You." Accessed September 5, 2012. www.simplesteps.org/eat-local.

OregonState.edu. "What Is the Relative Sweetness of Different Sugars and Sugar Substitutes?" Updated May 23, 2012. Accessed September 2, 2012. http://food.oregonstate.edu/learn/faq/faq_sugar53.html.

Philpott, Tom. "Big Ag Spends Big Bucks to Keep GMOs in Your Food Secret." *MotherJones*. August 7, 2012. Accessed September 5, 2012. http://www.motherjones.com/tom-philpott/2012/08/biotech-gmo-labeling-california.

Philpott, Tom. "What Has Massive Breasts, a Weak Heart, and a Lifespan of 42 Days?" MotherJones.com, June 12, 2012. Accessed September 2, 2012. www.motherjones.com/tom-philpott/2012/06/georgia-group-gives-bird-big-chicken.

PickYourOwn. "Crop Harvest Calendars." Last modified September, 2012. www.pickyourown.org/US_crop_harvest_calendars.php.

PickYourOwn. "Where to Find Pick-Your-Own Farms." Last modified April 23, 2012. www.pickyourown.org/index.htm#states.

Pollan, Michael. *Food Rules: An Eater's Manual.* New York: Penguin Books, 2009.

Roberts, Holly. "Benefits of Organic Eggs." Livestrong.com, August 11, 2011. Accessed July 31, 2012. www.livestrong.com/article/67236-benefits-organic-eggs/.

Schneider, Andrew. "Tests Show Most Store Honey Isn't Honey." Food Safety News.com, November 2, 2011. Accessed October 15, 2012. http://www.foodsafetynews.com/2011/11/tests-show-most-store-honey-isnt-honey/.

Shuman, Sue Kovach. "Cause for Concern in Chinese Blubs?" *The Washington Post,* June 20, 2007. Accessed July 31, 2012. www.washingtonpost.com/wp-dyn/content/article/2007/06/19/AR2007061900423.html.

Strom, Stephanie. "Has 'Organic' Been Oversized?" *The New York Times*, July 7, 2012. Accessed September 5, 2012. www.nytimes.com/2012/07/08/business/organic-food-purists-worry-about-big-companies-influence.html.

Sustainable Table. "Pasture Raised, Pasture-Based." Accessed August 25, 2012. sustainabletable.org/issues/pasture.

USDA. "Farmers Market Search." Last modified August 16, 2012. Accessed August 16, 2012. http://search.ams.usda.gov/farmersmarkets/default.aspx.

USDA. "Supplemental Nutrition Assistance Program." Last modified August 9, 2012. Accessed August 16, 2012. www.fns.usda.gov/snap/.

Union of Concerned Scientists. "Greener Pastures: How Grass-fed Beef and Milk Contribute to Healthy Eating." Last modified March 7, 2006. Accessed August 16, 2012. www.ucsusa.org/food_and_agriculture/solutions/smart_pasture_operations/greener-pastures.html.

United Press International. "Maple Syrup may help treat diabetes." ClassicalMedicineJournal.com, April 14, 2011. http://www.classicalmedicinejournal.com/the-classical-medicine-journal/2011/4/14/maple-syrup-may-help-treat-diabetes.html.

Watson, Linda. *Wildly Affordable Organic: Eat Fabulous Food, Get Healthy, and Save the Planet.* New York: DaCapo Books, 2011.

Watson, Molly. "10 Farmers Market Shopping Tips." About.com guide. Accessed July 31, 2012. http://localfoods.about.com/od/farmersmarkets/tp/Farmers--Market-Tips.htm.

Werner, Leo H. "Maple Sugar Industry." TheCanadianEncyclopedia.com. Accessed September 2, 2012. http://www.thecanadianencyclopedia.com/index.cfm?PgNm=TCE &ArticleId=A0005095.

Wilson, Scott J. "'Organic' Food Rule Could Have Up to 38 Loopholes." *The Seattle Times,* June 10, 2007. Accessed September 5, 2012. http://seattletimes.com/html /nationworld/2003741899_organic10.html.

WiseGeek.com. "What is Date Sugar?" WiseGeek.com, Accessed September 2, 2012. http://www.wisegeek.com/what-is-date-sugar.htm#.

WWF. "Sugar and the Environment." WWF, 2004. Available as PDF download at assets.panda.org/downloads/sugarandtheenvironment_fidq.pdf.

Resources for Working Class Foodies

For more information about farmers' markets, co-ops, and CSAs

http://search.ams.usda.gov/farmersmarkets: Search engine on the USDA website to find a farmers' market near you.

www.organickitchen.com: A great resource to find accurate information about organic foods—foods grown free of chemicals and pesticides.

www.organicconsumers.org: A nonprofit consumer advocate group that has excellent resources and information about buying organic.

www.eatwellguide.org/i.php?pd=Home: Eat Well Guide is a free online directory for anyone in search of fresh, locally grown, and sustainably produced food in the United States and Canada.

www.nrdc.org/health/farming/forg101.asp: The Natural Resources Defense Council website has many helpful tips and facts regarding sustainable living.

www.localharvest.org: Local Harvest gives people the opportunity to easily locate local organic food sources across the country.

www.organicgardening.com: Organic Gardening offers expert advice for people wishing to start growing their own organic produce.

http://michaelpollan.com/resources: Michael Pollan provides a number of links about affordable and sustainable eating habits.

www.coopdirectory.org: Excellent website that will help you find food co-ops near you.

www.ams.usda.gov/AMSv1.0/nop: This website details the USDA's nationwide organic food initiative and gives the facts about the standards that USDA organic food is held to.

A website that will help with food storage

http://www.fruitsandveggiesmorematters.org: Website that has helpful resources for eating more fruits and vegetables. It also has a useful chart that shows you how to store and clean produce.

Storing Fresh Fruits and Vegetables for Best Flavor

Store in the refrigerator

FRUIT	Berries	**VEGETABLES**	Belgian Endive	Cauliflower	Leafy Vegetables	Radishes
Apples	Cherries	Artichokes	Broccoli	Celery	Leeks	Spinach
(more than 7 days)	Cut Fruit	Asparagus	Brussel Sprouts	Cut Vegetables	Lettuce	Sprouts
Apricots	Figs	Green Beans	Cabbage	Green Onions	Mushrooms	Summer Squashes
Asian pears	Grapes	Beets	Carrots	Herbs (not basil)	Peas	Sweet Corn

1. Place fruits and vegetables in separate, perforated plastic bags.

2. Use within 1-3 days for maximum flavor and freshness.

3. Store each group in different produce drawers in the refrigerator to minimize the detrimental effects of ethylene produced by the fruits on the vegetables.

Ripen on the counter first, then refrigerate

Avocados	Kiwi	Nectarines	Peaches	Pears	Plums	Plumcots

1. To prevent moisture loss, store fruits and vegetables separately in a paper bag, perforated plastic bag, or ripening bowl on the counter away from sunlight. Ripening fruit in a bowl or paper bag can be enhanced by placing an apple with the fruit to be ripened.

2. After ripening, store in refrigerator and use within 1-3 days.

Store only at room temperature

FRUIT	Citrus fruits	Persimmons	**VEGETABLES**	Garlic*	Peppers†	Tomatoes
Apples	Mangoes	Pineapple	Basil (in water)	Ginger	Potatoes*	Winter Squashes
(fewer than 7 days)	Melons	Plantain	Cucumber†	Jicama	Pumpkins	
Bananas	Papayas	Pomegranates	Eggplant†	Onions*	Sweet Potatoes*	

1. Many fruits and vegetables should only be stored at room temperatures. Refrigeration can cause cold damage or prevent them from ripening to good flavor and texture. For example, pink tomatoes ripen to a better taste and red color if they are left at room temperature. In the refrigerator, they do not turn red, and even red tomatoes kept in the refrigerator lose their flavor.

2. Keep away from direct sunlight.

*Store garlic, onions, potatoes, and sweet potatoes in a well-ventilated area in the pantry.

†Cucumbers, eggplant, and peppers can be refrigerated for 1-3 days if they are used soon after removing from the refrigerator.

Cleaning Your Produce

Always keep produce separate from raw meat, poultry, and seafood. Never use detergent or bleach to wash produce. Instead, rinse produce under running tap water immediately prior to use, including those with skins and rinds that are not eaten. Washing too far in advance removes some of nature's natural preservatives. However, head lettuce or leafy greens remain crisper when washed right away and then refrigerated. Packaged fruits and vegetables labeled "ready-to-eat," "washed," or "triple washed" need not be washed. Refrigerate all cut, peeled, or cooked fruits and vegetables within 2 hours.

For information on how to store other fruits and vegetables go to **FruitsAndVeggiesMoreMatters.org**

Source: UC Davis Postharvest Technology

© 2012 Produce for Better Health Foundation.

Acknowledgments

Book writing—at least cookbook writing—is far from a solitary experience. It is collaborative in the truest, dirtiest, most gluttonous sense: Recipes must constantly be tested on new stomachs, and joys and complaints must constantly be shared with practically everyone you've ever met.

First and foremost I have to thank Kit Pennebaker, without whom there would never have been any Working Class Foodies, let alone a show and book so gorgeously photographed.

I pity anyone who doesn't have Kathleen Grace as their champion and couldn't think of a single person I'd rather have in my corner.

I am forever indebted to the generous contributions of my probably-not-adopted and definitely fantastic brother, Max Lando; the multitalented Daisy Edwards for her lively illustrations; Brendan McDermott, my frequent coconspirator and personal cooking guru; Theo Peck and Nick Suarez, the best confidence boosters a budding amateur cook could ask for; and Rachel Fershleiser, Cole Stryker, Meg Allen Cole, Jillian Nugent, and Marissa Nystrom for their recipes.

This book wouldn't be possible without the love, support, DNA, and willing stomachs of my family, but especially my parents, Ruth and Michael Lando; my eternally sharp-witted grandmother Shirley Lando, and the very-much-missed David Lando and Edith and Carl Mayle; Phyllis and Mark Rosenfield; Amy Rosenfield; and DA Pennebaker and Chris Hegedus, who make the term *generous* quake in their shadow.

None of this would have ever been possible without the support of the YouTube Next Lab, but especially the Next New Networks gang: Liam Collins, Lance Podell, Tim Shey, Vanessa Pappas, Ryan Nugent, Andres Palmiter, Ben Relles, Diane deCordova, and Pat Griffith, as well as Austin Lau and Sofia Sheth.

I must also thank, for their years of support, Tracy, Andy, David, Anna and Samantha Gardner; the Schwartzes; the Brocklebanks; the varied and lovely Pennebaker clan; Erik Beck; Justin Johnson; Will Cole; Rob and Corinne Czar; Fred Seibert; Carrie Miller; Todd Womack; Megan Iorio, Martin Edward Corwin Neuse-Braunlich, and Liana Schweiger; my ridiculously patient and supportive agent, Jessie Borkan, and everyone else at the wonderful Kuhn Projects; Sophia Muthuraj and everyone at Penguin/Gotham Books; and to the hardworking farmers and market managers and volunteers across the country, without whose dedication I might never have found my way out of the supermarket.

And to you, the reader, for whatever brought you to this book in the first place.

Index

agave nectar, 19
Alaea Hawaiian sea salt, 21
ales, 178–80
anchovies, 26
antioxidants, 19–20, 22
appetizers, 61–71
apples
   apple cake, 244–45
   applesauce with brisket, 195–99
   and efficient cooking practices, 16
   and pesticide residues, 23
   quesadillas, 224–26
   quiche, 229–31
apps for produce shopping, 7
apricots, 192–94
arugula, 27
asparagus, 23, 168–69
avocado, 23

bacon
   chicken and bacon pâté, 66–68
   as pantry staple, 25
   tomato sandwich, 223
   white bean and bacon dip, 68–70
   and zucchini pancakes, 76
bain marie, 73, 75, 140
baking, 47, 53–55. See also specific dishes
baking powder, 25
balsamic vinegar, 26, 36
barley, 116–19, 185–88
basic tomato sauce, 37–38, 149
beans, 21, 25, 68–70, 126–27
beef
   and Bolognese sauce, 39–41, 159–60
   brisket, 195–99
   cuts of, 9, 10

environmental impact of, 11
   golabki, 186
   and meat stocks, 35–36
   pastured vs. factory-raised, 11
beets, 64, 114–16, 155–57
bell peppers, 23, 78–80
Bernstein, Zach, 76
berries, 16, 23, 238–39
black beans, 127–28
blintzes, 135–37
blogs, 2–3
blueberries, 23
Bolognese sauce, 39–41, 159–60
bones, 9. See also meats
borscht, 114–16
braising, 178–80, 187–88, 192–94, 195–99
breads, 16, 27, 47, 53–54
breakfast dishes, 133–41
Brendan's Israeli Couscous, 78–80
Brendan's Moroccan-Spiced Lamb Meatballs,
   188–91
brining, 204–5
brisket, 195–99
brown butter sauce, 151, 152–54
brown sugar, 18–19, 25
budget for food, 5, 14, 18, 25–27
burgers, 218–20
burrata cheese, 147–48
butter
   brown butter sauce, 151, 152–54
   herb butter, 57, 58
   lemon butter, 155–57
   maple butter, 87
   new potatoes with butter and herbs, 82–83
   as pantry staple, 25
   and pie crusts, 56–57

butter lettuce and radish salad, 88–91
butternut squash, 226–28
buying clubs, 8

cabbage, 23, 184, 185–88
Caesar salad kale chips, 63–64
cage free chickens, 20–21
cake, 244–45
calzones, 142, 148–49
candied pumpkin seeds, 137–39
canning jars, 15
canola oil, 25
cantaloupe, 23
caramels, 18, 251–52
cardamom, 125
Carl's Latkes, 83–85
carrots
    and brisket, 195–99
    and couscous, 79–80
    and golabki, 186
    greens from, 13
    and inexpensive meal plans, 27
    and lamb shanks, 179–80
    and risotto, 170–72
    and roast chicken, 207–9
    roasted carrot salad, 101–3
    and sauces, 37, 39–40
    and slaws, 182, 184–85
    and soups, 117–19, 123–24, 129
    and stuffings, 74
    and tzimmes, 192–94
    variety of, 2
    and vegetable stocks, 33, 34
    and veggie burgers, 221–23
celery, 23, 27, 78–80
challah, 194–95
chanterelles, 169
chard, 15
cheddar cheese, 165–66, 229–31
cheeses
    blintzes, 135–37
    burrata, 147–48
    cheddar, 165–66, 229–31
    feta, 94–96, 161–62
    fontina, 170–72
    for French onion soup, 122
    goat, 230
    Gouda, 224–26, 230
    Gruyère, 170–72, 230
    mozzarella, 144, 147–48
    Parmesan, 25, 76–77, 144
    pecorino, 76–77
    quesadillas, 224–26
    Swiss, 230
    See also ricotta
cherry tomato and burrata pizza, 147–48
chicken
    cage free chickens, 20–21
    chicken and bacon pâté, 66–68
    and 5-dollar meal plan, 27
    Indonesian chicken wings, 181–85
    and meat stocks, 35–36
    roast chicken and vegetables, 206–9
chickpeas, 81, 130–31
chilies, 183, 220–23
Chinese-style leek and pork dumplings, 215–17
chipotle dipping sauce, 220–23
chocolate, 26
chorizo, 127–28
cider vinegar, 26
cider-brined pork chops, 204–5
cilantro-lime cream, 112–13
cobbler, 245–48
collard, white bean, and kielbasa soup, 126–27
Community Supported Agriculture (CSA), 7–8,
    14, 24, 183
composting, 14
condiments, 36–44
confectioners' sugar, 19, 136
cookies, 248–49, 250–51
co-ops, 8, 14, 24
corn, 23, 111–13, 220–23
cornmeal, 25
corporate food producers, 24
cost of foods, 29–30. See also specific recipes
couscous, 78–80
crêpes, 135
Crispy Roasted Chickpeas, 81
cruciferous vegetables, 125
cucumbers, 23, 92–93, 106–7

dairy, 21, 25. See also cheeses; milk
date sugar, 19
desserts, 235–52
    apple cake, 244–45
    honey-cornmeal cookies, 250–51
    jumble berry pie, 238–39
    oatmeal lace cookies, 248–49

pumpkin whoopie pies, 236–37
sea salt-honey caramels, 251–52
southern fruit cobbler, 245–48
toaster pastries, 240–43
dips, 68–70
doughs
and efficient cooking, 16
gnocchi, 150–52
pasta, 51–52
and pie crusts, 56–57
pizza dough, 143–46
dressings, 36–44. *See also specific dishes and salads*
dumplings, 215–17

eggplant, 23, 175–78
eggs
egg whites, 44–45
eggs *en cocotte* with tomato and shallot, 139–41
and mayonnaise, 43–44
as pantry staple, 20–21, 25
poached, 162–64
and quiche, 229–31
empanadas, 220–23
emulsions, 43–44
environmental impact of food choices
fruits and vegetables, 22–23
meats, 11–12
prepared foods, 14
seafoods, 11–12, 165
sugar, 20
Environmental Working Group, 22–23
escarole, 127–28
extra virgin olive oil, 22

fairy-tale eggplants, 175–78
farmers' markets
buying greens, 230
and organic foods, 24
quality and prices of, 1–3
and typical Working Class Foodie day, 14
USDA database of, 5
feta cheese, 94–96, 161–62
finishing salts, 26
fish, 12, 26, 210–11, 213–14. *See also* seafood
Fisher, M. F. K., 12
flanken, 192
fleur de sel, 21

flours, 20
and baking basics, 53–55
bread flour, 20, 143
buckwheat flour, 57
gluten-free, 57
as pantry staple, 20, 25, 26
for pie crusts, 57
for pizza, 143–45
See also breads; doughs; pasta
fontina cheese, 170–72
food blogs, 2–3
free range chickens, 20–21
fructose, 19
fruit cobbler, 245–48
fruits
and efficient cooking practices, 16
and gardening, 14
as pantry staple, 22–23
and tzimmes, 192–94

gardening, 14, 24
garlic
Brendan's Israeli Couscous, 78–80
and dressings, 36
and efficient cooking practices, 15, 27, 36–37
mussels in ale with garlic, 212–13
as pantry staple, 22, 26
and ratatouille, 178
with steamed greens, 15
and stocks, 33, 34
storing, 8
gazpacho, 107–9
gnocchi, 150–52
goat cheese, 230
golabki, 185–88
Gouda, 224–26, 230
Grace, Kathleen, 3
grains of paradise, 191
Grammy's Stuffing, 73–75
granola, 133–34
grapefruit, 23
grapes, 23
grapeseed oil, 26
Greek raita, 189–91
green beans and hazelnut salad, 91–92
greens
buying, 230
carrot, 13
collard, 126–27

greens (*cont.*)
  and efficient cooking practices, 15
  and inexpensive meal plans, 27
  mustard, 229–31
  and quiche, 229–31
  soups and stews, 125–26
  steamed, 15
grits
  eggs *en cocotte*, 141
  polenta compared to, 47
  and sausage, 167–68
  shrimp 'n' grits, 165–66
grocery stores, 14
Gruyère cheese, 170–72, 230

herbs
  and efficient cooking practices, 15
  and gardening, 14
  herb butter, 57, 58
  new potatoes with butter and herbs, 82–83
  as pantry staple, 25
  well-stocked pantries, 17
honey, 18, 19, 20, 25, 251–52
honey-cornmeal cookies, 250–51
hot sauce, 26
How to Cook a Wolf (Fisher), 12

Indonesian chicken wings, 181–85
iodine, 21
Israeli Couscous, 78–80

jumble berry pie, 238–39

kale, 15, 63–64, 98–100, 148–49
kasha, 185–88
ketchup, 42–43
kielbasa, 126–27
kiwi, 23
knives, 28
kosher salt, 21, 25
kumquats, 103–5

labeling of foods, 24
lace cookies, 248–49
lacinato, 63–64
Lahey, Jim, 53
lamb
  cuts of, *10*
  and meat stocks, 35–36
  meatballs, 188–91

and pasta, 157–58
  shanks, 178–80
lasagna, 39–41, 159–60
latkes, 83–85
leeks, 215–17
leftovers
  and golabki, 185–88
  grilled corn, 113
  maple-mustard roast pork, 201–2
  and pasta, 149
  sandwiches, 27
  in tarts, 227
  Thanksgiving pot pies, 231–33
lemons
  asparagus risotto with lemon, 168–69
  and dressings, 36
  lemon butter, 155–57
  lemon-pepper poppy beet chips, 64
  as pantry staple, 26
  and roasted trout, 210–11
lentils, 128–29
lettuce, 23, 88–91
local foods, 8, 20–21, 22–23

mackerel, 12
magnesium, 22
mangoes, 23
Manhattan, New York, 29
maple butter, 87
maple syrup
  and cheese blintzes, 136
  maple-mustard roast pork, 199–202
  as pantry staple, 19–20, 25
margherita pizza, 142–46
marinades, 46
marketing foods, 24
matzoh meal, 73–75, 84–85
Max's Cheddar Shrimp 'n' Grits, 165–66
mayonnaise, 43–44
McDermott, Brendan, 3, 42, 78, 159, 188
meats
  and Bolognese sauce, 39–41
  and efficient cooking practices, 15
  environmental impact of, 11
  meat stocks, 35–36, 50–51, 120–22, 180, 200
  off-cuts, 9
  shopping for, 8–11
  See also specific meat types
meringues, 45
milk, 18, 21, 25, 57, 59–60

Monterey Bay Aquarium, 12, 165
Moroccan-spiced lamb meatballs, 188–91
mozzarella cheese, 144, 147–48
Murray River flake salt, 21
mushrooms
    and barley soup, 116–19
    and golabki, 186
    as pantry staple, 26
    and pesticide residues, 23
    ragu, 163
    squash and mushroom tart, 226–28
mussels, 212–13
mustard, 26, 36, 199–202
mustard greens, 229–31

National Center for Home Food Preservation, 15
nectarines, 23
new potatoes, 27, 82–83, 192, 207, 210
Next New Networks, 3
noodles, 182, 184–85

oatmeal lace cookies, 248–49
oats, 25, 134
olive oil, 22, 25, 36, 41
olives, 26
omelets, 44
onions
    Brendan's Israeli Couscous, 78–80
    and brisket, 198
    French onion soup, 120–22
    and latkes, 83–85
    as pantry staple, 26
    and pesticide residues, 23
    roasted onion dip, 68–70
organic foods, 8, 11, 20–21, 24
orzo, 78–80

packaged foods, 24
pancake syrup, 19–20
pancakes, 75–77
pancetta, 172–74
pantries, 17–28
    and baking, 53–55
    and cost of meals, 30
    and efficient cooking, 13
    egg whites, 44–45
    grains, 46–47
    herb butter, 57, 58
    jarred sauces and condiments, 36–44
    pasta dough, 51–52

peanut butters and sauces, 46–47
pie crusts, 56–57
polenta, 47–49
ricotta, 59–60
risotto, 50–51
staple items, 25–27
stocks, 33–36
papalo, 13
pappardelle with lamb ragu, 157–58
Parmesan cheese, 25, 76–77, 144
parsnips
    golabki, 185–88
    as pantry staple, 33
    and risotto, 170–72
    and roast chicken, 206–9
    and salads, 88–89
    and soups, 68, 117–19
    storing, 8
    tzimmes, 192–94
pasta, 149–62
    dough for, 51–52
    lasagna Bolognese, 159–60
    as pantry staple, 25
    pappardelle with lamb ragu, 157–58
    pasta salad, 161–62
    ravioli, 149, 152–54, 155–57
    storing fresh pasta, 46–47
    sweet potato gnocchi, 150–52
pastries, 240–43
pastured livestock, 11
pâté, 66–68
pâte brisée, 56–57, 229–31, 231–33
peaches, 23
peanut butter, 25, 45–46
peanut noodles, 182
peanut sauces, 46–47, 184
pears, 16
peas, 169
pecorino cheese, 76–77
peppercorns, 25
pesticides, 23
pestos, 36–37, 58
pies
    crusts, 56–57
    jumble berry pie, 238–39
    pie crusts, 56–57
    pot pies, 231–33
    pumpkin whoopie pies, 236–37
pineapples, 23
pizzas, 141–48

poached eggs, 162–64
polenta, 25, 47–49, 162–64
poppy seeds, 64
pork
    and Bolognese sauce, 39–41
    cider-brined pork chops, 204–5
    cuts of, *11*
    dumplings, 215–17
    and golabki, 186
    maple-mustard roast pork, 199–202
    and meat stocks, 35–36
    tenderloin, 203–4
potassium, 22
potatoes
    and brisket, 198
    and inexpensive meal plans, 27
    latkes, 83–85
    new potatoes, 27, 82–83, 192, 207, 210
    as pantry staple, 26
    and pesticide residues, 23
    and roast chicken, 206–9
    and roasted trout, 210–11
    sweet potato fries, 86–88
    waxy, 7, 27, 196
    Yukon Gold, 84
    See also sweet potatoes
powdered sugar, 19, 136
prepared foods, 14
preservatives, 19
preserving, 15
price of foods, 29–30
prunes, 192–94
puff pastry, 226–28
pumpkin waffles, 137–39
pumpkin whoopie pies, 236–37
Purim, 192

quesadillas, 224–26
quiche, 229–31
quinoa, 98–100, 185–88

radicchio, 103–5
raita, Greek, 189–91
ratatouille, 175–78
ravioli, 149, 152–54, 155–57
recycling, 21
red peppers, 111–13
rice, 25, 27. *See also* risotto
rice vinegar, 26

ricotta
    cheese blintzes, 135–37
    and efficient cooking, 16, 57
    homemade, 59–60
    as pantry staple, 18
    and ravioli, 149, 152–54, 155–57
    and zucchini pancakes, 75–77
risotto
    asparagus risotto with lemon, 168–69
    basic recipe, 50–51
    pancetta, squash, and shallot, 172–74
    and roasted vegetables, 170–72
roast chicken and vegetables, 206–9
roasted trout, 210–11
roasted vegetables
    broccoli, 61–63
    carrot salad, 101–3
    and efficient cooking practices, 15
    onion dip, 68–70
    pot pies, 231–33
    red pepper and corn soup, 111–13
    and risotto, 170–72
    sandwiches, 15–16, 37
    tomato soup, 110–11
    veggie burgers, 218–20
Roberts, Adam, 215
rolled oats, 25
root vegetables, 170, 206–9. *See also* parsnips;
        potatoes

sage, 152–54
salads
    butter lettuce and radishes, 88–91
    cucumber, jicama, and seaweed, 92–93
    green beans and hazelnuts, 91–92
    grilled radicchio with kumquats, 103–5
    kale and quinoa, 98–100
    pasta salad, 161–62
    roasted carrot, 101–3
    spicy watermelon and feta salad, 94–96
    tomato salad, 96–97
    tricolor summer salad, 97–98
salmon, 213–14
salt
    and caramels, 18, 251–52
    finishing salts, 26
    as pantry staple, 25
    sea salt, 18, 21–22, 25, 251–52
    specialty salts, 22, 26

table salt, 21
sandwiches
    brisket, 199
    and carrot greens, 13
    dressings and spreads for, 68–70, 89
    grilled/roasted vegetables, 15–16, 37
    and homemade bread, 16, 53
    leftovers, 27
    maple-mustard roast pork, 201–2
    short ribs, 194–95
    tomato sandwich, 223
sardines, 12, 26
sauces, 36–44
    basic tomato sauce, 37–38, 149
    basic vinaigrette, 41
    Bolognese sauce, 39–41
    brisket, 197–98
    brown butter sauce, 151, 152–54
    Chinese dumplings, 215–17
    chipotle dipping sauce, 220–23
    hot sauce, 26
    ketchup, 42–43
    lamb meatballs, 189–91
    mayonnaise, 43–45
    peanut butter, 45
    peanut sauce, 46–47, 184
    pizza sauce, 144, 145
    Sriracha sauce, 183–84, 223
    See also tomato sauce
sausage, 167–68
sea salt, 18, 21–22, 25, 251–52
seafood
    and efficient cooking practices, 15
    mussels in ale with garlic, 212–13
    roasted trout, 210–11
    shellfish, 12
    shrimp 'n' grits, 165–66
    spice-rubbed salmon, 213–14
    sustainable practices, 12
Seafood Watch website, 165
seasonal foods, 6–7, 22–23, 130–31
seasonings, 17. See also herbs; salt; spices
semolina, 78
sesame, 65–66, 184–85
shallots, 139–41, 172–74
shellfish, 12
shishito peppers, 175–78
short ribs, 192–94
shrimp 'n' grits, 165–66

Sichuan peppercorns, 65–66
slaw, 182, 184
smoked cheddar, 230
snacks, 61–71
snap peas, 6, 65–66, 168, 182, 184
social element of cooking, 12–13
soups and stews, 105–31
    borscht, 114–16
    chickpea stew, 130–31
    chilled cucumber soup, 106–7
    collard, white bean, and kielbasa, 126–27
    curried spinach, lentil, and sweet potato soup,
        128–29
    escarole, black bean, and chorizo soup, 127–28
    French onion soup, 120–22
    gazpacho, 107–9
    mushroom barley soup, 116–19
    roasted red pepper and corn soup, 111–13
    roasted tomato soup, 110–11
    spiced squash soup, 122–25
    and vegetable broth, 16
southern fruit cobbler, 245–48
specialty oils, 26, 41
specialty salts, 22, 26
spices
    and Crispy Roasted Chickpeas, 81
    as pantry staple, 25
    and pork tenderloin, 203–4
    spiced squash soup, 122–25
    spice-rubbed salmon, 213–14
spinach, 23, 128–29, 224–26
spoilage, 57
squash
    and mushroom tart, 226–28
    and risotto, 172–74
    spiced squash soup, 122–25
Sriracha sauce, 183–84, 223
staples. See pantries
steel-cut oats, 25
stocks
    and efficient cooking, 9, 13–14
    and kitchen leftovers, 33
    meat stock, 35–37, 50–51, 120–22, 180, 200
    mushroom barley soup, 117–19
    as pantry staple, 26
    and polenta, 47–49
    and risotto, 50–51
    vegetable stock, 15–16, 33–34, 50–51, 120–22
strategies for food shopping, 5–16

strawberries, 23
Stryker, Cole, 183
stuffings, 73–75
sugar, 18–19, 25
supermarkets, 5
Supplemental Nutrition Assistance Program
    (SNAP), 5
sustainable practices
    efficient cooking practices, 13, 14
    and pastured livestock, 12
    and pork, 199–200
    and seafood, 12
sweet peas, 23
sweet potatoes
    curried spinach, lentil, and sweet potato soup,
        128–29
    empanadas, 220–23
    fries, 86–88
    gnocchi, 150–52
    as pantry staple, 26
    and pesticide residues, 23
    pot pies, 231–33
    tzimmes, 192–94
sweeteners, 18–19. See also sugar
Swiss cheese, 230
syrups, 19–20

table salt, 21
tacos, 201–2
tarts, 226–28
Thanksgiving leftovers, 231–33
toaster pastries, 240–43
tomato sauce
    basic sauce, 37–38, 149
    Bolognese sauce, 39–41
    and golabki, 186
    grits and sausage, 167–68
    and polenta, 49
tomatoes
    eggs en cocotte with tomato and shallot, 139–
        41
    gazpacho, 107–9
    grape tomatoes, 210–11
    heirloom tomatoes, 109
    kale salad, 98–100
    as pantry staple, 26

plum tomatoes, 38
ratatouille, 175–78
roasted tomato soup, 110–11
and roasted trout, 210–11
Roma tomatoes, 38
summer sandwich, 223
tomato salad, 96–97
tortillas, 224–26
tricolor summer salad, 97–98
trout, 210–11
truffle oil, 26, 169, 170
turkey, 231–33
tzimmes, 192–94

Union Square Greenmarket, 1–2, 5–6
U.S. Department of Agriculture (USDA), 5, 7

variety in food choices, 6, 12, 13
veal, 39–41
vegan foods, 19, 63–64
vegetable oils, 25
vegetable stock, 15–16, 33–34, 50–51, 120–22
vegetables. See roasted vegetables; specific
    vegetables and recipes
vegetarian foods, 19, 63–64, 78, 188, 218–20
veggie burgers, 218–20
vinaigrettes, 41
vinegar, 25–26, 36
virgin olive oil, 22

waffles, 137–39
watermelon, 23, 94–96
waxy potatoes, 7, 27, 196
whey, 59–60
white bean and bacon dip, 68–70
white vinegar, 25
whoopie pies, 236–37
window boxes, 14
wines, 178–80
winter vegetables, 170
World Wildlife Fund, 20

yeast, 54
Yukon Gold potatoes, 84

zucchini, 75–77, 78–80